Madhouse Movies

Also by Sharon Packer
and from McFarland

Neuroscience in Science Fiction Films (2015)

Cinema's Sinister Psychiatrists: From Caligari to Hannibal (2012)

Madhouse Movies

Essays on the Depiction of Psychiatric Institutions

Edited by
SHARON PACKER, M.D.

Foreword by H. Steven Moffic, M.D.

McFarland & Company, Inc., Publishers
Jefferson, North Carolina

This book has undergone peer review.

LIBRARY OF CONGRESS CATALOGING-IN-PUBLICATION DATA

Names: Packer, Sharon editor | Moffic, H. Steven writer of foreword
Title: Madhouse movies : essays on the depiction of psychiatric institutions /
edited by Sharon Packer ; foreword by H. Steven Moffic, M.D.
Description: Jefferson, North Carolina : McFarland & Company, Inc., Publishers, 2026. |
Includes bibliographical references and index.
Identifiers: LCCN 2026022215 | ISBN 9781476690926 paperback ♾
ISBN 9798368600352 ebook
Subjects: LCSH: Psychiatric hospitals in motion pictures | BISAC: PERFORMING ARTS /
Film / History & Criticism | PSYCHOLOGY / Mental Health | LCGFT: Film criticism
Classification: LCC PN1995.9.P776 M33 2026
LC record available at https://lccn.loc.gov/2026022215

ISBN (print) 978-1-4766-9092-6
ISBN (ebook) 979-8-3686-0035-2

Front cover photograph: Anthony Perkins as Norman Bates
in the 1960 film *Psycho* (Paramount Pictures/Photofest)

Printed in the United States of America

McFarland & Company, Inc., Publishers
Box 611, Jefferson, North Carolina 28640
www.mcfarlandpub.com

In memory of Philip Miller, Ph.D., A.M.L.S.,
of the Klau Library at Hebrew Union College.

Acknowledgments

My ever-patient editor, Layla Milholen of McFarland, deserves endless credit for her guidance on this collection, especially during the trying times of the pandemic and when McFarland's home state faced extreme natural disasters. My equally patient husband also merits kudos for his encouragement and his reflections. Most of all, I must acknowledge the many unnamed patients who shared their stories and their insights about mental hospitals and mental illness through the years. It is my greatest hope that their fortunes have changed for the better, their health has returned to a state of equanimity, and they will not need to enter a psychiatric hospital again.

Table of Contents

SECTION V: Politics and Polemics

SECTION VI: Supernatural Asylums

Foreword

H. Steven Moffic, M.D.

I have a confession to make. I'm not a movie critic, though I have been asked to publicly discuss movies shown with some presumed psychiatric impact. Even so, I'm not much of a moviegoer, and never have been. What, then, makes me qualified to write a foreword for a book about movies, and "madhouse movies" about psychiatric institutions at that?

At least I am a social psychiatrist. I suppose that I also have some outside confirmation, being designated as a "Hero of Public Psychiatry" by the speaker of the American Psychiatric Association in 2002 and recently receiving the Abraham Halpern Humanitarian Award from the American Association for Social Psychiatry in 2024.

I also have had the stimulating experience of getting to know Dr. Sharon Packer and her insights about patients, religions, and popular culture via her articles for *Psychiatric Times*, her chapters in my edited volumes on religion and psychiatry for Springer, and all her fascinating books on rarely covered popular culture topics that nevertheless have significant psychological impact.

I had the opportunity to experience such benefits—as I'm confident the other essayists in this book had—when I was asked to write on blind African American musicians for her recent book, *Lenses on Blindness.* Now we have this new book, which seems to have a connection to another from over a decade ago: *Cinema's Sinister Psychiatrists: From Caligari to Hannibal.* Being a lover and collector of masks, even the COVID kind, I have noted the one from 15 years back on the cover of *Superheroes and Superegos: Analyzing the Minds Behind the Masks.* There are many more such mental treasures in her collected works.

So perhaps I am qualified to comment on the social psychiatric value of movies in general, and this madhouse movie collection of essays edited and developed by Dr. Packer in particular, which have been sorted into Comics, Cults, Darkest Depictions, Incarceration, Politics, and the Supernatural.

I had a big smile and my heart skipped a beat when I noticed that probably my favorite movie of all time, the 1966 French film *King of Hearts*, was featured in one of the essays. At that time in the United States, the deinstitutionalization of the overcrowded state psychiatric hospitals had begun, but the communities the patients were released to often weren't ready to accept and help them settle in. We see the same progression in this movie, but under many different and absurd wartime circumstances. It became a beloved underground classic for its depiction of how lovable and fascinating severely ill mental patients can be if they have the right setting, as is also highly recommended when taking psychedelics.

King of Hearts is almost the opposite of the much more popular and well-known movie *One Flew Over the Cuckoo's Nest*. Even in 1965 and later in 1988, I visited state psychiatric hospitals in Michigan and Virginia that had remnants of *Cuckoo's Nest* still in place. If only this book could help reverse the popularity of these two movies! The closest I found to more of a lovable and beloved setting is the Grand Avenue Clubhouse in Milwaukee when I was president of the board. Clubhouses are community-based centers where adults living with mental illness are expertly guided toward more societal interaction and activities.

It's not any great insight to say that movies have become one of the public's great leisure time activities. No wonder, then, that movies can influence the public's perception of psychiatry and psychiatrists. Often, we are "mad" about our movie portrayals because they tend to be erroneously negative, but ironically it is the negative fears and fantasies that sell the best. Besides, we can learn something from these portrayals.

Therefore, I strongly recommend this book to anyone interested in the social aspects of psychiatry and mental health, any movie lover, and anyone interested in a scholarly examination of the particular madhouse movies covered. Whether on a big screen or little screen, in a movie theater or at home, on the go or on the couch, this book may well go straight to your hearts and minds as it did to mine.

H. Steven Moffic, M.D. *is currently a pro bono private community psychiatrist, previously based in academic institutions. National and international accolades include Exemplary Psychiatrist award from the National Alliance of the Mentally Ill (NAMI) (1993); "Hero of Public Psychiatry" commendation from the American Psychiatric Association (2002); Administrative Psychiatrist award from the American Psychiatric Association (2016); Creative Scholarship award from the Society for the Study of Psychiatry and Culture (2021); the Abraham Halpern Humanitarian Award from the American Association for Social Psychiatry (2024); and lead editor for a four-volume series on various religions and psychiatry (Springer, 2018–2024).*

Preface

Sharon Packer

This book about "madhouse movies" is not my first book about psychiatry and cinema or about mental illness and popular culture in general. Yet it has been the most difficult to assemble, despite being a collection of essays contributed by a wide variety of authors, rather than a single-author monograph.

As a practicing psychiatrist, I am accustomed to probing patients' reaction to perplexing events of the past, conflictual relationships in the present, or paralyzing fears of the future, reactions which still arise, even in these days of neuroscience, biological psychiatry, and psychopharmacology. And so, similarly, I must ask myself, "Why?" Why should a topic like this make me falter, second-guess myself, and induce such a stalemate, especially when film history includes so much rich material about "madhouse movies"? The answer may be as significant as the cinematic examples discussed in the essays that follow.

In short, I must confess that I am a fence-sitter on this topic. I am still uncertain of the "goodness" or "badness" of institutionalization or involuntary admission of people deemed to be harmful to themselves or others, or unable to care for themselves without further endangering their lives or their health (which are the criteria used in New York State). While I am far from the "mental illness deniers" like Szasz or Laing or Cooper, or others of their ilk, I still wonder if we help or harm people whom we incarcerate in mental institutions, especially against their will.

True, I spend my days practicing telepsychiatry and treating people who seek relief from various mental maladies, and by virtue of that alone, it is evident that I am thoroughly convinced that psychic suffering does indeed exist, and that it should be ameliorated as best and as safely and as quickly as possible. But should those "cures" include hospitals or asylums or "psych wards," especially when an individual does not request such confinement?

On one hand, I favor the more civil libertarian POV and loathe the idea of restricting individual freedom—provided that pursuit of such freedom does not infringe on the rights of others. Yet I hear other colleagues tout the benefits that they witnessed for unwilling patients who were remanded to treatment or forced to detox from potentially dangerous substances. Their poignant descriptions make me rethink my reflexive reactions, which are based on philosophy rather than observation. The most thought-provoking comments have been articulated by fellow appointees of the American Psychiatric Association's Council on Addiction Psychiatry.

At the same time, I cringe when I read about recent developments in New York

State, which expanded the powers of involuntary commitment to include practitioners with less intensive professional training than psychiatric physicians. The concept of the "2-PC" or the two-physician certificate, whereby two physicians must independently deem commitment necessary, is now null and void and no longer necessary under state law. And so, I must ask myself, is this a slippery slope? How long will it be before disgruntled citizens can call the authorities and demand that they remand their neighbors to hospital care, or when spouses can sign their mates into mental facilities, as happened to a specific minister's wife in the 19th century before she became a passionate advocate for the rights of women in similar situations?

There is good reason to debate these issues, not only from a clinical point of view, but also from a philosophical perspective. When does the state have the right to usurp an individual's freedom? Or when does the state have an obligation to intervene when someone with clearly compromised judgment puts themself or others at risk? We could debate these questions, seemingly endlessly, in any number of academic forums. Or we could watch movies that project our own anxieties onto the screen and thereby force us to confront these questions. We can mull over these ideas in our own minds or discuss them with people sitting next to us in a cineplex or compare our reactions to a film reviewer's conclusions. Fortunately, over the years, moviemakers have provided us with a wide variety of "cue cards" on screen, intended to elicit such responses, at the same time that their celluloid creations entertain us.

Those who are interested in less lofty questions but are still curious about the interface between psychiatry and cinema may want to read my previous books on the subject, which include *Dreams in Myth, Medicine, and Movies* (2002); *Movies and the Modern Psyche* (2007); *Superheroes and Superegos: Analyzing the Minds Behind the Masks.* (2010); *Cinema's Sinister Psychiatrists: From Caligari to Hannibal* (2012); *A History of Evil in Popular Culture: What Hannibal Lecter, Stephen King and Vampire Reveal about America* (2 volumes) (2014); *Neuroscience in Science Fiction Films* (2015); *Mental Illness in Popular Culture* (2017); and *Welcome to Arkham Asylum: Essays on Psychiatry and the Gotham City Institution* (2019).

In the interim, please enjoy the essays that follow, and feel free to share your suggestions with me at drpacker@hotmail.com.

Introduction

What's in a Name?

Sharon Packer

What shall I call this book? *Madhouse Movies*? *Insane Asylum Cinema*? *Funny Farm Films*? Each sounds like the name of a quirky production company, or maybe even an edgy musical ensemble, yet each is an equally accurate description of this project, and all are, in one way or another, politically incorrect at present. Appellations that were intended to be polite in a certain era can become pejorative at different times and places. It is not our intention to insult anyone, and we certainly do not want to disrespect current or past residents of those multi-named facilities. Our goal is simply to show you that there may be many manifestations of this type of film.

Let us begin by quickly explaining the differences—or the similarities—between "madhouses," "asylums," "mental institutions," "state hospitals," "psych wards," "sanitariums" (or "sanitoriums"), "funny farms," rest homes or residential facilities, and the less politically charged "retreats" (such as William Tuke's Quaker-funded York Retreat in the U.K., which introduced more humane "moral therapy" when it opened in 1792). Then we can decide if these facilities for the mentally ill evolved over time for the better or the worse, or if these name changes were merely marketing maneuvers to obscure the bad reputations of their antecedents.

In short, "madhouses" were 17th-century institutions that were replaced by 18th-century "asylums." The "mad," the indigent, and various kinds of criminals coexisted in these "madhouses." Although considered an archaic term, associated with inhumane treatment and unpleasant conditions, many medical historians and medical sociologists favor this emotionally evocative word, as evidenced by book titles that include Andrew T. Scull's *Madhouse: A Tragic Tale of Megalomania and Modern Medicine* (2005); *Madness in Civilization: A Cultural History of Insanity* (2015); or *Madhouses, Mad-Doctors, and Madmen: The Social History of Psychiatry in the Victorian Era* (1981). The late medical historian Roy Porter likewise employs this term in some of his many books, such as *Madmen: A Social History of Madhouses, Mad Doctors & Lunatics* (2004); *Madness: A Brief History* (2002); and *A Social History of Madness: The World through the Eyes of the Insane* (1988). Mike Jay writes of "madness" in *This Way Madness Lies: The Asylum and Beyond* (2016).[1] Many other examples appear in the endnotes of this essay and in the bibliography.

Michel Foucault, author of *Madness and Civilization: A History of Insanity in the Age of Reason* (1961), traces the evolution of attitudes to madness over the 17th and 18th centuries as industrial society emerged and demanded more conformity and discipline to meet shifting social and economic needs. In the earlier parts of his book, Foucault claims that 14th-century European leprosariums were "repurposed" to contain the insane after leprosy became less prevalent in Europe, diminishing the need for leper colonies. During the Age of Reason, erratic behavior became less acceptable, and out-of-control people who "lost their reason" were deemed to need containment. They were segregated from the rest of society and stigmatized, like lepers. Although Foucault's contentions about confining one group of social outcasts in facilities built for another include a kernel of truth, and the mad were indeed ostracized in more "civilized" Western society, his overall conclusions seem to be hyperbolic. While France and Denmark were better known for this trend than other countries, and some examples of converted leprosariums exist to this day, it is incorrect to aver that *all* European madhouses were once leper colonies—although this sensational accusation certainly attracts attention. More optimistic authors point out that mental illness was increasingly recognized as a medical condition and that belief in the treatability of such mental illness gelled over time, but an infrastructure for the delivery of treatments was needed. Leprosariums, with their existing infrastructure, seemed like logical choices.

Asylums, on the other hand, were initially intended to offer "asylum"—a place of refuge and protection—to those who needed to escape the pressures of outside society. These facilities focused on long-term care for people with severe mental illness. They sheltered those who were unable to function safely outside of institutional walls (although many of those overcrowded institutions became unsafe themselves). Sometimes asylums included treatments when available, but often they were warehouses, convenient locations for families to lock away inconvenient relatives.

Asylums started as a step up from madhouses, but even they deteriorated over time, to the point that the term "Bedlam," which was originally the truncated name of a British asylum, was appropriated for general use and came to signify "a scene of uproar and confusion."

To escape the taint of association with asylums, state hospitals emerged in the 20th century. State hospitals are publicly funded and operated by state governments, as the name indicates. Until deinstitutionalization began, these state hospitals served as the primary institutions for long-term care of people with serious and persistent mental illness (SPMI).

Eventually, care shifted toward hospital-based psychiatric units, and "psych wards" for the more acutely ill opened in general hospitals. Some freestanding and separate psychiatric hospitals appeared in due time, and then "community-based" (non-hospital) care became more common. Residential treatment facilities (RTFs)—as seen in *Girl, Interrupted* (1999)—offered transitional care for those who no longer needed hospital support but still required some supervision (hopefully better than the kind that was available to Angelina Jolie's victims). Facilities like RTFs might have been referred to as "rest homes" in the past.

In the interim, the sanitarium (also spelled "sanatorium" or "sanitorium") served as an alternative facility for "chronic care" of people with long-term maladies that did not respond to quick cures. The term comes from the Latin word "*sanare*," meaning "to heal." Sanitariums were commonly associated with unremitting medical conditions. Historically, they specialized in specific diseases, such as the highly contagious tuberculosis, but TB sanitariums became less common after effective antibiotics became available. Sanitariums were typically private, in contrast to publicly funded asylums such as Britain's notorious Bedlam.

Over time, the sanitarium's function expanded to include mental and emotional disorders. A private psychiatric sanitarium was usually located in a more secluded and comfortable setting than the typically overpopulated public mental asylums. They provided more humane environments for individuals whose wealthier families could afford attentive private care. Rest cures were commonly used in such settings, as they were for TB patients. Some scenes in *Now, Voyager* (1942) and Hitchcock's *Spellbound* (1947) are set in elegant and presumably expensive sanitariums. With the arrival of psychotropic medications in the mid–20th century, and the accompanying movement toward deinstitutionalization, the popularity of traditional psychiatric sanitariums waned. Most faded away.

In this essay, we will address each of these approaches and link them to various films, but first, let us look at an interesting outlier here, one which relates to the opening farm scene in Martin Scorsese's *Shutter Island* (2010), and which also makes us rethink current American approaches to people with serious and persistent mental illness and the dire housing situation that evolved in the wake of the "deinstitutionalization" movement. I am specifically referring to "funny farms." We will elaborate on *Shutter Island* later, but first, let us look at real life "funny farms" that possibly influenced this term. We will zero in on the "farms" in Geel, Belgium.

This facetious moniker may not be part of the medical lexicon, but farm-based and home-based adult foster care has been available to people with serious mental illness in Geel, Belgium, since the 13th century. Many say that Geel's centuries-old approach represents the greatest achievement in caring for and housing the mentally ill.

How Geel became associated with psychiatric disorders and so-called "funny farms" is a fascinating story. Since the 13th century, pilgrims seeking relief from neuropsychiatric symptoms flocked to the town that once welcomed St. Dymphna, who was a "simple" Irish princess before she was canonized. Living in the seventh century, Dymphna fled to Geel when her deranged father attempted to marry her, his own daughter, after her mother's death. In Geel, Dymphna dedicated herself to caring for the sick and mentally ill. Sadly, her persistent father followed Dymphna to the Belgian town—and beheaded her—when she refused his demands. To acknowledge her martyrdom and her dedication to the mentally ill, Dymphna was named the patron saint of the mentally ill. The townspeople of Geel have honored her legacy by caring for people suffering from mental disorders to this day.

In the mid–1300s, locals began building a church dedicated to St. Dymphna. The pilgrims who arrived in Geel lived in the homes of local farmers. The farmers helped the pilgrims with daily tasks and vice versa. In the mid–15th century, the church added a dormitory to house the pilgrims. However, reports of boarders being chained and beaten surfaced, so that the Belgian government took control of the church-sponsored program after 1850. In 1861, the government built a dedicated hospital in Geel. By the late 1930s, more than 3,700 patients were living with families or at the hospital campus. The "Geel system" became a model for community-based mental health care in many other towns in Belgium, France, and Germany[2] and has been the subject of many academic studies.

Unfortunately, most American and British attempts at alternative noninstitutional approaches to housing people with SPMI contrast dramatically with Geel's overall success (apart from the time-limited glitch in the mid–19th century). The experimental housing and treatment facilities promoted by high-profile anti-psychiatry activists in the U.K., such as the Scottish-born R.D. Laing or David Graham Cooper, the South African ex-patriot, did not hold up to their idealistic promises, even though they were revered by the 1960s and '70s counterculture. Places such as Kingsley Hall either closed of their own accord or were sometimes shuttered in response to local objections.

The absolute number of farm-based facilities that welcomed the mentally ill and treated them like family members has dwindled over time, but not because Geel's citizens disavowed their town's traditions. Rather, many farms closed as longtime residents relocated to urban areas in search of better-paying or more stable work. Contrast those enterprises with the homeless encampments that coalesced after the closing of massive state facilities in the U.S., and with the current "revolving door" policy that discharges people from inpatient treatment facilities before they are prepared to navigate life on their own.

Worse yet, let us contrast the genteel Geel approach with the tragic "transinstitutionalization" that followed the poorly planned deinstitutionalization movement, where people who had spent years in supervised state hospitals suddenly found themselves on the streets, later landing in jails or prisons after local criminals introduced them to dangerous and illicit street drugs and taught them equally illicit ways to procure such drugs. As a result, Rikers Island in New York, Los Angeles County Jail in California, and Cook County Jail in Chicago together house more mentally ill people than anywhere else. We will elaborate on this transition in later essays.

And so, we see that the antiquated 17th-century "madhouses" that lumped the mentally ill with indigents and criminals have resurfaced under a different guise and with a different label, the difference being that this time around, those facilities are identified as jails and prisons and are not disguised as mental institutions, asylums, or formal psychiatric hospitals.

The History of Asylums in Cinema

Asylums have appeared in cinema nearly since its beginning. Georges Méliès's first film appeared in 1896; the term "psycho-analysis" was coined by Freud a year later, in 1896. This chronological correspondence confirms that cinema and psychoanalysis were both born in the same bathwater of fin de siècle society.

In 1901, soon after those seminal cinema-related events, Méliès—the same French magician turned moviemaker who receives the most credit for movies' invention[3]—displayed a short silent film titled *L'omnibus des toques blancs et noirs* in its original French. The film was retitled as *Off to Bloomingdale Asylum* for American audiences and *Off to Bedlam* for the British. This short begins before the characters enter the asylum. In the span of a minute, the film combines comedy with science fiction, anticipating Méliès's better-known science-fiction fantasy film, *A Trip to the Moon* (1902), which would appear the next year.

In *Off to Bloomingdale Asylum*, white-costumed clowns ride in on a wagon drawn by a skeletal horse, performing acrobatic tricks and transforming back and forth between traditional white-faced circus clowns and ethically objectionable blackface. The figures are waving their arms and stomping their feet, as expected of out-of-control people who are being committed to an institution.

The blackface in the film demands an explanation. Blackface is and was associated with minstrel shows, which are disdained in the United States today. It also fell out of favor in France for different reasons. France's legacy of African colonialism—rather than the association with the slave trade in the Americas—eventually made this imagery taboo there as well. This switch of complexions was probably (and hopefully) intended as an inversion of the clowns' characteristic whiteface, rather than as an endorsement of racism. This transformation was also a way for Méliès the magician to showcase his special effects skills and his "movie magic."

On a less contentious note, *Off to Bloomingdale Asylum* offers a glance at the history of psychiatric institutions. Indeed, the Bloomingdale Insane Asylum enjoys a prominent place in New York City's history.[4] As detailed on the website of the present-day Bloomingdale Neighborhood History Group, the asylum was erected in 1821 in Morningside Heights in the northern reaches of Manhattan, home to Columbia University.[5] Named for its location on Bloomingdale Road, now Broadway Avenue, the facility was opened to serve an increasing number of mentally ill patients who were previously treated in the general medical wards of New York Hospital. In 1829 and 1834, more buildings were added.[6]

Besides providing fodder for Méliès's early film, what other functions did asylums perform? Asylums in general functioned as places of refuge from noxious external influences, whether untoward political forces, religious intolerance, or impending punishment. In this case, asylums offered custodial care for the mentally ill. There, such sick people could escape accusations of demonic possession and need not fear reprisals that followed from this misperception. Psychiatric asylums of the 18th century replaced the decrepit prison-like madhouses of the 17th century, which focused not on cure or care but on containment, which was perhaps accompanied by punishment, whether deserved or not.

Michel Foucault, who was friends with British anti-psychiatrist R.D. Laing, wrote about the reviled madhouses in his socially influential and politically charged (but factually inaccurate) book *Madness and Civilization* (1961). That much-read book was published in French as *Histoire de la folie à l'âge classique* (1961). When an abridged English translation appeared in 1965, Foucault's work reached American audiences. A complete English translation, *History of Madness*, was published in 2006.

In this book, Foucault examines the historical evolution of the concept of madness and the treatment of the mentally ill in Western society. He attributes the dramatic attitudinal shifts to the Age of Reason, with its attendant intolerance of those who "lost their reason," because of madness or anything else. Among other things, Foucault argues that madhouses and penal houses were essentially interchangeable, and so it came as no surprise when he later published *Discipline and Punish* (*Surveiller et Punir*) (1975), which specifically focused on prisons. Twentieth-century sociologist Erving Goffman, who also wrote as the counterculture coalesced, reifies Foucault's observations—but neither Goffman nor anyone else can confirm the existence of the "Ship of Fools," which is mentioned by Foucault. It turns out that this hypothetical "ship" was based on a fantastical painting from 1500, by the Dutch artist Hieronymus Bosch. Bosch's characteristic imaginative artwork in this painting and in many others retain cachet to this day.

Sadly, Foucault's conclusions about the conflation between mental institutions and prisons proved to be prophetic as much as historical, even if his contention about the existence of the "Ship of Fools" is chimerical. Transinstitutionalization often followed deinstitutionalization.

Audience Reactions to Mentions of "Madhouse Movies"

Whenever I mention "madhouse movies," or even the slightly more polite term of "insane asylum cinema," I hear stifled groans emanating from the audience. Listeners start grumbling, sub rosa, because they expect to hear about horror films and little else, except perhaps a fleeting mention of poignant docudramas that chronicle the mistreatment of the mentally ill. Yet such reflexive, all-consuming assumptions are not necessarily accurate—even though we have many examples of unsavory cinematic portrayals of psychiatric institutions and psychiatric practitioners. Most authors—even very impressive ones—who write about such topics emphasize the latter and gloss over examples that contradict this generalization.

For instance, the very title of Troy Rondinone's comprehensive 2019 monograph, *Nightmare Factories*, sums up that sentiment. He describes those fictional "madhouses" (or "funny farms, psychiatric hospitals, mental institutions") as "stark and foreboding … castles of despair and tyranny" [that] "symbolize mistreatment, fear, and imprisonment" [where] "treatments are torture, attendants are thugs, and psychiatrists are despots."[7]

Without denying that negative cinematic characterizations are more common than not, I must stress that positive representations of institutional treatments occasionally appear on screen. Ironically, in some instances where we would expect to find dismal depictions of psychiatric institutions—such as film noir, which typically focuses on dark plots, seedy settings, and subterranean activities—we can find positive messages about potential benefits of psychiatric institutions. (Admittedly, some staff members are not morally admirable, and may even be murderous, as occurs in Hitchcock's *Spellbound* [1945].) History professors Taylor and Harmon elaborate on such thought-provoking paradoxes in their essay on film noir.

Apart from the film noir genre, we find that some films are overly positive and go as far as to romanticize sanitarium life or rest-home cures and thereby invite other unintended adverse aftereffects. Such films set unreachable expectations that rarely if ever exist in real life, either then or now. Films that espouse over-the-top, unmitigated optimism ensure disappointment. There are enough examples of such films to merit an entire essay in this book (by this author) about "Romanticized Renditions vs. Realistic Depictions."

For instance, who could forget the sanitarium in *Now, Voyager* (1942), where Claude Rains plays the kindly psychiatrist who transforms Bette Davis's dowdy and downtrodden Aunt Charlotte into a self-assured woman of the world? (Rains gained even more fame for his equally admirable role as Captain Renault in *Casablanca* [1942], another wartime film that was released in the same year as *Now, Voyager* and deals directly with war-related themes.)

Okay, so it takes Charlotte two tries at the proverbial rest cure, instead of just one. And her story ends tragically, with an unrequited romance, in true tearjerker style, despite her substantial psychological success in the rest home. Charlotte's rest home is far removed from Charlotte Perkins Gilman's horrific, home-based experiences described in her much-discussed short story, "The Yellow Wallpaper" (1892),[8] which became a must-read in early feminist circles.

Now, Voyager is one of those wonderful 1940s "weepies" that were swept aside in the mid–1950s, when televisions appeared in most American homes and when daytime TV melodramas replaced World War II–era staples of the big screen. As we shall see in my essay "Romanticized Renditions vs. Realistic Depictions: The World of "Weepies," this film—as well as Charlotte's (pre–Prince Charming) Cinderella-like home life—has been subject to many divergent interpretations, as should be expected of an 80-year-old film that has survived several generations of spectators.

Theoretically, the women's film/weepie genre could have disappeared once World War II ended, or when the demand for tearjerkers was met by television soap operas a decade later. However, 1940s-era women's films and weepies were themselves reinventions from earlier eras. Weepies first appeared in the silent era, when "emotional acoustics" and histrionic, hyperbolic acting substituted for words and dialogue.

This genre plays on universal emotions, even if those emotions are magnified by external social, political, or economic situations. Dreams of a safe loving home, populated by kind and caring people—even if it is a so-called "rest home" or sanitarium—do not disappear from our imaginations. Similarly, fears of the exact opposite—of nightmarish images of malevolent "haunted houses"—are even more common than halcyon dreams of helpful houses. Madhouses and haunted houses are commonly conflated, at least on the silver screen, where such tropes comprise a separate subgenre.

Fast forward to 1966's *King of Hearts*, a French film with a soldier star (Alan Bates). The action occurs in World War I–era Europe, not in the Vietnamese jungles that were catalyzing campus unrest at the time. Even though *King of Hearts* is not American-made, and the action is not set in the U.S., it nevertheless reflects the rebellious spirit of the American anti-war era and the belief that the reigning authorities are wrong and that the counterculturists, iconoclasts, and insane asylum inmates are correct.

By the time this film hit the arthouse circuit in the U.S., the counterculture was in full bloom and anti-war protests were commonplace. It was all the better that the film illustrated the then-popular but subsequently discredited theories of R.D. Laing, the high-profile British anti-psychiatrist who claimed that the real world itself was insane, and that outside society needed more correcting than the patients who were locked inside the asylum.

In writing about "Countercultural Commentaries: *King of Hearts* and *Cuckoo's Nest*," sociology professor Laura E. Colmenero-Chilberg addresses the importance of *King of Hearts*, where the solider who is dispatched to deactivate a bomb falls in love with a jovial asylum inmate. By the time he arrives, the city is otherwise empty because "saner" citizens have fled for safety as enemy troops advanced. Yet the sanitarium's patients remain in town, playing gleefully.

Rather than condemning asylum life, à la *One Flew Over the Cuckoo's Nest* (1975), another cult film of the counterculture, this film applauds the paradoxical freedom afforded by a locked building that blockades noxious influences from the "real world" outside the asylum. That outspoken youth culture that embraced the ethos of *King of Hearts* was not the first generation to challenge the logic or the ethics of war. The carnage visited by World War I made many question the sanity of sending young soldiers to certain deaths. Important films about mental institutions or insane asylums, including *The Cabinet of Dr. Caligari* (1919), address the painful realities of the war by highlighting a psychiatric sanitarium, headed by a charlatan psychiatrist.

At the insane asylum in *The Cabinet of Dr. Caligari* (1919-20), where patients played by uncredited extras meander in the background, the white-robed Jane (Lil Dagover) is seated on the left, while Dr. Caligari's confederate Cesare (Conrad Veidt), the somnambulist encharged with kidnapping Jane, stands in the front right.

Standing in stark contrast to *Caligari*'s sinister asylum, which is exquisitely rendered in German Expressionist style and which became synonymous with this emerging aesthetic, is the sentimental asylum seen in *Rain Man* (1988). *Rain Man* was the highest grossing film of the year, despite its iconoclastic, groundbreaking storyline.

Tom Cruise stars as Charlie Babbitt, the insolent younger brother of the autistic savant Raymond, whom he remembers only as "Rain Man." Rain Man had been removed from the family home before Charlie was old enough to enunciate his name. Award-winning Dustin Hoffman plays Raymond, the progeny of a troubled family who apparently appreciated his long-term residential facility. His "kidnapping"-cum-road trip, initiated by Charlie, his "neurotypical"—yet neurotic—brother, drives the plot. Charlie hopes to reclaim a relationship with his mysterious older sibling and initially finds it inconceivable that institutional life is preferable to freedom. He dismisses warnings from Raymond's well-meaning and wise psychiatrist.

During their car journey, Charlie realizes that his impaired albeit brilliant brother needs his hospital setting for day-to-day survival far more than he needs his freedom—and surely more than he needs his estranged brother's affection. What a switch from Miloš Forman's *One Flew Over the Cuckoo's Nest*, which altered attitudes and even instigated California's anti–ECT laws, as explained in history professor Timothy W. Kneeland's essay on "ECT on Screen."

In this film still from Martin Scorsese's *Shutter Island* (2010), which begins with a scene of patient-inmates peacefully tilling the soil, Marshal Aule (Mark Ruffalo) stands behind the bald-headed psychiatrist Dr. Cawley (Ben Kingsley) as he speaks to U.S. Marshal Teddy Daniels (Leonardo DiCaprio), before Daniels learns that he is a psychiatric patient in the asylum and is not on the island in a professional capacity.

Comparable films about "old-fashioned funny farms" can carry kinder connotations—even if such motifs are embedded in more menacing settings. One such film, mentioned above, is Martin Scorsese's *Shutter Island* (2010), adapted from Dennis Lehane's 2003 novel of the same name. Much of the action of *Shutter Island* was shot in an actual psychiatric asylum, but Shutter Island itself is an isolated island that seems to be as far away from civilization as the proverbial Devil's Island, where convicted criminals were housed. When someone mentions secret "medical experiments" on the island, many may recollect filmic interpretations of H.G. Wells's 1896 *The Island of Dr. Moreau*, about a vivisectionist who was forced to leave England on account of his horrific scientific studies. John Frankenheimer's *The Island of Dr. Moreau* (1996), which starred Marlon Brando and Val Kilmer; or Don Taylor's film version from 1977; or the novel's first English language adaptation, *The Island of Lost Souls* (1932), come to mind.

As *Shutter Island* opens, unimposing inmates are tilling the soil and tending the garden of the fictional Ashecliffe Hospital for the Criminally Insane on the eponymous island. This name leaves no doubt that this is a film about a forensic psychiatric hospital, and that it is not an "ordinary" institution where patients seek help or escape the demands of the everyday world. As for the crossover between asylum cinema and prison themes, it is noteworthy that some film scholars say that mental hospital movies are a subgenre of prison films, even though both appear early in the silent era.

There is an enduring appeal to films about forensic facilities where inmates are mandated to care as well as incarceration—for several reasons. For one thing, films about forensic psychiatric facilities validate all-too-common fears about coerced incarceration. Because they admit only involuntary inmates, they lock their entries and exits. With their film fetishes, such as large locks, giant keys, iron bars on windows, and strong gates that encircle the institution, they are especially visually interesting on screen.

What's more is that they are truer to fact, given that involuntary incarceration for criminal activity continues to this day, even when managed care has otherwise minimized long psychiatric stays, and even when advocates for the civil rights of psychiatric patients have challenged most involuntary commitments outright and demanded court hearing for protracted stays on psychiatric wards or for administering medications against patients' wills.[9]

In this case, the psychiatrists who populate the superficially sinister *Shutter Island* turn out to be but "pseudo-sinister psychiatrists" who are misperceived by the film's protagonist, deluded U.S. Marshal Teddy Daniels (Leonardo DiCaprio). Daniels has been remanded to treatment on the island but is completely unaware of his status as a prisoner/patient.

In short order, we learn that Daniels is a drinker who hallucinates and who may be experiencing DTs (delirium tremens), or symptoms of alcohol withdrawal. Since we know that he is a World War II vet, we wonder if he is still reeling from the trauma of liberating Dachau, where he saw cadaverous, nearly lifeless concentration camp inmates clutching at barbed wire fences. When we witness the horrific images that he envisions, we attribute them to PTSD flashbacks (which was not yet named as "PTSD" in 1954, when the film was set), but we do not discount the phantasmagorical visions that can follow abrupt cessation of alcohol.

Despite such vivid wartime memories, Teddy cannot recall that he murdered his wife upon learning that she drowned their children. Instead, he believes that he entered Shutter Island to find a patient-prisoner who went missing. In his mind, he is acting in his official capacity as a U.S. Marshal. Neither he nor we are aware that the government agent-cum-"colleague" who accompanies him is his psychiatrist, who hopes to jar Daniel's memory through this unusual ruse.

There are vague allusions to experimental procedures performed at the Shutter Island lighthouse, perpetuating the precedent set by the fictional Dr. Moreau from late 19th-century literature. Alternatively, those hypothetical procedures may reference real-life lobotomies that were performed in the 1950s, when Dr. Walter Jackson Freeman II, a neurologist with no formal surgical training, touted his "miraculous" ice pick cure, which was performed more often in office settings, rather than in hospital wards.

Given that the action is set in 1954, when Dr. Freeman advertised the advantages of this simple yet permanent procedure, audiences who are versed in the history of psychiatry may conclude that this film reflects fact as much as fictional fears. The year 1954 carries other important connotations for psychiatry's history. In that year, chlorpromazine, the first phenothiazine-based antipsychotic medication of its kind, made its way from France to America. In time, under the brand name Thorazine, it would upend the American mental health care system when it freed patients from hallucinations and delusions and obviated the need for long hospital stays.

Regardless of their relationship to reality, Teddy's adventures on Shutter Island intrigue audiences, as he encounters curious characters during his foray there. He frets that one psychiatrist (Max von Sydow) who speaks with Germanic-accented English is a one-time Nazi collaborator. The doctor's appreciation of Viennese waltz music adds to

Teddy's suspicions about the doctor's Austrian roots and sets off flashbacks of Teddy's army days at Dachau.

One might say that the funny farm/forensic hospital setting of *Shutter Island* is reassuring for spectators, because it shows that a seemingly scary institution is merely a figment of an imperfect imagination. This then confirms that reflexive fears of psychiatric asylums are also based on fiction and can therefore be dismissed outright—after viewing this film.

Not all forensic psychiatric hospital settings in cinema are as benign as the one featured in *Shutter Island*. The forensic unit in the phenomenally successful, Academy Award–winning *Silence of the Lambs* features impenetrable glass cages that fail to prevent Hannibal Lecter's assaults on the facility's guards. Yet this hospital pales when compared to Lecter's own bizarre activities. For a more detailed discussion of Hannibal Lecter, sinister psychiatrist extraordinaire, please see my earlier monograph on *Cinema's Sinister Psychiatrists: From Caligari to Hannibal* (2012).

Another less celebrated film about a forensic psychiatric hospital deserves extra attention, if only because the actor who portrays the sinister psychiatrist and hospital administrator in *Batman Begins* (2005) gained even more fame for his Academy Award–winning role in *Oppenheimer* (2023). Cillian Murphy stars as the titular physicist who invented the atom bomb and who became both hero and villain to America. After appearing in *Batman Begins*, Murphy was "reincarnated" as the Birmingham-born Tommy Shelby, a charismatic war hero turned gang leader in BBC's *Peaky Blinders* (2013–2022), which spawned an American cult following when it resurfaced via streaming.

In *Batman Begins*, Cillian Murphy portrays Dr. Jonathan Crane, a peripheral character who is also known as the Scarecrow. Functioning as the asylum head, the villainous Dr. Crane works in an ordinary-appearing psychiatric institution. When alone with his charges, and while wearing a respectable suit and professional-style spectacles, Crane sprays patients with nerve gas and dons a scary mask that induces nightmarish visions in anyone who sees him. When he applies this technique while interviewing a mobster mandated to his mental hospital, the mobster appears to be hallucinating and so "flunks" the sham psychiatric exam.

The contrast between Crane's clandestine activities and the asylum's unspectacular interior makes the movie more unsettling. We see Murphy ascending the stairs in the guise of Dr. Crane or strolling through Arkham's internal corridors. However, Arkham's outside views project a very different sensibility, for the façade of the Arkham Asylum for the Criminally Insane is an archetypal Gothic institution that could double as a haunted house. Other Batman films (and several Batman comics) highlight Gotham's standalone psychiatric hospital.

Although it was late to appear in filmic renditions of the Batman universe, Arkham's permutations have multiplied since my earlier collection, *Welcome to Arkham Asylum: Essays on Psychiatry and the Gotham City Institution* (McFarland, 2019). This collection adds an entirely updated essay on Arkham in cinema, written by George Higham.

Unlike *Shutter Island*'s superficially welcoming Ashecliffe Hospital, Arkham is never inviting. It is a hyperbolic rendition of society's worst fears about psychiatric institutions, complete with high gates and iron bars. The mere fact that Batman is the most popular and most enduring superhero makes Arkham Asylum even more important to

American cultural history. Later films from the *Batman* universe that feature Arkham Asylum include the *Suicide Squad* (2016) series and the blockbuster *Joker* (2019) film and its follow-up.

The institution of Arkham is supposedly named for the fictional city in H.P. Lovecraft's 1929 story, "The Dunwich Horror." However, in the *Batman* comics and in several films based on the comics, we are told that Arkham is named for the Arkham family, which includes several psychiatrists who ostensibly inherited a gene that causes late-onset psychosis. Such genetic flukes do exist in real life (and occur in Edgar Allan Poe's 1839 story, "The Fall of the House of Usher"). While we can speculate about which inheritable neuropsychiatric disorders could conceivably cause such symptoms in middle-aged adults—and there are in fact several contenders—we can be confident that something is very wrong with some Arkham family members, for Dr. Amadeus Arkham, patriarch of the clan, has murdered his own mother.

As a counterpoint to George Higham's essay on "*Arkham Asylum:* From *Batman* Comics to Contemporary Cinema," which focuses exclusively on the DC Comics Universe, Jaq Greenspon writes a separate essay about "Gods and Mutants: Madhouses in Marvel Movies." Here, he shows us a very different side of the spectrum. Before proceeding, it should be noted that these comics-inspired essays about madhouses in movies are in no way funny. They are quite distinct from the humor—sometimes black humor—described by Professor Kristi Rowan Humphreys's essay on "No Laughing Matter: Comedies about Psychiatric Hospitals." There, she adds examples from antiquated (yet appealing) silent cinema and more recent renditions.

Although we can cite more examples of idealized asylums in cinema, we must admit that most movie madhouses are indeed malevolent—for several reasons. For one thing, media advertisers—who collect detailed statistics and demographics—confirm that bad news gets more clicks than good news. This implies that the public savors unsavory depictions of almost anything, and profit-oriented moviemakers pander to the public's sentiment. Adding villains to the plot makes for a more interesting storyline, and it is no accident that high-profile actors often vie for the opportunity to portray lowbrow criminals, such as the Joker.

Occasionally, social crusaders and yellow journalists join hands with filmmakers who mine exploitative or sensationalistic subject matter. Sometimes reformers owe their success to contemporaneous films depicting the same topics that they address in more serious venues. A notable example is *The Snake Pit* (1948), starring Olivia de Havilland, which reified accusations made by journalist Sidney Deutsch, as we shall see below.

The Snake Pit premiered two years after the equally historic film *Bedlam* (1946), which is a topic tackled by Bryan Senn in his essay, "The Historical Horrors of Val Lewton's *Bedlam*." Perhaps the fame of *The Snake Pit* played off the precedent set by this memorable horror film, which stars Boris Karloff. Karloff's name is synonymous with horror to this day, although Karloff himself objected to characterizing *Bedlam* as horror and insisted that it was historical, to acknowledge its roots in historical fact, as opposed to an invention of an author's overly active imagination. The film's name remains recognizable, not just because of the film or the enduring fame of its star, or even the subject matter, but because the word "bedlam" entered our lexicon and refers to a state of disarray or loss of control. Bedlam is short for "St. Mary's of Bethlehem." The real "Bedlam" was England's first mental hospital; the original building is still in Beckenham, Kent.

The Snake Pit helped to change psychiatric history because it catalyzed legal reforms.

Director Anatole Litvak based it on a semi-autobiographical memoir-cum-novel of the same name, written by Mary Jane Ward and published as a novel in 1947. In *The Snake Pit*, Olivia de Havilland plays as an unfortunate young woman who is unable to recall how she arrived in an overcrowded, understaffed mental hospital. Yet she retains vivid memories of shock therapy, hypnotherapy, and hallucinations endured while incarcerated in "Juniper Hill State Hospital." The fictional Juniper Hill represents the real-life Rockland State Hospital, which stands to this day, due north of NYC, just a quick car ride away from Manhattan's towering skyscrapers.

De Havilland's character, Virginia Cunningham, fondly recollects her pipe-smoking psychiatrist, who "helps" her return to her "normal" role in life: as a wife, rather than as a writer. Although this transformation was normative by 1948 standards, feminist critics later deconstructed the perceived "cure," whereby Cunningham dismisses her dreams of succeeding as a writer and accepts her role as homemaker and wife of her husband, a role that was more socially acceptable and even expected in post–World War II America.

An essay by history professors W. Harrison Taylor and David Andrew Harmon tells us much more about this film and about the film noir genre overall in "Film Noir: Dark Dramas about Insane Asylums." *Snake Pit*'s plot is revealed via flashbacks, as was typical of psychoanalytically inspired films of the late 1940s and of film noir. The protagonist's recollections result from "narco-synthesis," or the use of sleep-inducing drugs to unlock repressed secrets that, according to Freudian (or Jungian) lore, promised insights into conflicts that supposedly caused psychological distress. Narco-synthesis themes were common in late 1940s films. An offshoot of this technique is the "amytal interview," also called "truth serum," but it is rarely used in contemporary psychiatry.

The Snake Pit won many accolades, including an Academy Award for Best Sound Recording. It was nominated for Best Actress in a Leading Role (Olivia de Havilland), Best Director, Best Music, Best Scoring of a Dramatic or Comedy Picture, Best Picture, and Best Adapted Screenplay. When it won the International Prize at the Venice Film Festival in 1949, it was identified as "a daring inquiry in a clinical case dramatically performed." Despite his many supporters, Anatole Litvak did not win an Oscar of his own for this film.

Some say that Litvak's own encounters with two different totalitarian governments sensitized him to the totalitarianism of mental asylums. Litvak was a Russian-born Jew who left Communist-controlled Russia after the government nationalized its theaters and took control of film production, among other things. In the 1920s, he escaped to Germany, which he subsequently fled in the 1930s, shortly before the Nazis took power and before they had a chance to implement the stringent restrictive Nuremberg Laws, which laid the groundwork for the Holocaust. Had he remained, his livelihood, as well as his very life, would have been at risk.

The emotional impact of *The Snake Pit* was amplified by Albert Deutsch's book, *The Shame of the States*, published by Harcourt Brace while *The Snake Pit* was still in production. A remarkably erudite autodidact, Deutsch was the medicine and social welfare columnist of the *New York Star*. While Deutsch's book was not as gripping as Ward's firsthand memoir, his publication received attention from magazines and journals, thanks to his well-established media connections. Reviews of Deutsch's book amped up that attention.

Anti-psychiatry activists, sometimes speaking on now defunct Madness Network

News radio shows, would become more vocal two decades later, as detailed by Ashley Barry in her essay on "Mad Studies Perspectives on Madhouse Movies." Those passionate activists would rail against psychiatrists who acted as "agents of the state," who deprived patients of their agency and elevated the status of the psychiatrist at the expense of the patient. In contrast to the latter-day social activists chronicled by Barry, Deutsch did not impute bad hospital conditions to the psychiatrists who practiced in those hospitals. In fact, his opinion was the polar opposite. Deutsch advocated for expanding the role of psychiatrists in state hospitals and for adding more psychiatrists to the inpatient wards of those institutions. He attributed these unacceptable hospital practices to the system's inefficiencies and the lack of adequate hospital staff. He claimed that state hospitals did not hire enough psychiatrists, along with trained nurses and other professionals. According to Deutsch, America needed more psychiatrists—not fewer.

Deutsch showed how patients were warehoused in state hospitals that could be compared to the fictional Juniper Hill. Deutsch wrote in first person, stating that "I was reminded of the pictures of the Nazi concentration camps at [Bergen] Belsen and Buchenwald.... I entered buildings swarming with naked humans herded like cattle and treated with less concern.... I saw hundreds of patients living under leaking roofs, surrounded by moldy, decaying walls, and sprawling on rotting floors for want of seats or benches."[10] His words were as dramatic as the Litvak's movie, which premiered after the publication of the book. A seasoned journalist, Deutsch dramatized visual imagery with words, in much the same way that Litvak dramatized concepts on celluloid. The comparison of state hospitals to concentration camps was especially hard-hitting at a time when the public was just learning about the horrors of the Holocaust.

Deutsch was not content to impugn his home state of New York alone, which housed Juniper Hill/Rockland State Hospital. He argued that no state met the American Psychiatric Association's minimum spending recommendation of $5/day per patient for treatment, food, and housing. The national average in 1948 hovered at $1.25/day. Deutsch attributed psychiatric patients' low recovery rates to such insufficient funding, which in turn led to inadequately trained ancillary staff and delayed the hiring of fully trained psychiatrists.

It was *The Snake Pit*'s cinematic depiction of conditions in mental hospitals that directly prompted reforms of conditions that Deutsch had railed against. In response to *The Snake Pit*, 26 states passed legislation demanding upgrades in state hospital procedures. Once again, a picture says a thousand words, and a moving picture says exponentially more.

Fifteen years later, we encounter Hall Bartlett's film, *The Caretakers* (1963). *The Caretakers* is arguably equally relevant to the history of psychiatry (even if it is not as well-remembered) as *The Snake Pit*, for this film was released when seismic shifts in psychiatric care settings were set in motion by JFK's Community Mental Health Act bill, signed in that same year. Set in an overcrowded hospital ward, this film stars Robert Stack as a reform-minded psychiatrist who promotes more humane treatments over the "old school" restraints and shock therapy favored by Joan Crawford's oppositional head nurse. Stack had recently won an Emmy for his portrayal of "G-Man" Elliot Ness in television's *The Untouchables* (1959–1963). Crawford's role as head nurse Lucretia Terry does not push as many buttons as Louise Fletcher's Nurse Ratched in *One Flew Over the Cuckoo's Nest*, but there is a continuum between these hostile head nurses.

A Banner Year

The year 1963 apparently was a good year for riveting psychiatric film themes. *Shock Corridor* (1963) chronicles the activities of a newspaper reporter who enters an institution with the intent to solve a murder committed there. Aided by a friendly psychiatrist and the reporter's girlfriend, who pretends to be his sister, he feigns insanity and is hospitalized. Soon enough, he realizes that the murderer is none other than a hospital orderly. By then, the reporter has been "made" by the orderly, who then torments him to induce his mental collapse. The orderly nearly kills the reporter and overdoses him with drugs that turn him catatonic. At that point, his sham "sister" sees his deterioration and so she signs a consent for ECT. Devastated, the reporter remains in the hospital, taking little solace in his success at identifying the murderer he sought.[11] The message is straightforward: psychiatric treatments, and the hospitals that offer such treatments, and members of their staff, may be more harmful than helpful.

We encounter a similar plot a year later in *Shock Treatment* (1964), in which Lauren Bacall plays an evil psychiatrist and hospital administrator. She torments an undercover actor (Stuart Whitman) who entered the mental hospital in search of a million dollars that went missing there.

Crawford is better remembered for her more glamorous roles, yet her rendition of mental instability in *Possessed* (1947) earned her an Academy Award nomination for Best Actress. This film was released a year before *The Snake Pit* sent cinematic shock waves in 1948. In *Possessed*, Crawford's distraught character wanders the streets in search of a lost lover who does not reciprocate her affection. She eventually collapses into a near-catatonic state. An ambulance arrives and delivers her to the emergency room, and she is whisked away to the hospital's "Psychopathic Department," where the doors are locked and the windows barred.

Joan Crawford resurfaces once again, a year after *The Caretakers* opened in 1963, in a psychological horror film, *Strait-Jacket* (1964), produced by William Castle, horror maestro supreme. He based the film on a screenplay by Robert Bloch, one-time protégé of H.P. Lovecraft, and author of the novel *Psycho*, on which Hitchcock's 1959 film of the same name was based.

The action in *Strait-Jacket* begins after the protagonist is released from a psychiatric hospital. She had been confined there for the last two decades, having axe-murdered her husband and his lover. She had been discharged under the belief that she was cured of whatever ailment induced her to resort to murder, but she is now suspected of committing a new series of axe murders. This psychological thriller revolves around forensic psychiatric questions that linger to this day and is a prime example of films that begin after escape or (in this case) release from the asylum. It also anticipates the premise of John Carpenter's history-making *Halloween* franchise.

The Joan Crawford films mentioned above are significant to film fans and to film history, but it is John F. Kennedy's Community Mental Health Act of 1963—signed in the same year that *The Caretakers* was released and that Kennedy died—that has monumental implications for the history of mental health care. Some say that *The Caretakers* is a fictionalized exploration of the same hospital-related problems and growing philosophical conflicts that Kennedy hoped to solve with the CMHA. Kennedy's bill aimed to shift patients into community-based resources, and to steer them away from large and often isolated institutional settings.

Kennedy's motivations behind this bill were not necessarily politically motivated, for he was the brother of a young woman who had been rendered nonfunctional by a lobotomy performed many years earlier. In response, JFK was apparently propelled to improve conditions for other mentally ill people. His concern for society's underdogs was consistent with the ethos of the times, for this was the dawn of the civil rights era, when efforts were made to ensure equal access to education and housing opportunities. In hindsight his deinstitutionalization program was overly optimistic, underfunded, and probably doomed to failure from the get-go. It did not consider the willingness of families to welcome lost relatives, or their abilities to subsidize another soul. Those of us who see homeless encampments of mentally ill people in metro areas are well aware of the sad aftermath of those deinstitutionalization initiatives.

Because Kennedy's tragic assassination occurred less than a month after he signed his last bill into law on October 31, 1963, the public may be less familiar with this initiative. That overarching event eclipsed the significance of this landmark legislation. Perhaps *The Caretakers*' cinematic significance was also diluted by the larger-than-life drama that unfolded in Dallas of the same year. The film faded into relative oblivion, at least when compared to *The Snake Pit*'s high-profile depiction of state hospitals.

Another film which might have made a major impact on mental health care reform, had it been available for public viewing, is discussed in Professor Ashley Barry's "*Titicut Follies:* What Was and What Could Have Been." As "Mad Studies" professor Barry explains, this disturbing 1967 black-and-white documentary about a forensic state facility was pulled from distribution and banned for 20 years. The law professor-turned-filmmaker who produced it was brought up on legal charges. After a series of court battles, the State of Massachusetts agreed to allow the film's airing to professional audiences for didactic purposes only. In her essay, Barry uses *Titicut Follies* as a touchstone for tracing the evolution of the anti-psychiatry, critical psychiatry, and ex-patient movements, which surfaced both before and after *Titicut Follies*' premiere.

Reasons for the Public's Intrigue with Mental Hospital Movies

There are many reasons why movies such as *The Snake Pit*—and others like it—impacted the public's imagination so strongly. To this day, "madhouse movies" attract audiences—even when the likelihood of being admitted to a psychiatric ward is minuscule compared to 1955, the year when more Americans were hospitalized than ever before or since. In fact, many hospitals, even some with long histories and close community ties, have closed their psychiatric wards because their beds went unfilled.[12]

While psychiatric hospitalization—much less involuntary admission—is unlikely, a strikingly high percentage of Americans seek psychiatric treatment in office or clinic settings. Many more take psychotropic medications, which are more often prescribed by primary care physicians than by psychiatrists. With the rapid expansion of telepsychiatry during the COVID pandemic, more Americans have been able to access mental health care. Fully half of all Americans enter therapy at one point of their lives or another. Even the British, with their stiff-upper-lip ethos, seek psychotropic meds.

According to 2019 statistics from the National Institute of Mental Health (NIMH), approximately one in five American adults lives with some form of mental illness—

and those numbers were compiled before the pandemic started, after which pandemic-related social isolation, along with realistic fears of contagion and bereavement reactions in response to lost loved ones (or even casual acquaintances), set psychiatric symptoms skyrocketing. As of April 2022, an American Psychiatric Association news bulletin confirmed that half of all Americans cited current concerns with their mental health (partly predicated upon the pandemic). Post-pandemic, a significant percentage of people who contracted COVID continue to suffer from protracted neuropsychiatric complaints. For lack of a better term, this syndrome is commonly called "long COVID." As of July 16, 2024, long COVID is said to affect at least 7 percent of those who contracted COVID, regardless of the intensity of their original illness. The estimates for enigmatic post–COVID syndrome are regularly increasing and may possibly impact as many as a third of those who contracted it.[13] Even more recent data links "long COVID" to a profound uptick in dementia diagnoses that are made not necessarily immediately, but within the five years that follow infection.

The Snake Pit *(1949) Compared to* Frances *(1982)*

We can compare the theme of *The Snake Pit* to the biographical film *Frances* (1982), which chronicles the downward trajectory of once promising but obviously troubled actress Frances Farmer, whose alcohol use disorder and amphetamine abuse were apparently overlooked by her hospital-based treatment team. The psychiatric sequelae of her substance use led to lengthy treatments in psychiatric facilities. Perhaps her symptoms were compounded by preexisting personality issues and family stressors. Literature professor Eric J. Sterling devotes an essay to her sad story: "*Frances:* Memoir Movies (and Made-Up Madhouse Memories)."

This *Frances* film should not be confused with Arthur Lubin's comedic black-and-white *Francis* from 1950, a film based on stories by David Stern. That *Francis* revolves around an American military officer who is hospitalized when he insists that an army mule named Francis speaks to him. Importantly, Professor Sterling's essay, as well as *Frances*, reminds us that even the rich and famous can fall victim to psychiatric abuse and neglect, though current concerns in psychiatry largely revolve around substandard treatment of underprivileged poorer people and more marginalized people, and especially people of color.

At this point, it is worth mentioning that women who manifest out-of-control or threatening behavior are more likely to be remanded to psychiatric treatment, whereas men who show similar behavior are more likely to be arrested and their behavior criminalized. Men of color who display inappropriate or aggressive behavior are at even greater risk of being confronted by the police and jailed (or worse) than white men, even if they have prior psychiatric diagnoses that might otherwise merit automatic transfer to treatment facilities.

Timing Is Everything: Dr. Caligari and the Aftermath of World War

Sometimes the timing of such themes is critical to the film's impact on the public. *The Cabinet of Dr. Caligari* (1920) is a case in point. Even though it is an artistic masterpiece, and is often considered to be one of the most important movies of the 20th century, its trope about mental hospitals and sinister psychiatrists was especially salient in the aftermath of World War I. The charlatan psychiatrist of *The Cabinet of Dr. Caligari* is more than mere fiction; Dr. Caligari is a stand-in for the much-hated Austrian military psychiatrists who forced fearful soldier-patients to return to the front without showing any sympathy for underlying psychological suffering that propelled supposedly fictitious symptoms.

Those doctors administered painful aversive (but not therapeutic) "Kaufmannization" shock treatments, intended to goad patients into "giving up" their supposedly "hysterical" deficits of deafness or paralysis. With few exceptions, such as future psychoanalyst Ernest Simmel, those unempathic military psychiatrists did not consider the contribution of unconscious distress that translated into medical manifestations.[14]

While *Caligari*'s sinister charlatan psychiatrist remains well-remembered by the film world, there is another prominent German Expressionist psychiatrist, or psychoanalyst to be more exact, who is arguably better remembered by Europeans. Fritz Lang's Dr. Mabuse faced incarceration in an inpatient psychiatric ward in Lang's second sound film, *The Testament of Dr. Mabuse* (1933). One of several films about this criminal mastermind and self-described psychoanalyst who is believed to represent Freud, or perhaps the hypnotist Svengali, or possibly Jewish psychoanalysts in general, *Testament* was in postproduction when Hitler came to power. This prophetic movie carries political connotations that extend far beyond its chronological link to Hitler's ascendence.[15] More information about the *Dr. Mabuse* franchise can be found in two McFarland books: David Kalat's *The Strange Case of Dr. Mabuse* (2005) and Sharon Packer's *Cinema's Sinister Psychiatrists: From Caligari to Hannibal* (2012).

There is yet another rarely discussed but increasingly important reason to fear incarceration in psychiatric institutions. Alzheimer's disease—or any other form of dementia—is a less common motif for movies, although some films, such as *Still Alice* (2014)[16] or *Rise of the Planet of the Apes* (2011),[17] have given us glimpses of the future that awaits a substantial number of people as they age. Television shows are more likely to tackle this thorny topic. Some fantasy films focus on sudden increases in intelligence—an unlikely event except in SF stories—but realistic renditions of the dreaded dementia apparently do not attract audiences, as discussed in my earlier book *Neuroscience in Science Fiction Films* (McFarland, 2014).

More Reasons for Concern with Mental Illness–Related Movies

Fear of loss of cognitive capacity looms large as our population ages. (At age 85, half of all people show some degree of dementia.) This impending epidemic induces intense trepidation. The average person's concerns revolve around memory loss, rather than behavioral or perceptual changes that often accompany dementia and are prevalent enough to merit their own acronym: BPSD or "behavioral or psychiatric symptoms of dementia." Some types—such as Lewy body dementia (LBD)—are more likely to be accompanied by psychotic symptoms or hallucinations and sometimes begin with such symptoms. Robin Williams's struggles with the disorder heightened public awareness of LBD.

Whatever the etiology or the neuropathology, the fact remains that the most common catalyst for placement in supervised settings outside the family home is behavioral outbursts or aggression. Like the title character in *Still Alice*, the individual has no agency and loses control or capacity to make major life decisions, which include custodial placement. Sometimes behavioral disinhibition requires admission to psychiatric wards where trained staff are more readily available than in nursing homes. If that is not cause for concern, then what is?

Involuntary commitment is uncommon in today's America, and psychiatric hospitals, as well as psychiatric wards in general, have dwindled over time as the demand for those institutions has diminished. Cost concerns are often blamed for these shifts, but advances in treatment techniques and changes in societal values also contributed to their closings. The preference for the "least restrictive settings" means that outpatient day programs are favored over in-hospital overnight stays, whenever safe and available. To ensure that even exploitative films about psychiatric asylums contain some semblance of credibility, themes pertaining to "cinematic insane asylums" have shifted in response to these real-life shifts in care settings.

As mentioned above, films about forensic psychiatric hospitals persist because those facilities still exist. Plus, highly publicized (albeit sensationalized) reports about "serial killers" or so-called "psycho killers" lead people to believe that such unhinged perpetrators are much more prevalent than they are. As proof of their persistent popular appeal, note that some very successful television shows, such as *Dexter* (2006–2013), which portray fictionalized serial killers (and charming ones at that), persist for many seasons and spawn many spin-offs, whereas other "true crime" shows, such as the two-season *Mindhunter* (2017), are based on actual events, albeit extremely rare ones. These shows pander to the public's intrigue with such rarities and play on the American intrigue with "true crime"–inspired entertainment and podcasts overall, as documented by a Pew Research study from 2023.[18]

Yet films about forensic institutions that restrain potentially dangerous patients offer solace to fearful audience members who react to media hype about mental illness and mass shootings. How else to explain the phenomenal success of *Halloween* franchise films about Michael Myers and his escape from his institution? Those movies afford opportunities for "dress rehearsals" about ways to react, should spectators encounter a Michael Myers–kind of character in their own backyard. Relief awaits the audience after the movie concludes, when viewers see that they are safe in their theater seats or on their sofas. Media professor, horror film scholar, and sound editor Jeffrey Bullins elaborates on these issues in his essay, "John Carpenter's Career: From *Halloween* to Lovecraft."

Abandoned Asylums, Shuttered State Hospitals, and the Supernatural

Apart from the forensic hospital trope, three other subgenres of "madhouse movies" deserve mention: the theme of the abandoned asylum recurs (which is completely credible, considering how many state hospitals have closed). The psychiatric asylum-cum-haunted house, where supernatural activities occur, seems to enjoy a timeless appeal. Sometimes these two above-mentioned memes overlap, and supernatural activities can occur in abandoned asylums, or even in otherwise secure forensic facilities, as is the case with both *Gothika* (2003) and the 1999 remake of *House on Haunted Hill*, which was based on William Castle's original 1959 version, which starred Vincent Price. The updated *House on Haunted Hill* is set in a ghost-infested abandoned asylum—for the "criminally insane," no less—in contrast to Castle's film, which occurs in a mansion owned by an eccentric millionaire, back in the days when millionaires—rather than billionaires—represented the pinnacle of wealth.

Another ploy makes such movies even more plausible: movies about mental institutions can be set in the distant past, such as Clint Eastwood's *The Changeling* (2008), which we discuss in greater detail below. Even much older films, such as *Where Is My Child?* (1937), have been backdated to 1911, thereby assuring spectators from the late '30s Roosevelt Depression that immigrant life is much improved compared to the early 20th century, when the film's action occurs. More on this tactic is available in my essay, "*Where Is My Child?*: A Weird Welcome to America."

Conflating psychosis with the supernatural, in relation to the madhouse-cum-haunted house or otherwise, deserves special attention, and so George Higham's essay on "*Dracula*: The Supernatural in the Asylum" examines this time-honored theme. Some cultural subgroups in contemporary American society continue to attribute psychosis to spirit possession—and in some regions of the world, this explanation is more the norm than the exception—but the average American does not openly endorse such beliefs and is more likely to attribute mental disorders to neurotransmitters, and possibly adverse social circumstances, although parental abuse was the most popular culprit in the heyday of psychoanalysis. Nevertheless, enough self-described nonbelievers patronize movies with such plots to make them worth producing.

There is ample historical precedent to link psychiatry with the supernatural to make this theme credible and to encourage audiences to suspend disbelief while the film rolls. It was not so long ago when doctors of the church, rather than doctors of medicine (or "doctors of the soul," as psychiatrists were sometimes called), were responsible for explaining—even exorcising—mental maladies or neurological disorders such as seizures.

Appeasing the spirits when behavior is affected is not unique to non–Western cultures, as evidenced by the enduring popularity of the classic Yiddish folklore about the dybbuk. *The Dybbuk, or Between Two Worlds* premiered as a 1920 play by S. An-sky. The play was subsequently made into several film versions and has been adapted for opera, puppetry, and television. The best-known example of the crossover between psychiatry and the occult occurs in the movie made from William Peter Blatty's novel, *The Exorcist* (1973), which was produced by Blatty himself. *The Exorcist* is often listed as the most remembered—or sometimes as the scariest—film of all time. With a psychiatrist-priest as a pivotal character, *The Exorcist* dramatizes the long-standing link between psychiatry and the supernatural—with the latter winning out in the end. It is worth noting that none of the action in either *The Exorcist*, *The Dybbuk* (1937), *The Vow* (1937) (a later rendition of *The Dybbuk*), or Sydney Lumet's 1960 made-for-TV version of *The Dybbuk* takes place in a psychiatric asylum, confirming that this time-tested theme need not occur within the confines of an institution. A cemetery, or a marriage *chuppah* (canopy), works just as well when it comes to dybbuks.

Keeping pace with trends in deinstitutionalization, some newer mental hospital movies blend supernatural elements with standard asylum settings. *In Dreams* (1999) shows the dagger-wielding psychiatric nurse (played by Robert Downey, Jr., in drag) as she enters the dreams of disturbed patients and traipses between the real world into the netherworld. *Gothika* (2003) adds a supernatural touch to this sensationalized blaxploitation film, where Halle Berry stars in a role that that won her a Teen Choice Award (2004) for Choice Movie Actress in Drama/Action Adventure. She was also nominated for Outstanding Actress by Black Reel Awards, Outstanding Actress in a Motion Picture by NAACP Image Awards, and Outstanding Actress in a Motion Picture and for Best Female Performance by MTV Movie Awards. The film itself was nominated for Best Horror/Thriller at the Golden Trailer Awards (2004), despite bad reviews from critics. Berry plays a psychiatrist who believes that she is visited by ghosts but is diagnosed as psychotic because her colleagues—apart from a psychiatrist played by Robert Downey, Jr.—refuse to believe that the so-called ghost carves messages on her arms. They are convinced that her cuts are self-inflicted. As the film ends, Dr. Miranda Grey's sadistic psychiatrist husband is revealed to be the clandestine culprit who is more fiendish than the ghouls who haunt his wife.

To expand the appeal of madhouse movies beyond the supernatural thriller and horror crowd, Hollywood moviemakers turned to the abandoned asylum motif, another tried-and-true technique that was a win-win even before the advent of managed care and the transfer of most psychiatric treatment to outpatient settings. For instance, video games that revolve around abandoned asylums—such as *Silent Hill*—inspired a 1999 film adaptation by the same name. The remake of *House on Haunted Hill* (1999) appeared in the same year. In that updated rendition of the 1959 original, the action occurs in a long abandoned (and haunted) asylum—the Vannacutt Psychiatric Institute for the Criminally Insane. Vannacutt is overrun by ghosts of tortured patients who died in a fire they set in 1931, when they revolted against the sadistic psychiatrist who incarcerated them.

Session 9 (2001) is one more turn-of-the-millennium thriller that takes place in an abandoned mental hospital, as historian of medicine Brenda S. Gardenour Walter tells us in her aptly titled essay, "*Session 9*: Danvers State Hospital is the Star of the Show." In this film, a cleaning crew encounters unexpected challenges as they remove asbestos. That film was set and shot at the actual Danvers State Hospital in rural Danvers, Massachusetts. The hospital is believed to have inspired some H.P. Lovecraft stories, which in turn inspired Arkham Asylum in the Batman world. The role of the supernatural in *Session 9* itself is ambiguous and allows the spectator to speculate about the strange goings-on in the hospital.

Managed Care and Mental Hospital Movies

It is worth exploring the realistic reasons for the uptick in "abandoned asylum" films around the turn of the millennium, even if those reasons had little relationship to the millennium (which has been blamed for whole host of film themes that emphasize doom and gloom, confusion, and catastrophe). These contributors are linked to the economic and political climate, which in turn prompted major administrative and policy changes—one might say upheavals—that had been put in motion well before the 20th century ended. Half a century had already elapsed since the JFK's "deinstitutionalization" movement began as an earnest—albeit failed—effort to free patients from coercive or crowded conditions at state hospitals.

Both patients and practitioners demonize financially motivated managed care, which may have dealt the final blow to asylums, sanitariums, rest homes, or "retreats, but which did not start the process. Those wheels had been turning for decades before the much-maligned MCOs (managed care organizations) arrived in the early 1990s and became the standard of health care delivery by the end of the decade. Psychiatric care was not singled out for belt-tightening, although the lengthy and expensive and questionably effective psychoanalytic treatments were targeted, as were protracted stays for substance use disorders. Still, psychiatric institutions felt the squeeze more than many medical fields because psychiatrists care for a disproportionately high number of chronic patients, many of whom remain in custodial care, or asylums.[19]

In retrospect, some cynics suspect that the original deinstitutionalization movement itself was also financially motivated; that it was not exclusively ideologically driven, and surely not as altruistic as typically portrayed. More detailed studies are needed to confirm or refute such claims. Managed care, in contrast, was based on monetary motivations from the start, leaving no ambiguity about its purpose. As a result of these administrative shifts, some seriously ill people were deprived of needed hospital care, even if they were previously deprived of personal agency and possibly also stripped of their civil rights, as claimed by anti-psychiatry activists and others. However, it should be noted that encouraging independence among those who can use that independence constructively can confer great clinical advantages over fostering dependency on "the system" and the co-optation of free will and decision-making authority.

Erving Goffman's *Asylums: Essays on the Social Situation of Mental Patients and Other Inmates* (1961), alluded to earlier, masterfully explains the impact of long-term custodial treatments. The mere fact that he equates patients' detention in state hospitals with inmates' detention in prisons makes a profound statement. Seasoned psychiatrists who treated patients who transitioned from state hospitals to less restrictive community hospitals also commented on the lamentable conditions of such patients and winced at the deference they displayed toward hospital staff, which was acquired during protracted state hospital stays.[20]

To maintain credibility in the face of these sea changes in psychiatric treatment, and to ensure that spectators could reliably "suspend disbelief" long enough to enter "movie mode," more and more moviemakers set madhouse movies in the past, when risks of involuntary incarceration without recourse to the court system were more real. In response to these shifts, several 21st-century films about sinister asylums (and the sinister psychiatrists who staff them) are backdated, even if it appears that the film's action is taking place in the present. But that technique is not entirely contemporary, as *Where Is My Child?* from 1937 proves.

An ideal example is *Changeling* (2008), directed by Clint Eastwood and starring Angelina Jolie and John Malkovich. As mentioned, this film shows how an unscrupulous psychiatrist bows to the demands of politicos who want to discredit Jolie's character, Christine. The psychiatrist is an unimportant player in the plot, even though he locks Christine away in a mental ward, demands that she sign false statements, looks away as aids hose her down, and supposedly subjects her to ECT (electroconvulsive therapy), which was not available when the action occurs. The film is set in 1928 and continues into the mid–1930s. Jolie's costume shows that Christine exists in the flapper era, even though details about psychiatric treatments do not conform to historical fact. Inspired by a real-life case, the movie eventually ends well when John Malkovich, in his

Moses-like preacher role, demands that the Pharaoh-like hospital head "let his people go." With this plea, he frees Christine from her incarceration.

As we watch *Changeling*, we may remember Jolie's related role in *Girl, Interrupted* (1999), another backdated film that chronicles events that occurred in the 1960s, over 30 years before the movie's release. The sorority-like atmosphere of the pricey halfway house of *Girl, Interrupted* was already a rarity in 1999 and became even rarer over time. Facilities like that have historically been reserved for the wealthy, who can pay out-of-pocket, without approval of third-party payers that typically refuse to reimburse lengthy "luxury" stays. Similar institutions have closed in real life, including the one seen in *I Never Promised You a Rose Garden* (1977), as will be discussed in "Romanticized Renditions vs. Realistic Depictions."

Other films fit this bill equally well. *The Jacket* (2005), starring Kris Kristofferson as a drugged-out doctor, and with Adrien Brody as the hapless Gulf War veteran who finds himself first in a time warp and then in a morgue-like box in a state hospital basement, may be the most disturbing film of the lot. In this film, orderlies are more abusive than the indifferent psychiatrist who presumably approves Brody's drug studies, solitary confinement, and straitjackets.

Perhaps the most memorable sanitarium or rest home (one which is worlds away from the hideous institution in *The Jacket*) is Green Manors in Alfred Hitchcock's *Spellbound* (1945). This opulent institution treats its patients well, offering them regular sessions with staff, along with lovely living quarters attended by maids, waitresses, butlers, and doormen. Unfortunately, "upper management" does not treat its professional staff well at all. As the film concludes, the aging hospital head pulls a gun on psychiatrist Dr. Constance Petersen (Ingrid Bergman) after she accuses him of murdering a missing doctor. Surprisingly, she turns around and walks away. He then turns his gun away from Dr. Petersen and points it at his own head. We never see him pull the trigger, but we hear shots fired. This scene is much more dramatic because the action takes place in such an elegant sanitarium. This is the first film that employs psychoanalysis to drive the plot. *Spellbound* is one of the lesser-known Hitchcock films, but is a prime example of film noir, as discussed by history professors Taylor and Harmon in their essay.

I would be remiss to omit an old and time-honored trope: "when the inmates take over the asylum," which is the premise behind *Caligari*, and which peppers later film plots as well. That trope did not begin with the movies, which themselves officially began only as the 19th century was ending. Edgar Allan Poe deserves credit for introducing this plot-driving device via his story "The System of Doctor Tarr and Professor Fether" (1845), written before the Civil War shook the foundations of American society. The underlying conflicts that led to this war prodded the country to question the legitimacy of the "existing order." Many historians saw parallels between the rigid roles in antebellum America and the traditional hierarchy in the insane asylum, as Poe described, but almost anything that turns the existing order upside down can produce a compelling drama or a funny farce. Professor Humphreys's essay covers comedic representations of madhouses in movies, but this specific story was never intended to be funny or farcical.

Writing in 1845, two decades before America's Civil War ended, Poe begins by telling us, "During the autumn of 18—, while on a tour through the extreme southern provinces of France, my route led me within a few miles of a certain Maison de Sante or private mad-house, about which I had heard much in Paris, from my medical friends."

Given that Poe's story is set in France, it should not surprise us to learn that a

French production company turned Poe's short story into a silent short. Éclair's *Le système du docteur Goudron [Tarr] et du professeur Plume [Feather]* from 1913 is fairly true to Poe's original, although the film was adapted from Parisian Grand Guignol's more gruesome version. The French film was later renamed *The Lunatics*, making the title more memorable and easier to pronounce but more politically incorrect for contemporary sensibilities. Interestingly, the director of this silent short was Maurice Tourneur, the father of Jacques Tourneur, creator of *Cat People*, a cult classic about a deceptive and seductive psychiatrist. The elder Tourneur's own film resume was impressive, even if the fame of the son eclipsed that of his father. In 1915, Maurice Tourneur directed *Trilby*, a film about the evil hypnotist Svengali who begs comparison with Freud—but Tourneur senior is better remembered for a later movie, *The Last of the Mohicans* (1920), than for his earlier psychiatric themes.

Even before Éclair's French production company interpreted the Poe story, Edison's *Lunatics in Power* (1909) added a farcical touch to this theme. J. Searle Dawley, whose one-reel *Frankenstein* (1910) is more celebrated than this little film, directed *Lunatics in Power*. Although Robert Wiene's *Cabinet of Dr. Caligari* is typically (incorrectly) credited for launching the "inmates take over the asylum" theme, the 1913 French film modeled after Poe's short story was first, with Edison's one-reel comedy as the runner-up.

Lunatics in Power appeared one year after Clifford Beers published his autobiographical account about *A Mind That Found Itself* (1907). Beers's book launched the mental hospital reform movement, also known as the "mental hygiene movement." Beers himself probably suffered from manic depression (bipolar disorder), rather than schizophrenia, for the former condition could fuel the seemingly endless energy deployed in his campaign against the abuses and indignities inflicted on mental patients, whereas the latter diagnosis is characterized by a decline in mental acuity. Comedies such as those mentioned above, which dissed dreaded asylum directors, likely fortified Beers's accusations.

Why We Worry So Much About Psychiatric Symptoms

Yet there is still more to the story—much more. Psychiatric symptoms differ from ordinary physical symptoms that send patients to medical doctors. They are easier to misinterpret and may be evident to trained professionals only. Most of the time, a prospective medical patient feels dizzy or notices a rash or experiences an ache or a pain or a strain and so is aware that something is amiss before he or she schedules an appointment with the doctor. They have subjective experiences—and sometimes also objective "signs"—that something is not right. Admittedly, some cancer or cardiology diagnoses arise out of nowhere, without any prelude, appearing incidentally in imaging studies, and perhaps that is one more reason why those diseases are so scary, apart from any life-threatening implications.

With a medical diagnosis, suspicions can be confirmed with objective findings. One need not rely on mere conjecture or perception on the part of the professional, as occurs in psychiatric diagnoses. The radiologist can point to a lesion on the lung, or the gastroenterologist can forward laboratory tests listing abnormal liver functions, or the dermatologist can read pathology reports about skin biopsies. Such concrete data leaves little ambiguity that something is amiss (even if there is often variability in how pathologists or radiologists interpret the same slides or scans).

In contrast, in the case of psychiatric diagnosis, objective findings are rarely available. Most currently available objective tests are not clinically useful or are too cumbersome or expensive for everyday use. (Some brain imaging studies and quantified "mental status exams" may support certain neuropsychiatric diagnoses, but those are exceptions rather than the rule.) It becomes one person's word against another's, and the opinion of the professional almost invariably trumps the excuses of the patient, making it all too easy to be railroaded, or gaslighted, or scammed. How scary that is. Films about gaslighting exist for good reason.

No wonder so many people seek out madhouse movies, not necessarily for entertainment, but possibly also as a "dress rehearsal" should the need for admission to a psychiatric facility arise. Yet madhouse movies' appeal—and importance—extends beyond clinical issues or diagnostic debates. Broader philosophical concerns are at play, concerns that revolve around the role of the state in the life of the individual, or the priority accorded the individual over society (or vice versa). Debates about when the state has the right—or the obligation—to intervene in an individual's life, and to curtail his or her freedom by forcing incarceration in a hospital or by mandating psychotropic medications over objections, are unending. Some say that answers to these life questions lie at the cornerstone of a free society.

When viewing these films, we are forced to question the functions of the hospital, both implicit and explicit. Does it perform a police function or a clinical function or a little bit of both? And what are the qualifications of the individuals delegated to decide if someone deserves to be stripped of their personal freedom and mandated to enter a physical space that is not of his or her choosing? Moreover, if people deemed to possess certain psychiatric symptoms can be coerced into a psychiatric asylum, or subjected to potentially harmful or at least unpleasant treatments within that institution, how soon will "ordinary citizens" be stripped of their personal freedoms and confined within other institutions? We know that the Soviets sent political dissidents to mental hospitals, which discredited objectionable ideas de facto. That amounted to much more than a disinformation campaign. Years later, the People's Republic of China mandated psychiatric hospitalization for members of the religious movement Falun Gong. Other examples of politically motivated institutionalization exist. Even in pre–Civil War America, enslaved Black people who escaped bondage were diagnosed with "drapetomania," implying that a desire for freedom signified psychopathology.

Hospitalization in psychiatric institutions co-opts personal freedom. It robs individuals of the right to move about as they choose. It compromises personal dignity, since it often forces individuals to forfeit their wardrobe and replace their own clothes with institution-issued garments, as occurs in prisons. It pigeonholes patients into a mental hospital hierarchy, where their personal value and their individual desires are pushed to the bottom of that hierarchy and are governed by hospital administrators or treating physicians or nurses or even orderlies.

A more extreme example arose in Nazi Germany, when mental patients, "incurable alcoholics," people with same-sex preferences, and others who were deemed to live lives that were "not worth living" were exterminated through Operation T-4. Psychiatrists determined which institutionalized patients should live and which should die; sometimes the psychiatrists themselves carried out these killing mandates. After that heinous policy ended in response to protests by clergy, the same killing machines and gas chambers were reappropriated for the genocide of the Jewish people, the Roma (Gypsy) people, and Seventh-day Adventists (who opposed Hitler). History tells us that the boundaries between government-sanctioned mass murder of mental patients and the mass murder of entire "races" or nations or peoples is porous, and that such boundaries can be breached under the right circumstances.

What appears to be a simple hour or two of entertainment on the surface may carry many centuries' worth of debates about individual rights, or about a given government's obligations, and related political and philosophical ramifications that extend far beyond the psychiatric symptoms of any single patient. Equally importantly, each madhouse movie implicitly comments on the behaviors or perceptions that a given society deems sane versus insane at a particular point in time. We know that some societies—and even some centuries—have venerated the very same behaviors that can instigate involuntary commitment to mental institutions, via a Baker Act in Florida or a 2-PC in New York state, or with whatever acronym applies in other states. The Surrealists who emerged in the wake of World War I, the 18th-century Romantic era artists and writers who followed in Goya's footsteps, and the 1960s counterculture all esteemed psychosis and aspired to "go crazy." Those movements, whether they were artistic, cultural, or political, emulated the antics of people whose perceptions are not governed by reason and rationalism, either by choice or by chance.

In short, some people whom we label psychotic in our contemporary American society could have been saints, prophets, or seers at different places and times. As an example, the biblical prophets whose words are sanctified by many in the Western world—and who perceived the presence of the divine and claimed to have heard otherworldly communications—would be dismissed as schizophrenic by today's standards. So, each movie about madhouses is a portal to social anthropology as much as a commentary on clinical psychiatric care. Sometimes, this conflation lies at the crux of the plot. Distinguishing between sanity and insanity (which are legal rather than medical terms) is even more fluid, partly because doctors of law—rather than doctors of medicine or doctors of psychology—construct those definitions.

Films such as *One Flew Over the Cuckoo's Nest* and *The Jacket* show what happens when weak-willed or drugged-out psychiatrists allow the Nurse Ratcheds of the world—or ordinary orderlies—to take charge and pour their frustrations onto powerless patients. Perhaps the most enduring trope of all is the role reversal, when the inmates take over the asylum and turn the world topsy-turvy. Madhouses offer unbridled opportunities for diabolical drugging, romantic seduction or forcible rape scenes, confinement via straitjackets, even morgue-like lock boxes (as happened in *The Jacket*). Yet the rubric of madhouses includes romanticized sanitariums headed by handsome and suave—yet caring and competent—doctors played by the likes of Claude Rains or fictionalized accounts based on idealized portraits of real-life doctors as depicted in *I Never Promised You a Rose Garden*, the film or the memoir.

Movies can change attitudes toward science and sociology far more quickly and intensely than pure text. For instance, Miloš Forman's film, *One Flew Over the Cuckoo's Nest*, revolutionized the public's—and even professionals'—attitudes toward ECT (shock therapy). In response, the state of California outlawed ECT altogether, at least temporarily. Ken Kesey's 1962 book of the same name, which inspired the film did not incite such incendiary responses from readers, even though his book became a bestseller and had already been parlayed into a successful Broadway play before the film debuted. *Cuckoo's Nest* (the film) became a cult classic. The former Oregan State Hospital, where it was filmed, is essentially a shrine, having been converted into the Museum of Mental Health.[21]

Admittedly, social media venues such as Facebook and TikTok and X stand accused of galvanizing public opinion, and of spreading misinformation about mental illness to vulnerable segments of the population (especially to adolescents), to the point that in 2024 the surgeon general of the United States called for a warning label on social media platforms. Australia is currently contemplating more extreme measures.[22] Yet the so-called silver screen (and the small screen, and definitely the streaming screen, which makes so many movies more available and more affordable) continues to capture attention and influence the masses and sway opinion.

In the essays that follow, we will explore many topics that revolve around madhouse movies, or "insane asylum cinema"—but bear in mind that terms that appear polite at a certain point in time are often viewed as grossly impolite in other eras. And so, our use of the word "madhouse" is not intended to disparage, only to describe, and to mirror the terminology of many respected sociologists and historians.

These essays represent the views of artists, filmmakers, and scholars from a wide variety of fields. They have been divided into categories—Comics and Comedies; Cult Classics; Darkest Depictions; Incarceration, Voluntary vs. Involuntary; Politics and Polemics; and Supernatural Asylums. In our closing section, "Before and After the Asylum," we will remind readers that the story of the asylum does not necessarily end after the outer doors close (or open), and that the real action of some films may be situated outside of the asylum.

For the sake of full disclosure, essays that undermine the value of the individual—whether sane or psychotic—have not been included, because it is our intention to show respect to the people who populated these asylums or institutions, regardless of how the institutions are shown in cinema.

Notes

1. Introduction Andrew T. Scull's well-received sociological and historical books, such as *Madhouse: A Tragic Tale of Megalomania and Modern Medicine* (Yale University Press, 2005); *Madness in Civilization: A Cultural History of Insanity* (Princeton University Press, 2015); and *Madhouses, Mad-Doctors, and Madmen: The Social History of Psychiatry in the Victorian Era* (University of Pennsylvania Press, 1981) also use this well-recognized word. Historian of medicine Roy Porter likewise employs this same term in some of his many books, including *The Anatomy of Madness: Essays in the History of Psychiatry*, Vol. 3; *The Asylum and Its Psychiatry*, edited by W.F. Bynum, Roy Porter, and Michael Shepherd (Routledge, 1988); *Madmen: A Social History of Madhouses, Mad-Doctors and Lunatics: Revealing History* (Tempus, 2006); *Madness: A Brief History* (2002); *A Social History of Madness: The World through the Eyes of the Insane* (Weidenfeld and Nicolson, 1988). Mike Jay writes about "madness" in his books *This Way Madness Lies: The Asylum and Beyond* (Thames & Hudson, 2016) and *A Visionary Madness: The Case of James Tilly Matthews and the Influencing Machine* (North Atlantic Books, 2014). Sander L. Gilman alternates his terminology, as in *Seeing the Insane: A Visual and Cultural History of Our Attitudes Toward the Mentally Ill* (Echo Point Books and Media LLC, 2014) and *Disease and Representation: Images of Illness from Madness to AIDS* (Cornell University Press, 1988), whereas Canadian historian of medicine Edward Shorter entitles his treatise *A History of Psychiatry: From the Era of the Asylum to the Age of Prozac* (Wiley, 1997). Many more excellent examples by historians of psychiatry are listed in the bibliography.
2. Ilvy Njiokiktjien, "The Belgian town where families take in people with psychiatric conditions," *The Guardian*, May 10, 2024.
3. The Lumiere Brothers and Edwin S. Porter also merit mention in early film history.
4. *Off to Bloomingdale Asylum*'s original French title is *L'omnibus des Toqués Blancs et Noirs*, which

translates to "the omnibus of white and black 'crazies.'" In the short film, the performers switch back and forth between blackface characters and white clowns.

5. "The Bloomingdale Insane Asylum," Bloomingdale History, January 10, 2016, https://bloomingdalehistory.com/2016/01/10/the-bloomingdale-insane-asylum/.

6. Scull, ed., *Madhouses, Mad-Doctors, and Madmen*; Benjamin Reiss, *Theaters of Madness: Insane Asylums and Nineteenth-Century American Culture* (University of Chicago Press, 2008); Gerald N. Grob, *Mental Institutions in America, Social Policy to 1875* (Routledge, 2008); Constance M. McGovern, *Masters of Madness: Social Origins of the American Psychiatric Profession* (University of Vermont Press, 1985); and Walid Fakhoury and Stefan Priebe, "Deinstitutionalization and Reinstitutionalization: Major Changes in the Provision of Mental Healthcare," *Psychiatry* 6, no. 8 (August 2007): 313–316.

7. Troy Rondinone, *Nightmare Factories* (Johns Hopkins University Press, 2019).

8. Charlotte Perkins Gilman, "The Yellow Wallpaper," *The New England Magazine*, January 1892.

9. At the time of this writing, American Psychiatric Association's Council on Addiction Psychiatry is considering publishing recommendations for involuntary commitment for unremitting substance use disorders, and New York State's governor is weighing the merits of legislation that will expand privileges for psychiatric commitment, to allow nurse practitioners and possibly clinical social workers to "commit" potential patients to involuntary confinement, rather than restricting such assessments and decisions exclusively to psychiatric physicians.

10. Albert Deutsch, *The Shame of the States* (Harcourt Brace, 1948).

11. Samuel Fuller, *Shock Corridor* (Allied Artists, 1963).

12. Sharon Packer, "Beth Israel's Nathan Perlman Place and its Place in History," *Psychiatric Times*, July 30, 2024, https://www.psychiatrictimes.com/view/beth-israel-s-nathan-perlman-place-and-its-placein-history.

13. Liyad Al-Aly and Clifford J. Rosen, "Long Covid and Impaired Cognition—More Evidence and More Work to Do," *New England Journal of Medicine* 390, no. 9 (February 29, 2024).

14. Sharon Packer, *Cinema's Sinister Psychiatrists* (McFarland, 2012).

15. Jay Hoberman, "An Evil Doctor Who Casts a Spell on Subjects and Viewers Alike," *New York Times*, May 6, 2020, https://www.nytimes.com/2020/05/06/movies/drmabuse-the-gambler.html.

16. Sharon Packer, *Still Alice* film review (*Psychiatric Times* 32, no. 4, April 23, 2015).

17. Sharon Packer, *Neuroscience in Science Fiction Films* (McFarland, 2014).

18. Sarah Naseer, "True crime podcasts are popular in the U.S., particularly among women and those with less formal education," Pew Research Center, June 20, 2023.

19. Personal communication from Mel Thrash, M.D., Medical Director of Magellan Health, NYC.

20. The late Ralph O'Connell, M.D., former clinical director of psychiatry at St. Vincent's Hospital in Greenwich Village, was quick to comment on the servility seen among former state hospital patients.

21. Kirk Johnson, "Once a '*Cuckoo's Nest*,' Now a Museum," *New York Times*, March 31, 2013.

22. Vivek H. Murthy, "Surgeon General: Why I'm Calling for a Warning Label on Social Media Platforms," *New York Times*, June 17, 2024.

SECTION I

Comics and Comedies

1

Gods and Mutants

Madhouses in Marvel Movies

JAQ GREENSPON

At the beginning of the 1972 film *The Ruling Class* (1972), the character of Jack, the 14th Earl of Gurney, is quite mad, thinking himself to be the personification of Jesus Christ. His actions bear out the idea, as he is nothing but kind and benevolent, with feelings of love for all. Then, due to the machinations of his relatives, he is "cured" of his insanity by being converted into a cold-blooded killer, a manifestation of Jack the Ripper. At the end of the film, it is this persona who is in control, a manipulative murderer who happily takes his rightful place in the welcoming House of Lords.

This film is not unique in this concept. There are plenty of jokes that use this concept as a premise—if the second coming were to happen, the messiah would be locked up, since there is no way he could really be who he claims to be. For example, in *Man Facing Southeast* (1986) and the similar *K-Pax* (2001), characters are institutionalized for having the audacity to believe they are from another planet. In other words, they are delusional, and regardless of the fact that they are shown as harmless, they are locked up "for their own good." What is more, in both films, the ambiguity of the endings leaves the viewers to at least entertain the notion that the characters were telling the truth: that they were indeed from other planets.

It is not just aliens who get this treatment. In *Miracle on 34th Street*, both the 1947 and 1994 versions, Kris Kringle, who claims to be the true Santa Claus, resides in a home for the mentally ill. He is there despite never being diagnosed with any type of mental illness and regardless of displaying magical powers, albeit in such a way as to have them not draw attention to themselves. No, Kringle is institutionalized merely because of his belief in an identity the rest of the world deems too fantastic to be real.[1]

And then there are superheroes. For some reason, in worlds which have verified aliens, gods, and fantasy figures, it is with alarming frequency that these selfsame characters find themselves locked up in asylums for claiming to be something that has been proven to exist within the context of the stories being told. So where is the line?

DC Comics, for example, has not one but two different places for their superpowered criminals to be locked away, over and above the idea of a regular prison. Both Arkham Asylum and Belle Reve[2] keep villains away from their respective heroes for a period of time, without ever really locking them up. They are deemed criminally insane and therefore can redeem themselves by getting rid of the delusion that they possess powers or come from another planet or realm, despite the reality that these things exist as part of the world-building inherent in the field.[3]

Marvel, on the other hand, has taken a slightly different approach. Instead of treating their superpowered criminals as insane, they lock them into highly secure facilities like the Raft or the Vault or Seagate (or Ryker's Island, if one lacks sufficient or, more likely, any superpowers) and save the asylums for the heroes whose loyalty is in question and who need a bit more in the way of control. In this way, the idea of mental instability leads not to crime, but to disobedience. The comic universe, particularly under the Marvel banner,[4] understands that crime happens, that criminals are to be punished, but ultimately, their actions are not only explainable, but understandable. However, heroes who do not conform to the ideals of the system within which they operate are considered "crazy" and need to be rehabilitated until they fall in line with societal norms.

Two recent examples illustrate how comic book movies have taken the idea of madhouses from two different directions, yet created situations with strikingly similar results. In Marvel's *Moon Knight* series (2022), nearly half of the production takes place, ostensibly, within the walls of an unnamed asylum, while the film *The New Mutants* (2020) spends almost the entirety of its 90-minute run time within the Milbury Hospital facility.

The New Mutants is based on a graphic novel of the same name, created by Chris Claremont and Bob McLeod, originally released in 1982. The book featured five younger mutants, initially designed to be a new class of students at Professor Xavier's School for Gifted Children, long the home of the original X-Men. Within the world of the comics, the X-Men, who were created by Stan Lee and Jack Kirby in 1963, were mutants, people with some sort of extra ability,[5] designed to be stand-in representations for any marginalized group.[6] Over time, the initial group, and those mutants who joined later, had aged out of the school motif and so Claremont and McLeod were tasked with creating a new set of teenage mutants to become students of the school. Of the five presented in that initial outing, four made the transition to the big screen, with the fifth, Illyana Rasputin, having been on the periphery of the original X-Men,[7] joining the New Mutants officially with issue #14 of the original run of the comic. Illyana possesses the power to create metal armor and a sword when fighting, as well as the ability to transport into a dimension known as Limbo. The remaining four members of the group are Rahne Sinclair, a shapeshifter who can become a wolf; Roberto da Costa, who can channel the power of a sun; Sam Guthrie, who can project himself like a cannonball; and Dani Moonstar, who can psychically discover a person's deepest fears and manifest them into reality.

It is mostly through Dani's point of view that we experience the film. She is the outsider among a group of outsiders, brought to Milbury Hospital after an opening sequence in which she sees her father die, killed by an unseen monster. She wakes up strapped to a hospital bed and is immediately told she is in a "facility for people like you." The speaker is Dr. Cecilia Reyes, administrator of the hospital and, as will be shown, the only person in the facility other than the young mutants themselves. She demands complete obedience from her charges, ostensibly to help them. In fact, at the first group meeting, where the rest of the group are introduced to Dani and Dr. Reyes's authority is questioned, Reyes explains, "I'd like all of you to think very carefully about how you'd like to use your time here." She immediately uses her position and authority within the hospital to place the onus of release on the patients themselves, implying they are being held until they see things the way Reyes wants them to be seen. She solidifies this point by intoning that "the program can't help you if you refuse to participate." However, she never explains what the program is. At best, Reyes implies that the program is a kind of purgatory, a way station toward a future with Charles Xavier as a member of the X-Men, but never actually says so explicitly. Reyes always speaks in vague generalities and leaves herself open to plausible deniability. This is the first indication that things may not be what the viewer is being led to believe.

Things are made abundantly clear soon enough, when Illyana is tasked with the job of showing Dani around the place. This begins with Illyana stopping before the locked front door and yelling up at the sky for Reyes to disengage the locks. The feeling of total control Reyes has here feels almost godlike in its totality.

As the pair step outside, the exterior of the facility is revealed as something more of a rundown country estate rather than a typical hospital. In fact, the only time the name of the hospital is revealed is in this sequence, like a scratched and faded painting on the arch above the doorway. This leads to understanding the decay which will be revealed within. During the tour, which lasts all of the 15 steps it takes to exit the building and walk to the central courtyard, Illyana casually points out the dorms and a chapel, "If you believe in that shit." It seems as if the location itself is trying to be an idyllic setting, but the ultimate impression, despite the blue skies and sunshine, is one of subjugation and depression. In the front courtyard stands a sculpture of an angel, wings spread, in the middle of a dry fountain. The metaphor of dry and ineffectual spiritual context is obvious.

Dani looks around and sees no walls. She questions the apparent lack of restraint and Illyana explains that Reyes has told them all "the nearest town is twenty miles away, but she could be lying. To keep us from trying to escape." And when Dani, who is a member of the Cheyenne Tribe and used to wide open spaces, tries to make a run for it, she is stopped by an invisible force field. It is this appearance of freedom dangled before her which sets Dani off, sending her into a suicidal spiral, which is the first seed in the eventual destruction of the facility and Reyes herself.

Dani climbs the clock tower of the church building to get a better view of her surroundings; then, when she realizes there is no escape, she decides jumping to her death is her best option. Suicide is a means of escape. Ironically, she is saved by Rahne, who tells her, "It's going to get better, I promise." This rhetoric hits on two levels. The first is that this is a promise Rahne cannot possibly keep. It is an empty platitude designed to create a temporary respite for the sufferer. The second is that the rhetoric echoes that of the LGBT movement.

It is this second level which begins to illuminate the facility these teenagers find themselves in. This is a place where people who are different from the rest of society are sent to be "cured" of some defect they are born with. Once Rahne gets Dani back down to ground level, she literally spells it out for the new inmate. She explains that Roberto, who comes from a wealthy Brazilian family, was sent here, by his parents, to be cured. He is an embarrassment to them the way he is. Furthermore, Rahne, among all the teens, seems to understand her predicament the best, telling Dani she will "get out of here. Probably before the rest of us cuckoos." Rahne self-identifies as mentally ill.

As for Dani getting out, that is entirely up to Reyes. Within the facility, her word is law. She is always a presence, even when she's not physically present. There are points when she leaves the kids to have a group therapy session on their own, which builds a bonding sense of camaraderie; however, even though the kids think she is not there, she is watching through hidden cameras from a high-tech control room. She says, "It's crucial I know you can be trusted," but at no point does she reciprocate this trust. When the kids question how they know they are better, Reyes tells them, "You're better when I say so." There are no guidelines or benchmarks to be reached. In effect, the kids are "better" when they no longer have independent thought.

Not an easy task to accomplish, though. These five teens are in a state of flux, trying to understand their identities as both mutants and people while Reyes seeks to control both. From her perch in the control room, Reyes watches them surreptitiously, allowing them just enough rope to find things to use as leverage. Thankfully, the facility has the requisite horror trope rooms: the swimming pool illuminated solely by the underwater light and the rec room, which, in this case, shows nothing but *Buffy the Vampire Slayer* on the TV. In fact, Rahne is watching the episode "The Body"[8] where Willow and Tara share a lesbian kiss. This foreshadows Rahne's future relationship with Dani, as well as driving home the metaphor of mutants as marginalized people who need to be controlled.

Because there is no one in the building besides the five kids and their warden, it does not take long before Illyana spikes Reyes's evening drink, leaving the inmates free to run the asylum. It is at this point that the true nature of the kids takes over, as if Reyes is the personification of the building (as has been noted, she is the only adult present), and when she is asleep, subconscious desires are free to reign. Without conscious, active control, four of the five inmates begin to express their sexuality, here used as a metaphor for transitioning into adulthood as well as the wanton proclivity often seen at that time.

Illyana takes Roberto to the swimming pool, where she taunts him into losing control, exposing both his raw power and his need for a guiding hand in learning to control his impulses. At the same time, Rahne literally helps Dani to come out by showing her a secret means of escaping from the building, one not controlled by Reyes. Physically leaving the building allows for a release of inhibitions and the reveal of their true identities, both sexually and physically. Rahne leads Dani to the graveyard on the grounds, where they lie down and look up at the red force field of the sky. Dani acknowledges the unrealness of the situation, expressing to Rahne the fear that "sometimes it feels like I made you up." The two share an intimate moment, a first for both, before their powers take over. As if their sexual awakening leads to an uncontrolled moment of release, Rahne begins to transform into her wolf persona,[9] while Dani, letting her guard down, sends psychic bolts across the grounds, forcing each of the kids to face their worst fears.

With this awakening, however, comes the return of external control in the form of Reyes and the asylum itself. At this point we learn that Reyes is working for an unseen superior and is ordered to terminate Dani. The line separating Reyes and the hospital blurs until it seems that they share a singular identity, that of enforcer for the status quo. The institution, through Reyes, is not there to help, but to control. Reyes even states that her actions are not her own idea, but that she is simply following orders. The hospital exists merely to stamp out any trace of uniqueness and individuality found within its charges.

It is finally Roberto who puts words to the central theme when he says, "This place is designed to keep us inside. All our powers won't work. It's hopeless."[10] As with any form of imprisonment, the removal of hope is the final step to total control.

However, in this case, it backfires. The idea that those who are being subjugated will meekly accept their predicament or, at the very least, will become docile once they are shown resistance is one that many authoritarians rely on. Indeed, for Reyes and the Milbury Hospital, this was working well until Dani arrived and allowed her fellow inmates to face and conquer their greatest fears, thereby making Reyes's threats impotent. In the end, it is the inmates, using their combined abilities, without the prerequisite fear of authority, who walk freely away from their imprisonment, ostensibly having "cured" themselves by understanding their power is manifest in precisely what the hospital was trying to destroy.

This is contrasted by what happens to Marc Spector, Moon Knight, at the Sienkiewicz[11] Psychiatric Hospital in *Moon Knight* (2022). In this case, the idea of the institution is just that, an idea. In *The New Mutants*, even if the hospital is used as an extended metaphor, there is never any doubt about the veracity of the location and the inhabitants' place within it. The same cannot be said for Marc Spector.

Since Spector, an American soldier of fortune, is only one of three different personalities inhabiting this particular body (the others being Steven Grant, a mild Englishman who works in the gift shop outside the Egyptian exhibits at the British Museum, and Jake Lockley, a Hispanic cab driver with questionable morals and a violent streak), it can reasonably be stated that he deserves to have his mental state questioned. Even so, despite recurrent fugue states as he slips between personalities with no memory overlap, he doesn't actually enter the asylum until near the end of the fourth episode, when he is shot in the chest at point-blank range by the show's antagonist, Arthur Harrow, a leader of a cultlike group that worships the Egyptian goddess Ammit. This is the second time when death paradoxically brings more life to the character. The first time was when he was revived to be the "fist of Khonshu," i.e., the material plane avatar of the Egyptian moon god, tasked with meting out justice for the wronged of the world.

In this second instance, though, Spector wakes up as Grant in an asylum that looks like an all-white, antiseptic version of a fast-food restaurant. The only color in the place comes in the form of the desserts being handed out by the orderlies. Here, everything is slightly askew. An inmate calling bingo insistently calls out numbers which do not exist on a normal bingo board, and *Wizard of Oz*–like, everything Steven sees is a touchstone to something seen previously in the show, including a Moon Knight action figure. The impression given is that everything that has gone before is merely a reflection of the present. "What's past is prologue," as Shakespeare said.[12] Even Steven himself is in the deception, seeing Marc in his reflection. Ostensibly, this is a breakthrough. In fact, his doctor, with the face of Harrow, explains to Grant/Spector and to the viewer, "I know you're having a great deal of difficulty being able to differentiate between what's real and what's in your head," and later, "your mind is violently vacillating between sense and nonsense." But it is Harrow himself who is keeping Spector psychically off balance.

In reality, or as close as this production ever comes to reality, Spector is being gaslighted. He is constantly asked to forgo the evidence of his own eyes and told he is crazy. Harrow continues the victim-blaming seen in *The New Mutants* when he tells Spector, "Remember, you're only sedated because of your own behavior." That "remember" is important, since it is one of the things Spector cannot do. Therefore, it makes sense that Spector will blame himself for the trouble he is in. Harrow further complicates matters when he repeatedly puts the onus of recovery on Spector by spitting such platitudes as "All I'm asking of you is an honest assessment of your situation" and "I can't help you if you don't help yourself." This becomes Harrow the doctor's primary modus operandi. Naturally, it is in the best interest of Harrow.

Like Reyes and, it seems, in the MCU, the asylum, and by extension the psychiatrist, is set up as the villain. In both cases, it is within the walls of the hospital where the characters, while fighting back against the help being offered, find the help they need.

Things come to a head for Spector when he starts to question the reality of the asylum itself. He is told, "You're doing everything and anything possible not to look within." And yet, that is almost entirely what he is doing. He is manifesting his other self until the two meet and can confront the obstacles ahead of them together. Because of this, Marc is easily able to postulate that Harrow is "not really a doctor" and yet Spector is still bound by the socially accepted conventions of what is real and what is not. When he sees the Egyptian god of birth and fertility, a talking hippopotamus called Taweret, Spector's initial reaction is disbelief. Obviously, if this is not real, then maybe he is "crazy" after all, and Harrow, when he says, "The struggling mind will often build places to seek shelter for different aspects of the self," is right.

Ultimately, the hospital becomes a portal to the past, with each door of a long corridor opening onto various memories, some long hidden, and the two personalities, Spector and Grant, fighting over what should be remembered and what should be left hidden. Like *The New Mutants*, *Moon Knight* veers off into areas of identity. How one defines themselves matters just as much, if not more so, than how society defines us. The question, in this case, is "who is the real person?" Did Spector create Grant or did Grant create Spector? In Peter Coogan's *Superhero: The Secret Origin of a Genre*, the author talks about the need for a superhero to have an identity separate from their everyday life.[13] With Moon Knight, not only is there a secret identity, but there are in fact two. But since the man has died, twice, is the superpowered figure the true identity while the human form is just a hiding place?

Two of the most popular superheroes deal with this same issue. With Batman, there is a theory which states the costumed persona is the real one, while billionaire Bruce Wayne is merely a means to an end. Conversely, Clark Kent is the self-identified real person, while Superman serves a specific purpose.

The same is true in both stories being looked at here. The mutant kids are dealing with a psychiatrist who is trying to control their powers and thereby their identities, while Spector is trying to stop his other personalities from discovering the veracity of their own origin. At one point, when Grant is trying to open a specific door, Spector stops him, asking, "You want to remember the truth?"

This is the crux of the matter. The heroes in the Marvel universe must constantly reassess what passes for reality. In both stories, they grapple with questions about perceptions of reality, as compared to "actual" reality. In other words, reality is what you believe it is, and the kids in *The New Mutants* eventually understand that they are enough exactly as they are. They embody the "it gets better" rhetoric of the LGBT movement, knowing it will get better as long as they themselves decide it.

For Spector, it is even more visceral. After the traditional big battle against the primary antagonist, Spector can leave the dreamscape he has repeatedly been put into merely by thinking himself out of it. Harrow tells him that the "imagination is a powerful thing," without comprehending that it is precisely this advice that allows Spector to prove his sanity, to himself if nothing else, and to be free from all his alternative identities.

In both cases, the heroes have come out on the other side as stronger, more capable characters who are willing to play the game and appear normal and obedient—even if, deep down, they know better.

Notes

1. F.A. Fenning, "Voluntary Submission to Treatment and Custody in Hospitals for the Insane," *JAMA* LVIII, no. 15 (1912): 1104–1107, doi:10.1001/jama.1912.04260040120005.
2. Sharon Packer and Daniel R. Fredrick, eds., *Welcome to Arkham Asylum: Essays on Psychiatry and the Gotham City Institution* (McFarland, 2020).
3. J. Goodwin and I. Tajjudin, "'What Do You Think I Am? Crazy?': The Joker and Stigmatizing Representations of Mental Ill-Health," *Journal of Popular Culture* 49 (2016): 385–402, https://doiorg.ezproxy.vdu.lt:2443/10.1111/jpcu.12402.
4. While the Marvel Cinematic Universe is produced under the Marvel Productions banner, a number of characters had previously been licensed out to other studios to make filmed entertainment. The source material, however, all comes from the same publisher.
5. Stan Lee, *Son of Origins of Marvel Comics* (Simon and Schuster, 1975).
6. P. Andrew Miller, "Mutants, Metaphor, and Marginalism: What X-Actly Do the X-Men Stand For?" *Journal of the Fantastic in the Arts* 13, no. 3 (2003): 282–90, http://www.jstor.org/stable/43308614.
7. Her brother is Piotr Rasputin, *Colossus* from the New X-Men, and she was first seen in *Giant Size X-Men #1*.
8. *Buffy the Vampire Slayer*, season 5, episode 16, "The Body," written by Joss Whedon, Rebecca Kirshner, and Steven S. DeKnight, directed by Joss Whedon.
9. Meg-John Barker, "Plural selves, queer, and comics," *Journal of Graphic Novels and Comics* 11, no. 4 (2020): 463–474, DOI: 10.1080/21504857.2020.1774403.
10. I.N. Korner, "Hope as a method of coping," *Journal of Consulting and Clinical Psychology* 34, no. 2 (1970): 134–139, https://doi.org/10.1037/h0029004.
11. Bill Sienkiewicz was the main artist on the original Moon Knight comic run. Even though he did not create the character, he was instrumental in its popularity. He was also an early illustrator on the New Mutants comic series.
12. William Shakespeare, *The Tempest*, Act 2, Scene I.
13. Peter Coogan, *Superhero: The Secret Origin of a Genre* (MonkeyBrain Books, 2006).

2

Arkham Asylum

From Batman *Comics to Contemporary Cinema*

George Higham

Arkham Asylum is what it needs to be.

Sometimes a joke, sometimes an institution of mind-bending horror, Arkham Asylum continues to grow in popularity throughout the Batman intellectual property (IP) since its first comic book appearance in 1974. A fitting base for many of Batman's psychiatrist-villains,[1] the madhouse exists as an easily versatile structure ready to serve the narrative at hand. As a revolving-door asylum for the criminally insane, it allows apprehended villains to constantly reappear to commit more murder and mayhem, forcing Batman to once again battle and capture them.

The *Batman* films were slow to adapt Arkham to the big screen, but since the 1990s, the inclusion of Arkham Asylum in other Batman IPs such as cartoons, television, and perhaps most importantly video games has become central to not only Batman stories but to other successful DC comic book films as well. Interestingly these movies often showcase the DC villains, such as the *Suicide Squad* movies (2016, 2021) and the blockbuster Joker-centric *Joker* (2019) and its sequel, *Joker: Folie à Deux* (2024).

This essay traces the rise of the infamous madhouse, focusing on the big-screen appearances of Arkham Asylum and the influence of other *Batman* media which made it possible.

Asylum, Home for the Criminally Insane, State Hospital—call it what you will, Arkham Asylum is a malleable location appearing throughout all media of the Batman mythos.

Geographically, the institution may be situated within Gotham City, on the outskirts of the city, in a tower, on an island, or even within Wayne Manor itself. Founded by Amadeus Arkham in the 1920s, the asylum has been destroyed, rebuilt, and redesigned numerous times—most often at the whim of DC Comics, the long-running publisher of the *Batman* comic books.

Even though the Batman character has been around since his 1939 premiere in *Detective Comics* #27, it was not until 1974 that Arkham first appeared in the *Batman* comics. Among the writers tasked by DC Comics in the early 1970s to bring Batman back from the campy pop-culture phenomenon of the 1960s was Dennis O'Neil, who tapped into his appreciation of H.P. Lovecraft's weird tales to subtly infuse some darkness into the tales of the Dark Knight. The most obvious, and everlasting, element was introducing the name of "Arkham" into the Batman universe. For Lovecraft, Arkham

Arkham Asylum, sometimes called "Arkham Hospital" or "Arkham State Hospital," appears in several film adaptations about the *Batman* universe but is most prominent in *Joker* (2019), which gained fame for its cinematography but was denounced by some for its unsavory depiction of persons with psychosis, such as the eponymous Joker.

was the fictional New England town which was home to his darkly strange tales. Arkham had a university and, yes, an asylum bearing the name of the town.

O'Neil introduced Arkham without a backstory. It would be 15 years before the secret origin of the place was revealed. For O'Neil's purposes, Arkham was the "Arkham State Hospital," where Batman's iconic villain Two-Face was imprisoned. Exemplifying multiple personality disorders, Harvey Dent and his evil alter ego was most definitely mad, and having him confined to a mental institution was a no-brainer. Serving as little more than a backdrop location from which he escapes, Arkham already exhibited the key characteristic that would haunt all future renditions of the madhouse—the easily defeated security protocols, which inevitably enabled the proclivity of recidivism among those held there.

Arkham slowly built its reputation over the years until taking center stage in the highly acclaimed graphic novel *Arkham Asylum: A Serious House on Serious Earth* (1989). In the *Batman* comics, the "State Hospital" had become an "Asylum," routinely housing the large number of Batman's colorful foes deemed too insane for incarceration at the local Blackgate Prison. Chief among them was the Joker. Writer Grant Morrison concocted a tale which sees Batman fall into a trap set by his arch-nemesis within the walls of Arkham Asylum, now a full-blown gothic nightmare of a place. Adding to the atmosphere of dread, artist Dave McKean supplied fully painted artwork for the graphic novel which was destined to influence the *Batman* universe for decades to come. Morrison's story detailed the creation of the asylum amid tragedy and violence within the Arkham family that gave the institution its name, building on the bits of history hinted at in the *Batman* comic books in the years leading up to his graphic novel.[2]

The year 1989 was a pop-culture bonanza for Batman as Tim Burton brought his vision of *Batman*, the Dark Knight, to the silver screen—and *dark* it certainly was. Casting Michael Keaton as Bruce Wayne/Batman was a controversial choice for Burton. Known for his comedic roles while lacking the physical menace expected from Batman, fans were outraged at Keaton's casting. It had been a long time and several generations since a live-action Batman had appeared, and the fans feared a reprisal of the campy Batman of 1960s television and film starring Adam West in the titular role. Burton's unconventional approach paid off for everybody. Michael Keaton's serious and edgy performance nailed Bruce Wayne in a way never seen. Jack Nicholson provided marquee star power by appearing as the Joker. The critics loved it, and more importantly so did the paying audiences. Not only did Warner Bros. reap profits from the film, but some very lucrative merchandising deals also fattened their coffers.

Hoping for lightning to strike twice, Burton and Keaton were brought back for *Batman Returns* (1992). The studio had loosened the reins on Tim Burton a bit, allowing him more creative control based upon his previous success ... but the film was too weird for the all-important aspect of merchandising, and proved to be too dark for even fans of the Dark Knight. Danny DeVito appeared as the villain Penguin in a performance marred by black bile drooling from his wretched mouth. Michelle Pfeiffer as Catwoman was a bit too fetishistic for the younger audiences. Batman (Keaton) appears to indiscriminately kill lesser villains with his arsenal of weapons loaded into the Batmobile.

Surprisingly, Burton avoided any inclusion of Arkham Asylum in his films—which is admittedly strange since Arkham would have been a perfect fit for his dark *Batman* cinematic world. But 1992 would feature Arkham Asylum in an unlikely place—on the small screen—in *Batman: The Animated Series* (1992–1995). Following *Batman Returns*, Warner Bros. was desperate to keep the Batman IP relevant and made the good choice of producing a quality animated series that would go on to not only influence changes in the *Batman* comics but also feature films and video games into the next century.

Paul Dini (writer) and Bruce Timm (art) created a show which not only routinely featured Arkham Asylum but built upon its importance in the *Batman* universe. They created a character whose origin was tied to the asylum itself, one destined to overshadow even Batman sometimes in her eventual adaptation to the big screen—Harley Quinn. Originally a minor character meant to appear only once as the Joker's moll, her popularity was immediately evident, and a legend was born.[3] Fan approval secured the character's inclusion in the *Batman* comic books, a rare transitional occurrence for a fictional character. Dini and Timm crafted *Mad Love* in 1995, a graphic novel highlighting Harley Quinn's origin story as psychiatrist Harleen Quinzel, assigned to treat the Joker within Arkham Asylum.[4] She falls in love with him, facilitates his escape, and becomes insane herself along the way. In turn, *Mad Love* was cyclically adapted back into animation in 1999 for the television follow-up to *Batman: The Animated Series*. *The New Batman Adventures* (1997–1999) retained not only Dini and Timm on the creative end but continued to use the fan-favorite voice acting of Kevin Conroy as Bruce Wayne/Batman, Mark Hamill (of *Star Wars* fame) as the Joker, and Arleen Sorkin as Harley Quinn. Sorkin's voice became synonymous with the character, setting the stage for all actors (voice and live action) to follow, short of Lady Gaga's interpretation in 2024 ... but more on that later.

While Batman continued to enjoy success on the small screen and on the printed page, Warner Bros. wanted to give the movies another shot ... but not with Tim Burton.

They handed the property over to Joel Schumacher, who helmed *Batman Forever* in 1995. Val Kilmer replaced Michael Keaton as Bruce Wayne/Batman, which was merely the first of a countless series of bad choices. Jim Carrey stole the show as the Riddler, while Tommy Lee Jones turned in an embarrassing performance as Two-Face.[5] Rounding things out, Nicole Kidman appears as Dr. Chase Meridian, a staff psychiatrist at Arkham Asylum, in the first appearance of the madhouse on the silver screen.

Schumacher was enamored of Arkham Asylum and wanted to include it in his film. His version is a Gothic haunted-castle structure fronted by humungous gargoyle-adorned stone pillars supporting an iron arch spelling out "Arkham Asylum," seemingly set atop a mountain. After apparently killing Two-Face, Batman destroys the Riddler's mind, leaving him a horrifically deformed mess. The brain damage he suffered prevents him from recalling the secret identity of Batman being Bruce Wayne. To be sure of this, Wayne (who has conveniently been having a tryst with Dr. Meridian) sends Dr. Meridian into Riddler's cell in Arkham to ask him who Batman is. Pathetically flapping his straitjacket arms, Riddler proclaims that he himself is the Batman, while prancing about his cell. The film ends on this depressing note, but Schumacher was far from done with Batman, or Arkham Asylum.

In 1997, Schumacher effectively drove a stake through the heart of the *Batman* movie series with *Batman and Robin*. George Clooney donned the cowl this time around, with the infamous detailing of nipples, protruding buttocks, and a bulging crotch now added to the Batman costume.[6] Arnold Schwarzenegger appeared as Mr. Freeze, and Uma Thurman took on the role of Poison Ivy. The film remains notorious on every level—so much so that Schumacher has publicly apologized for destroying the franchise with his over-the-top campy antics that must have seemed like a good idea to someone at some point.

Once again, his Gothic Arkham Asylum appears onscreen, but this time surrounded by a moat of sorts in its mountainous setting. Its function is more in line with some of the comic book renditions, which depict the asylum as a customized series of cells specifically designed to hold crazed supervillains by limiting/foiling their superpowers. Following Batman's apprehending of Mr. Freeze, the icy villain is stripped of his protective suit, which keeps him alive at subzero temperatures. Prey to the taunting guards of Arkham Asylum, Mr. Freeze is forced to exist within the small confines of a cold-blast ray projected from the ceiling within an unusually large cell. Poison Ivy breaks him out to team up with him, upon which he gets his vengeance upon the taunting asylum guards. She eventually secretly betrays him and in the end is strangely remanded to the same cell within Arkham, as he promises to make her life a living hell.

Schumacher references the use of Arkham Asylum in his previous film by showing an evidence locker (!?) within the institution stocked with costumes and props of both the Riddler and Two-Face, indicating their presence within the madhouse … even though Two-Face perished while battling Batman.

More cartoonish than the animated *Batman* series, which was concurrently running on the small screen, the Arkham Asylum of Schumacher's films served as mere gag within a series of very unfunny jokes. As enamored as he was of Arkham, Schumacher never got to shoot his third *Batman* film—which was to have been centered around the asylum and its colorful selection of mad villains. *Batman Unchained* was to feature Harley Quinn's big-screen premiere (reimagined as the Joker's daughter, played by Courtney Love) along with Dr. Jonathan Crane, aka the Scarecrow (Nicolas Cage), another crazy

In *Batman Begins* (2005), future Academy Award–winner Cillian Murphy plays the irredeemably evil Dr. Crane, aka Scarecrow, a one-time psychology professor who now heads Arkham Asylum, where he conducts unethical experiments and sprays inmates with his fear gas while he wears scary masks to make patients believe they have gone insane.

Arkham psychiatrist. Following a blockbuster start, after nearly a decade of diminishing box office returns, Warner Bros. opted out of bringing Batman back to the big screen—especially under Schumacher's control—until a complete reboot would occur in Christopher Nolan's *Batman Begins* (2005), when Christan Bale would redefine Bruce Wayne/Batman for a new generation.

Before that, however, Arkham Asylum made a brief appearance in the *Birds of Prey* live-action television series (2002–2003), a short-lived show set in Gotham City after Batman abandons the city. Dr. Harleen Quinzel (Mia Sara) also appears, but hardly in her Harley Quinn persona and more as herself, hiding her criminal past as well as her own psychosis while she plots against the heroes attempting to fill the crime-fighting void left by the Dark Knight's departure.

The Batman cinema IP had a rocky road back to the big screen, plagued by fits and starts—but the wait paid off. Nolan's vision of Batman coupled with Bale's performance brought a level of realism never heretofore experienced in any version of Batman in any form of media. A military/tactical aesthetic was introduced into Batman's costume and gadgets. The Batmobile was now a repurposed military vehicle. Challenged by several villains, Batman faced off against both Ra's al Ghul (Liam Neeson) and Dr. Jonathan Crane/The Scarecrow (Cillian Murphy). And Arkham Asylum finally got to play a significant role in the adventure!

In Nolan's film, Arkham Asylum was "played" by the National Institute for Medical Research Laboratory in Mill Hill, London, for the exterior shots and part of the Midland Grand Hotel, an intricately lush Victorian structure located in Kings Cross, for interiors. The asylum was positioned within Gotham City, no longer a castle set upon a mountaintop outside the city limits. The imposing structure houses a range of interiors, including an impossibly high, elaborately adorned open staircase, empty hallways, and a subterranean area resembling a water treatment plant. Arkham Asylum is home to Dr. Jonathan Crane, allowing his free rein over the inmates for his fiendish experiments in fear. Those not subjected to his chemical tests are forced into slave labor, manufacturing his fear-inducing concoction. Crane plans to use the chemicals to poison Gotham City's water supply at the behest of Ra's al Ghul.

Crane has perfected his fear-chemical in both a gaseous and a liquid form. He has weaponized the gaseous form, known as "fear gas," for close-quarters combat and intimidation. It instantly besets his victims' minds with terrifying hallucinations and distorts their perspectives. He protects himself from its effects using a special mask equipped with his own oxygen supply, in the form of a stitched-together face, which gives him the criminal moniker of the Scarecrow. Crane has outfitted his briefcase and suit jacket with pressurized canisters, enabling him to fire fear gas at his opponents. With his mask on, they hallucinate his visage as a pulsing, maggot-encrusted, corpselike face while their sense of reason slips away. Crane can adjust the dispersal amount to induce a temporary psychosis on up through a fatal brain meltdown.

Crane uses a mid-range dose to induce a psychotic break in the double-crossing mobster Carmine Falcone (Tom Wilkinson) while interrogating him in prison. His plan to have Falcone remanded into his care at Arkham Asylum succeeds ... but it draws the attention of Rachel Dawes (Katie Holmes), the assistant district attorney of Gotham City. Dawes confronts Crane within Arkham Asylum. He tricks her into following him into the asylum's depths where she sees an army of his patients manufacturing the fear-chemicals while dumping them into an exposed pipe connected to the city's water supply. Crane has no fear of being caught as he poisons her with a fatal dose of his fear gas.

When Crane realizes that Dawes was followed there by Batman, he calls the police, who are currently hunting the Dark Knight as a wanted vigilante. Batman breaks in and forces a blast of Crane's psychoactive gas into the villain's own face, causing him to lose his mind. The asylum serves as a spectacular set piece while the action continues as the police arrive, storming the building. Sergeant Jim Gordon (Gary Oldman), destined to become police commissioner one day, aids Batman in getting the deathly ill Dawes out of the building while Batman distracts the police with some high-flying tactics, eventually backed up by a huge swarm of ... bats. Arkham Asylum is besieged by the dense swarm, which serves as cover for Batman's escape. Whew.

Nolan uses Arkham Asylum to bring plot points together, to reveal some secrets and motivations, and as a playground for a spectacular action sequence. While Crane would reappear in bit parts in Nolan's follow-ups, *The Dark Knight* (2008) and *The Dark Knight Rises* (2012), Arkham Asylum would not.

In the meantime, Arkham Asylum came into its own in 2009 when Rocksteady Studios, a little-known game developer, launched *Batman: Arkham Asylum* as a home video game. Paul Dini (writer of the Batman animated series) was brought in to provide the narrative content of the game, while the top voice talents from the animated series also reprised their roles. Kevin Conway is Batman, with Mark Hamill as the Joker and Arleen Sorkin as Harley Quinn.

Rocksteady's approach, however, was worlds away from the animated series. Hyperrealistic renderings created a very dark, very run-down, and very frightening Arkham Asylum.[7] Borrowing a plot cue from the 1989 graphic novel *Arkham Asylum: A Serious House on Serious Earth*, Batman is lured into the asylum by the Joker, soon finding himself fighting off all the villains he has incarcerated there. The gameplay is very fight-centric, and much effort was put into the 3D graphics to get Batman's cape to realistically flow during his countless acrobatic moves and battles. The asylum itself is suggestive of a nightmarish prison, but the game environment sets the asylum on an island with a startling amount of scenery to explore and interact with while immersed in the game environment.[8] Harley Quinn was given a more "mature" upgrade, her costume now being that of a sexy "nurse" while sporting a corset and miniskirt, having given up the traditional harlequin outfit featured in the animations and comics.

The success of *Arkham Asylum* cannot be overstated. The bestselling and best-reviewed game of 2009 put Rocksteady on the map while ensuring numerous follow-ups over the following years. It also cemented the name "Arkham Asylum" into the public consciousness by virtue of popularity. It reinvigorated interest in Harley Quinn, who after her initial burst on the scene in the late 1990s had been coasting along as a secondary character in the comics.

Her redesign would inspire her big-screen premiere in 2016's *Suicide Squad*. Played by Margot Robbie, Harley is already imprisoned as the film begins, but it is not in Arkham Asylum as one might expect. The Belle Reve Maximum Security Prison in New Orleans houses the weirdest, most dangerous semi-superpowered villains, chosen by intelligence officer Amanda Waller (Viola Davis) to form an expendable team of criminals to serve as she sees best to protect national security. The character introductions are shown as flashbacks highlighting their powers, exploits, and eventual apprehension. Harley's flashback plays as an homage to the *Mad Love* story (both comic and animated), showing a rapid-fire sequence of her work at Arkham Asylum, falling for the Joker (Jared Leto), facilitating his machine-gun escape from the madhouse, and subsequently being abused and humiliated by him. For this sequence, director David Ayres recreates the iconic artwork created by Alex Ross for the back cover of a *Mad Love* reprint of a tux-wearing dapper Joker dancing with Harley Quinn in her iconic harlequin/jester outfit within Arkham.[9]

Margot Robbie nailed the character, bringing the voice and the look of Harley Quinn to the film in a spectacular, fun way. Robbie would reprise her role in *Birds of Prey* (2020) as well as the soft reboot of *Suicide Squad* titled.... *The Suicide Squad* (2021).

A void was left when Christopher Nolan completed his *Batman* trilogy in 2012 with *The Dark Knight Rises*. Up until then, the *Batman* movies had existed in a vacuum, featuring solo adventures without recognizing the existence of other DC superheroes (excepting of course Robin and Batgirl from the Schumacher films), but this was about to change. Zack Snyder reintroduced Superman to the big screen with *Man of Steel* in 2013 with the intent of building a DC cinematic universe which would eventually bring Superman together with Batman, Wonder Woman, the Flash, and Aquaman. He pushed further into this world with *Batman v Superman: Dawn of Justice* (2016) while laying the groundwork for his *Justice League* film in 2017. Ben Affleck took on the role of Bruce Wayne/Batman in what many considered to be the most comic book-accurate portrayal of the Dark Knight to appear in the movies. He retained the "tactical" edge established in Nolan's films but was now thrust into the more fantastical world of superheroes, supervillains, and even aliens. Without a solo effort of his own, Batman became part of the Justice League, caught up in catastrophic events that threatened the world. While there was little time for Arkham Asylum while Batman was assembling the Justice League and saving the world, he did use incarceration there as a threat to Lex Luthor

(Jesse Eisenberg) in *Batman v Superman: Dawn of Justice*. "I still have some friends there," he tells the supervillain, causing Luthor to blanch with fear.

Affleck reprised his Batman role for cameos in a few other DC films but had planned on headlining in a Batman solo film to be set within Arkham Asylum … but the generally lukewarm response to the DC cinematic universe sparked yet another reboot, bringing Batman back to his solo roots with a younger actor playing a younger Bruce Wayne/Batman.

But prior to that drastic change in the DC movies, DC was also producing live-action superhero content for television. Surprisingly, one of the popular shows was a Batman show … without Batman! Recall that this had been tried in *Birds of Prey* (2001–2002) by setting the story after the Dark Knight had left Gotham City—but without much success.

The concept for *Gotham* (2014–2019) was to set it *before* young Bruce Wayne becomes Batman, focusing on Jim Gordon's (Ben McKenzie) days as a police officer while things start to get weird with the advent of numerous supervillains coming into their own.

The series featured Dr. Hugo Strange (BD Wong) as chief psychiatrist of Arkham Asylum. True to the comics, Dr. Strange is a mad scientist villain with a penchant for experimenting on his patients to create monster-men. Arkham Asylum not only provides a cover for his nefarious work but also hides a secret research facility called Indian Hill deep below the asylum.

The show's concept proved to be a tricky balance, forcing reinterpretations upon existing Batman characters to coexist while much younger while set against a ticking clock as young Bruce Wayne inevitably takes up the Batman mantle as the show concludes.

Back in the movie theaters, concurrent with both this show and the DC cinematic universe, was the lighthearted *Lego Batman Movie* (2017), an animated romp through the Batman mythos which also featured Arkham Asylum as a location that Batman and Robin infiltrate and humorously get trapped in. Merchandising for the film included a Lego model of Arkham Asylum, which was the third toy variation of the madhouse put out for children since 2008.

While the DC cinematic universe was on the ropes, filmmaker Todd Phillips had a radical way to tap into the Batman IP—a Batman film without Batman. While this may seem to echo television's *Gotham* series, his approach would be the most serious adaptation of the Joker ever undertaken. In *Joker* (2019), Phillips cast Joaquin Phoenix as the lead in a Gotham City that harkens back to the notoriously squalid NYC of the 1980s, while also recalling such cinematic classics as *Death Wish* (1974) and *Taxi Driver* (1976). Phoenix excels as Arthur Fleck, the Joker before he becomes the Joker. Phillips created a very depressing world setting, which was most definitely not part of the DC cinematic universe, in his standalone effort.

While Arkham figures prominently in the plot, a decision was made to intentionally not refer to the institution as Arkham *Asylum*, as that word harkened back to bygone days and hinted at a more fantastical approach. Instead, Arkham reached back to its roots from its first appearance in 1974, appearing as the more progressively titled Arkham State Hospital.

Joker was met with both praise and backlash regarding its depiction of mental illness on screen. The film remains open to interpretation, as most of the story is shown through Arthur Fleck's experiences—and he is a *most* unreliable narrator, in a vein recalling the twist of David Fincher's *Fight Club* (1999). Some viewers have hypothesized that Fleck is a patient within Arkham State Hospital for the entire duration of the film, and that the increasingly violent narrative is all in his head. Contradictory visual appearances of the Arkham's interiors—varying from dingy yellow to bright white hallways, along with background clocks that always display 11:11—have been cited as proof that the audience's perspective is skewed through Fleck's subjective experiences.

Either way, Arkham in *Joker* is the most depressingly realistic version of the fictional madhouse ever committed to film. The arched exterior was shot at the Brooklyn Army Terminal in New York. Some of the lobby/interior was also a location shoot, occurring at NYC's Metropolitan Hospital. Fleck/Joker remains committed within Arkham as the film concludes, setting up the sequel *Joker: Folie à Deux* (2024). Todd Phillips returns to direct, with partial story credits, and Joaquin Phoenix reprises his role as Arthur Fleck/Joker.

Translated from French as "madness for two" while suggesting "shared delusions," *Joker: Folie à Deux* brings Harleen Quinzel, aka Harley Quinn, into Joker's life. Lady Gaga steps into the role, offering a new take on the now classic character. Musical numbers have been added to the story, perhaps further blurring the line between their "shared delusions" and reality, if any reality at all exists within the walls of Arkham State Hospital.

Maintaining the "State Hospital" designation, *Joker: Folie à Deux* utilized a different building for the exterior shots of Arkham. New Jersey's abandoned Essex County Isolation Hospital (aka the Overbrook Asylum) shuttered its madhouse doors in 2006, yet remains an imposing structure and the perfect stand-in for a realistic Arkham, because it really was a giant asylum.

While the *Joker* films stand apart from the rest of the DC cinematic universe, the name changes back to Arkham State Hospital and has been maintained for the latest entry in the Batman movies. *The Batman* (2022) occurs in a rainy, wretched Gotham City that takes some obvious cues from David Fincher's *Se7en* (1995), both stylistically and thematically. The Riddler (Paul Dano) serial murders his way through Gotham's rich and famous via an overly complex plan based purely on envy. The film takes a turn toward *Silence of the Lambs* (1991) when the Batman (Robert Patterson) has nowhere to turn but to an incarcerated psychotic person for advice.

A scene cut from the theatrical release (but available for streaming/home viewing) has the Batman visit Arkham State Hospital to question an "Unseen Arkham Prisoner" (Barry Keoghan) whom he previously apprehended. Shown only in out-of-focus cut aways, glimpses of a pale, hideously scarred face and scraggly green hair tell viewers this is in fact the Joker. A large glass wall equipped with a bank-like pass box deviates from any attempt at architectural reality for the setting, also mimicking the holding cell of Hannibal Lecter in *Silence of the Lambs*.

No exterior of Arkham appears, and the interior cells appear to be set within a disorienting black void. This is where the defeated Riddler eventually lands, forming an impromptu friendship with the "Unseen Prisoner" in a nearby cell as the film concludes.

The recent more realistic movie appearances of Arkham as a "State Hospital" certainly reflect the progressive nature of mental healthcare. Even comic book–based fantasy films recognize the advancements made in psychopharmacology as far back as the mid–1950s which signaled the eventual end of "asylums" in favor of outpatient treatments.

Time will tell if this approach to the terminology used on the big screen lasts, but DC has already announced a television series as part of the rebooted DC cinematic universe titled.... *Arkham Asylum*.

Yes ... as always, Arkham Asylum is what it needs to be.

Notes

1. Sharon Packer, *Cinema's Sinister Psychiatrists: From Caligari to Hannibal* (McFarland, 2012), 210–212.
2. Grant Morrison, *Batman: Arkham Asylum—The 25th Anniversary Edition* (DC Comics, 2014), *Notes* (no page number).
3. Robert Greenberger and Matthew K. Manning, *The Batman Vault* (Running Press, 2009), 165.
4. Sharon Packer, "Harley Quinn and the Joker: Pitfalls of Doctor-Patient Romances," in *Welcome to Arkham Asylum: Essays on Psychiatry and the Gotham City Institution*, ed. Sharon Packer and Daniel R. Fredrick (McFarland, 2020), 101–109. Dr. Packer authoritatively analyzes the Harley Quinn/Joker relationship, citing real-life parallels along with other examples from cinema.
5. Les Daniels, *Batman: The Complete History* (Chronicle Books, 1999), 186–187.
6. Sharon Packer, *Superheroes and Superegos: Analyzing the Minds Behind the Masks* (Praeger/ABC CLIO, 2010), 184.
7. Matthew K. Manning, *Batman: Arkham Universe, the Ultimate Visual Guide* (Penguin Random House, 2015), 98–105.
8. Daniel Wallace, *The Art of Rocksteady's Batman* (Abrams, 2015), 59–106.
9. Paul Dini, *Batman: Mad Love* (DC Comics, 2009).

3

No Laughing Matter

Comedies About Psychiatric Hospitals

Kristi Rowan Humphreys

In analyzing Charlie Chaplin's slapstick comedy, philosopher Theodor W. Adorno wrote, "Incessant and spontaneous change: in Chaplin, this is the utopia of an existence that would be free of the burden of being-one's-self."[1] Originating centuries ago on the theatrical stage, slapstick comedy uses exaggeration, physical gags, and sometimes violence to make audiences laugh. Like Adorno, many scholars have examined the relationship between slapstick and laughter. Walter Benjamin, for one, wrote multiple texts throughout the late 1920s and 1930s that mention the subject. Steven Jacobs and Hilde D'haeyere note that Benjamin seemed to believe slapstick's appeal had much to do with the idea that "cinema developed in tandem with a new reality characterized by the constant exposure to shocks as a result of [modern industrialization]" ... and emphasized "the link between the overstimulation of the senses induced by modern technology and the development of a mass culture with a strong preference for thrills."[2] Social trends always seem to be a continuation of and a reaction to what came before, so slapstick, as it evolved throughout the 20th century, can reveal insights regarding the desires and needs of audiences in reality. In a poignant study on the violence of slapstick, Muriel Andrin quotes distinguished film archivist and historian Eileen Bowser: "All things that the moral melodrama [of the 1910s and 1920s] was meant to suppress appeared again in slapstick comedy: anarchy, amorality, eroticism, vulgarity, fantasy, cruelty, the total disrespect for the forces of organized society."[3] Thus, slapstick provided an escape while simultaneously addressing a changing world. In addition to these two appeals, though surprising, slapstick provided the comfort of repetition in the form of, as Jennifer M. Bean claims, a "seemingly endless recycling of gags and scenarios—even whole story treatments"[4] for these early 20th-century audiences. Clearly, slapstick comedy had a multitude of characteristics that appealed to audiences for a variety of reasons.

Despite decades of changing realities, slapstick comedy has retained much of its popularity. What interests me is how slapstick has allowed audiences, old and new, to laugh at matters that are sensitive. Chaplin and the early cinema slapstick masters certainly applied this treatment to issues such as poverty, homelessness, and rejection, but this essay argues that slapstick has also functioned to allow audiences to laugh at a different not-so-humorous phenomenon: the insane asylum. Beginning with silent films like *Off to Bloomingdale Asylum* (1901)[5] and *Modern Times* (1936)[6] through vehicles including *Love Crazy* (1941),[7] *The Pink Panther Strikes Again* (1976),[8] *High Anxiety*

(1977),[9] *The Ninth Configuration* (1980),[10] and *Good Burger* (1997),[11] the filmic medium continues to use slapstick comedy to inspire audiences to laugh at the subject of the asylum institution, but representation in this context also encourages viewers to consider how it reflects, interacts with, challenges, and even programs our realities.

In his autobiography *My Wonderful World of Slapstick*, famous deadpan comedian Buster Keaton discusses the discomfort in finding his slapstick reputation entering events in his own reality. He describes a story from his time in the army when he passed out, awakened, and asked his fellow soldiers, "Did we win?" Keaton recalls, "I spoke in all seriousness. But nobody knew that, and everyone laughed, which is the sort of thing that often gets a man an undeserved reputation for being a wit. I was not amused at all to find slapstick flowing over into my new life in the Army. I took being a soldier quite seriously."[12] Even though Keaton is speaking of his real life, I argue that there are complicated similarities in using slapstick to address serious topics in film, including institutions of mental illness, as representation—in any form—almost always bleeds into reality in some way. Consequently, the relationships between slapstick, insane asylum representations, reality, and social commentary deserve further analysis.

It is important to note that this is not a new phenomenon; thus, to establish trends or inconsistencies, I have chosen to analyze films chronologically. In 1901, groundbreaking French director Georges Méliès created a short film titled *Off to Bloomingdale Asylum*.[13] According to the current Bloomingdale Neighborhood History Group's website, the Bloomingdale Insane Asylum was erected in 1821 in the Morningside Heights area of Manhattan, where Columbia University now resides.[14] The facility served 120 patients at a time and was created in response to an increasing number of mentally ill patients, who were previously being treated alongside all other patients at the New York Hospital. It received its name because of its location on Bloomingdale Road, which is now Broadway Avenue. In 1829 and 1834, additional buildings were constructed to house the noisier and more violent patients. I include this detail about the additions because of its relationship to the film. At just a minute in length, *Off to Bloomingdale Asylum* presents a skeleton horse pulling an "omnibus," or stagecoach-type wagon in this case, carrying five visibly active and restless individuals who are waving their arms and stomping their feet. The title implies these are mentally ill individuals being committed, but the only indication of their need for the asylum is their unruliness, which is communicated throughout the short film by slapstick comedy. Without the title, this detail would be very unclear—a feature that could also speak to the complicated issue of labels and mental illness. However, this essay will focus primarily on the institution of the asylum, rather than on representations of the illnesses themselves.

Modern Times, one of Charlie Chaplin's most famous films, was written and directed by Chaplin and was a part-silent, part-talkie hybrid film released in 1934. In the film, Chaplin's Tramp character is working on an assembly line in a factory—a line on which the boss continues to require increased speed. Unable to take the pressure of the working conditions any longer, the Tramp begins to behave wildly, running around, changing gears, flipping switches, and spraying people in the face with oil. The supervisors determine he is mentally ill, so an ambulance is called. This scene is followed by an intertitle that says, "Cured of a nervous breakdown but without a job, he leaves the hospital to start life anew."[15]

The next brief scene is inside the front office of the asylum. The Tramp, walking toward the camera with his signature bumbling, duck-waddle gait, is accompanied by his doctor as he is being discharged from the asylum. Even though the scene is brief, Chaplin's famous slapstick is still employed to drive the action. As the doctor is instructing the Tramp to "take it easy and avoid excitement" (intertitle), the doctor slaps him on the back.[16] The Tramp pretends to nearly fall to the ground. He then exits the asylum steps, giving a morning stretch. The use of slapstick in *Modern Times* is not only used to make the filmic asylum more palatable, as I will argue with later films, it provides strong support for Benjamin's assertion that slapstick's appeal could be viewed as society's response to the "constant exposure to shocks" that was a natural part of adapting to industrialization.[17] The Tramp is doing his best to adjust to the factory demands, but slapstick enables Chaplin to address industrialization's societal impact in general, which Benjamin claims underscores the reason slapstick was so popular at the time.[18] Slapstick provides an acceptable bridge from social commentary in the factory to the need for an asylum to the jobless streets. The Tramp's physical stretch as he leaves the asylum is juxtaposed with a montage of images displaying a society now dependent on and subject to industrialization, furthering the function of physical comedy in this capacity.

The 1941 film *Love Crazy*, directed by Jack Conway, introduces a twist in how slapstick is applied to the filmic asylum. The plot involves a couple who is getting a divorce, but the husband, Steve Ireland (William Powell), does not want the divorce from Susan (Myrna Loy), so he pretends to be insane in an effort to buy him some time to convince Susan to stay married to him. In the divorce hearing, the judge decides Steve is indeed insane and gives Susan the option to either take him into her custody or have him placed in an asylum. Knowing Steve is not being truthful, she has him placed in the asylum, and slapstick comedy is used throughout the asylum scenes.

The film includes many examples, so I will include just a few here. In one scene, the asylum gardener is using a ladder to trim a tree. When the gardener leaves with the tree limbs, Steve tries to run away with the ladder so that he can jump the asylum fence and escape to see Susan; however, the ladder is chained to the tree (likely a realistic detail regarding the asylum experience), and Steve consequently trips, flips, and ends up with his head stuck in the ladder. Later, Steve tries to climb the fence again, this time using a net attached to a tree. He gets his foot caught in the net and is found hanging upside down, and the asylum doctors believe he has tried to commit suicide. Steve wants them to understand this is not true and attempts to show one of the doctors what he was trying to do with the net, but this time, the doctor gets his own foot caught and is left dangling from the tree. Asylum officials then believe Steve has tried to kill the doctor and begin calling him a "homicidal maniac."

Love Crazy's use of slapstick in the asylum is significant. First, it functions to remind audiences that even though most of the film takes place in an insane asylum, it is still a comedy. This perspective of "not taking things too seriously" connects the film to Adorno's belief that slapstick comedy presented for audiences a "utopia of an existence that would be free of the burden of being-one's-self."[19] It also likely appealed to audiences who were adapting to an ever-changing world that they often did not want to have to "take too seriously." Second, *Love Crazy*'s slapstick is used to enter the dialogue of the extent to which sanity and insanity are matters of social convention. Steve is not actually insane, but if his behavior is deemed by others (asylum staff) to be insane behavior, then he will be deemed to be mentally ill and in need of the asylum. In this case, slapstick is the method through which the film connects these ideas to the cinematic insane asylum.

The Pink Panther series of films is unique in that most audience members know to expect slapstick comedy before they begin the movie. The fifth in its series, *The Pink Panther Strikes Again*, is a 1976 film directed by Blake Edwards that provides many examples for this analysis. The plot picks up when Chief Inspector Charles Dreyfus (Herbert Lom) is soon to be released from a mental hospital, after spending three years there because he was driven "insane" by the bumbling Chief Inspector Jacques Clouseau (Peter Sellers). Knowing that Clouseau was Dreyfus's initial trigger, the asylum psychiatrist asks Dreyfus one final time about his ability to deal with Clouseau again in reality. Dreyfus feels confident that the asylum staff has healed him. As Dreyfus awaits discharge, seated on a bench by a small river running through the asylum grounds, Clouseau walks across the asylum lawn to visit Dreyfus on his final day. First, Clouseau finds a cricket set on the ground, takes a mallet, and hits a ball, which bounces off a tree and knocks Dreyfus in the head and into the river. Clouseau attempts to retrieve him by extending the mallet; but when Dreyfus grabs it, the end of the mallet comes off, and he is forced back into the river. Undeterred, Clouseau then extends a nearby rake to Dreyfus and successfully pulls him out. The two men eventually sit on the bench together, and Clouseau reveals to Dreyfus, "We have made quite a few changes since you went crazy." As Clouseau stands, the bench tips over and Dreyfus spills back into the river. When Dreyfus is finally out again, he assures doctors that he is perfectly all right but then steps onto the rake, which hits him on the head; he falls back into the river. In anger, Dreyfus runs after Clouseau, and the asylum staff determine he is not ready to leave the asylum.

Even though physical comedy is ultimately used in this filmic asylum to retain Dreyfus as a patient, it functions slightly differently than it does in *Love Crazy*. In *The Pink Panther Strikes Again*, Dreyfus is the passive player in the slapstick routine. Clouseau drives the action, while Dreyfus is compelled to respond. It is Dreyfus's inability to tolerate the slapstick antics (to be able to "roll with the punches" of life) that causes asylum staff to deem him unfit for society and lands him back in the asylum. This connects the film to Andrin's assessments regarding slapstick and violence.[20] With slapstick, audiences not only are encouraged to laugh at sensitive subject matter but are also allowed to release emotions that they suppress in reality. In real life, violence in any form is not considered funny; yet in the filmic asylum, the physical comedy signals to viewers that even though this is a patient in a mental health facility, it is acceptable to laugh at the slaps, knocks, and pushes. In this context, the character who can master and manipulate the slapstick maneuvers is considered less in need of an asylum than the one who cannot.

The plot of *High Anxiety*, a 1977 satirical film by Mel Brooks, takes place in an asylum called the Psycho-Neurotic Institute for the Very, Very Nervous. Dr. Richard H. Thorndyke (Brooks) has been hired as the new "head shrink" of the asylum, and while he is getting adjusted to the institution, various forms of slapstick are employed to introduce him to the facility and its patients. In this film, when slapstick appears, it typically functions to reveal how the asylum is intentionally making patients worse to keep them there and to continue to take their money. For example, in one of the first scenes, Dr. Thorndyke is looking at patient files and realizes a patient, Mr. Cartwright (Ron Clark), should have been discharged months earlier. He asks resident asylum psychiatrist Dr. Montague (Harvey Korman) about it, and they both bring in the patient for assessment. Mr. Cartwright explains that he believes he is healed because when he arrived, he had terrible neck pains and nightmares about werewolves; however, he no longer suffers

In *High Anxiety* (1977), comedian Mel Brooks spoofs several Hitchcock films simultaneously as he showcases a *Spellbound*-style sanitarium for the "very, very nervous" (and the very, very rich), where he himself plays the anxious patient, Professor Thorndyke, who is bombarded with pigeon poop in a parody of *The Birds* (1963).

from those events. As Dr. Thorndyke continues to ask Mr. Cartwright about the reasons he feels he is ready to leave the asylum, and without Dr. Thorndyke noticing, Dr. Montague begins sling-shotting paper clips into the patient's neck (to cause the neck pains again) and terrifying him with vampire teeth (to recreate the nightmares); Cartwright is so affected by these actions, generated through slapstick comedy, that he becomes hysterical and must be carried out of the room by orderlies. Making patients appear ill when they are not is foundational to the plot, but the methods used to achieve this almost always involve slapstick. Even though it is a spoof, it is important to note how the film comments on the actual efficacy of mental health facilities, furthering questions about whether they help or hurt. Like the Bloomingdale Asylum in reality, which eventually added buildings for violent patients, the "Psycho-Neurotic Institute for the Very, Very Nervous" also has wings for "violent" patients. There, patients are locked in cells, much like a prison, which reflects a common stereotype about insane asylums in general, both in film and in reality. Thus, even though *High Anxiety* is clearly satirical, it uses slapstick to underscore and even make laughable the ways in which we perpetuate asylum stereotypes through visual and popular culture.

Many of these stereotypes are also furthered in the 1980 comedy *The Ninth Configuration* (1980), but of all the films included in this analysis, it may be the most difficult to ascertain if and when laughter is appropriate in this film, even with the use of slapstick.

The asylum in this film is an abandoned castle, and the film opens with the following statement: "Toward the end of the war in Vietnam, an unusually high percentage of American servicemen suddenly manifested symptoms of psychosis. Most were in combat and had no prior history of mental disturbance. Government wondered if the men were faking. To prove this, the US government set up multiple facilities, one of which was highly experimental in this abandoned castle in the Pacific Northwest."[21] This sets a very serious tone that initially feels uncomfortably disrupted by the slapstick comedy; the film then adds to this uncomfortable juxtaposition by furthering the asylum-as-prison trope. Throughout the film, patients are referred to by asylum staff as "inmates." Furthermore, the trope is established firmly by the opening song, "San Antone" by Denny Brooks—a song made famous by the 1977 film *Rolling Thunder*[22] about a veteran who spent time as a prisoner of war. The film also uses comedy to address the various ways in which these veterans are dealing with postwar trauma; most of the slapstick comedy functions to reveal how each patient is navigating reality by masking himself with various alternative identities. This echoes Adorno's assessment of the "incessant and spontaneous change" aspect of slapstick comedy that creates "the utopia of an existence that would be free of the burden of being-one's-self."[23] It seems this is precisely how this filmic asylum is functioning. Characters (patients) assume diverse identities, and actors use slapstick to bring the personalities to life. These identities include pirate, French painter, theatrical director, scuba diver, and nun, to name a few. This filmic asylum is quite layered in the way the conflicted actions of its characters, as they work through psychological challenges, parallel the feelings of a conflicted film audience, as they decide when it is or is not appropriate to laugh at postwar trauma.

Lastly, the 1997 film *Good Burger*[24]—a film about teenagers trying to save a burger joint—may be unexpected for a scholarly analysis. However, in many ways, *Good Burger* combines most of the points discussed in this essay: asylum slapstick, violence, stereotypes, false identities, and asylum-as-prison tropes. In the film, Ed (Kel Mitchell) and Dexter (Kenan Thompson) work at the fast-food restaurant Good Burger and decide to disguise themselves as employees of the competing burger place, Mondo Burger, in an effort to go undercover and find the secret recipe that is making their burgers so popular.

When the two teenagers are discovered by Mondo Burger staff, Ed and Dexter are committed to "Demented Hills Asylum." There, slapstick comedy prevails, as they are placed in straitjackets, thrown into an ambulance, and then forced into an asylum room with padded walls.

Ed is excited about all of this and begins throwing his body into the padded walls for fun, saying, "Look the walls are padded!" He does this in addition to other forms of physical comedy, including gymnastics and dancing. When Ed and Dexter join fellow patients for games during free time, additional forms of slapstick are revealed. For example, other patients think that "go fish" means to eat the playing card or that the primary function of the paddle in the game of ping pong is to hit oneself in the head. At one point, when Ed removes the straitjacket of another patient, the patient begins wildly destroying the facility. Eventually, someone yells, "It's medication time!" Ed changes the asylum music to a Funkadelic song, "(Not Just) Knee Deep," and encourages all patients—some of whom are still in straitjackets—to dance like zombies. Some of the song lyrics include the following: "She's a freak. The girl is a freak." Incidentally, it could be argued that the film's combination of medication, song lyrics, and choreography

In William Peter Blatty's *Twinkle, Twinkle, Killer Kane* (1980) (also known as *The Ninth Configuration*), the delusional Vietnam vet Colonel Vincent Kane (Stacy Keach), also known as "Killer Kane," believes that he heads the military psychiatric hospital before he learns that he is a patient in the hospital and that it is his brother—not he—who is the real psychiatrist.

extends another asylum stereotype involving medicated, zombie-like patients. Regardless, while the patients (as well as a few guards) are dancing, Dexter uses slapstick to enable an escape from the asylum. He elbows the guards in the crotch, stomach, and face and steals the keys. They ultimately escape by busting through glass windows.

It is challenging to ascertain much depth or insight from *Good Burger*, but it is a good final example. It reveals that by 1997, cinema and audiences were willing and able to treat the filmic asylum as pure escapist entertainment. In *Good Burger*, we find the asylum stereotypes of the straitjackets and padded walls (and the use of the word "freak" in the music), the violence of the body blows and window escapes, the use of false identities both in the institution and beforehand, and the asylum-as-prison trope of Ed and Dexter being committed to an asylum as a form of formal punishment—and all of this is made palatable and entertaining for audiences through slapstick comedy.

In the book *Currents of Comedy on the American Screen: How Film and Television Deliver Different Laughs for Changing Times*, Nicholas Laham brilliantly analyzes the screwball comedy. In discussing how the genre functioned as a diversion from reality for audiences, he quotes the work of film critic Duane Byrge and Professor Robert Milton Miller: "Life for much of the original audience of [screwball] comedy films was undeniably hard. The screwball fantasy offered to them on the screen implied that life should be fun.... The 'real world' depicted in the fantasy was ultimately nonsensical. Yet, it was a more appealing world than the one outside the theatre's doors."[25] Every decade encounters and navigates its own unique challenges, but for many, regardless of circumstance, slapstick comedy offers the same fantasy during hard times, the same "life should be fun" mentality, and the same "nonsensical" escapist entertainment, described of the screwball comedy in Laham's book. That said, slapstick used to communicate aspects of the filmic asylum specifically adds layers of meaning to the fantasy, fun, and nonsensical. Audiences of asylum slapstick are not just encouraged to laugh at the jokes, gags, and skits; in the asylum context, they are also forced to grapple with the extent to which our realities inform (or don't) our visual cultures and, most importantly, to consider the magnitude of how our consumption of representation programs our realities.

Notes

1. Theodor W. Adorno, "Chaplin Times Two," trans. John MacKay, *The Yale Journal of Criticism* 9, no. 1 (1996): 60.
2. Steven Jacobs and Hilde D'haeyere, "Frankfurter Slapstick: Benjamin, Kracauer, and Adorno on American Screen Comedy," *October Magazine* 160 (2017): 32–33.
3. Muriel Andrin, "Back to the 'Slap': Slapstick's Hyperbolic Gesture and the Rhetoric of Violence," in *Slapstick Comedy*, ed. Tom Paulus and Rob King (Routledge AFI Film Readers Series, 2010): 226.
4. Jennifer M. Bean, "The Art of Imitation: The Originality of Charlie Chaplin and Other Moving-Image Myths," in *Slapstick Comedy*, ed. Tom Paulus and Rob King (Routledge AFI Film Readers Series, 2010): 236.
5. *Off to Bloomingdale Asylum* (1901), directed by Georges Méliès.
6. *Modern Times* (1936), directed by Charles Chaplin.
7. *Love Crazy* (1941), directed by Jack Conway.
8. *The Pink Panther Strikes Again* (1976), directed by Blake Edwards.
9. *High Anxiety* (1977), directed by Mel Brooks.
10. *The Ninth Configuration* (1980), directed by William Peter Blatty.
11. *Good Burger* (1997), directed by Brian Robbins.
12. Buster Keaton, *My Wonderful World of Slapstick* (Pickle Partners Publishing, 2015), 53.
13. *Off to Bloomingdale Asylum*'s original French title is *L'omnibus des Toqués Blancs et Noirs*, which translates to "the omnibus of white and black 'crazies.'" In the short film, the performers switch back and forth between blackface characters and white clowns.
14. "The Bloomingdale Insane Asylum," Bloomingdale Neighborhood History Group, January 10, 2016, https://bloomingdalehistory.com/2016/01/10/thebloomingdale-insane-asylum/.
15. Chaplin, *Modern Times*.
16. *Ibid.*
17. Jacobs and D'haeyere, "Frankfurter Slapstick," 34.
18. *Ibid.*
19. Adorno, "Chaplin Times Two," 60.
20. Andrin, "Back to the 'Slap,'" 226.
21. Blatty, *The Ninth Configuration*.
22. *Rolling Thunder* (1977), directed by John Flynn.
23. Adorno, "Chaplin Times Two," 60.
24. Robbins, *Good Burger*.
25. Nicholas Laham, *Currents of Comedy on the American Screen: How Film and Television Deliver Different Laughs for Changing Times* (McFarland, 2009), 26.

SECTION II

Cult Classics

4

ECT on Screen

The Continuing Cultural Impact of Cuckoo's Nest

TIMOTHY W. KNEELAND

Electroconvulsive Therapy, also known as electroshock, or by the initials ECT, is the use of electricity to induce a seizure to ameliorate the symptoms of mental illness. The treatment plays an outsized role as a metaphor for psychiatric oppression and torture in films made in the United States. Although ECT has appeared in many movies since *The Snake Pit* (1947), the 1975 film *One Flew Over the Cuckoo's Nest* had the most significant impact on the public perception of ECT and psychiatry, one that healthcare professionals are still battling today. In *One Flew Over the Cuckoo's Nest*, the setting—in this case, a state hospital—is as significant as the treatment itself, those who administer it, and those who receive it—the patients.

A review of Hollywood's dramatized view of electroshock reveals elements of the history of the treatment and popular fears about psychiatry and psychiatric treatment facilities, specifically fears that such facilities might impose such treatments on patients confined within their walls, without regard to the patients' wishes or concern for their welfare.

The Origins of Electroshock Therapy

The origins of ECT lie in the period between the world wars, when mental hospitals in Europe and America were filled with chronically ill patients who had little or no hope of being cured. European psychiatrists and neurologists responded by developing new somatic treatments they believed would cure the insane and restore them to the community.

Julius Wagner-Jauregg designed the first treatment to garner widespread approval. Wagner-Jauregg injected neurosyphilis patients suffering from general paresis insanity with plasma from the blood of malaria victims. This procedure induced a mild form of malaria that led to high fevers in the patients. The patients remained in a fever for a week or more, after which they were given quinine, the standard cure for malaria. The results were uneven; some patients died, but others recovered and left the institutions. Until the invention of penicillin, fever therapy became the standard treatment in Europe and the United States for general paresis and other chronic mental illnesses. Malaria supplanted mercury, which had been used for centuries, and which carries its own dangers, both mental and physical. Considered a breakthrough at the time, Wagner-Jauregg received one of only two Nobel Prizes in Medicine ever given to psychiatrists.[1] The prize was awarded in 1927.

Wagner-Jauregg's success inspired others to seek somatic treatments for psychological ailments, which led to the development of so-called shock treatments. Manfred Sakel pioneered insulin coma to treat schizophrenic patients in his Vienna clinic. The procedure was labor intensive and required daily introduction of insulin into patients until they fell into a coma and nearly died; this stage was followed by infusions of intravenous glucose, which revived them. The procedure took weeks and required attendants to closely monitor patients to avoid accidental fatalities. Even with around-the-clock care, 1–2 percent of patients died during the treatment. Despite the risks, insulin shock became a standard treatment for schizophrenia from the 1930s until it was replaced with pharmaceutical treatments such as chlorpromazine in the 1950s.[2]

Convulsive therapy was pioneered by Ladislas von Meduna, who became convinced that people with epilepsy were naturally resistant to schizophrenia due to the abundance of glial cells in their brains. Following Wagner-Jauregg and Sakel, he used a chemical agent to induce an artificial convulsion in hopes of curing schizophrenia. The procedure was less labor intensive than insulin shock, but it was difficult to predict the intensity of the seizures. Furthermore, patients became filled with fear and dread about the experience after just one treatment. Despite patient objections and the inability to control the seizures, psychiatrists reported mental health improvement for both psychotic and depressive patients. Like insulin, the treatment remained in regular use until the 1950s, when it was discarded in favor of psychopharmacology.[3]

Intrigued by the results claimed by Meduna, the Italian psychiatrist Ugo Cerletti sought a more efficient and effective method of inducing convulsions and invented electroshock. Cerletti had followed with professional interest reports that indicated that causing a convulsion would alleviate or cure patients diagnosed with mental illness. He used chemical agents but was aware that electricity could be applied non-fatally to hogs and thought this might be a better means of controlling the seizure and also be less time intensive. He and his colleague Lucio Bini experimented on dogs to develop a safe technique for using electricity on humans. They found that if they applied electricity directly to the head and not through the body and heart, they could induce non-fatal convulsions.

In April 1938, Cerletti had an opportunity to try his technique on a schizophrenic patient brought to his clinic in Rome. After a series of electrical jolts that were non-convulsive, the patient achieved a grand mal seizure that led to violent convulsions. The patient had 11 treatments from April through June 1938, when Cerletti pronounced him cured and returned him home.[4] Thus, electroconvulsive therapy was born.

History of Electroshock Therapy, 1938–Present

ECT was widely used after World War II for depression, mania, and psychoses, with patients ranging in age from early childhood to octogenarian. During its heyday in the 1940s and 1950s, electroconvulsive therapy differed significantly from what patients experience today. Patients were lined up to undergo ECT early in the morning and moved in and out of treatment rooms as if on an assembly line. They were strapped to their beds, their heads were smeared with a glycerin ointment, and a rubber mouthguard was placed between their teeth to protect them from shattering during the convulsive phase. Finally, electrodes were placed on their heads either through forceps or via a belt tightened across their temples. Electricity was sent through their brain by an alternating current of up to 150 volts until seizure was reached. The tonic and clonic spasm led to violent convulsions that made patients' eyes bulge and stopped their breathing, turning them cyanotic. Some shook so violently that they cracked their teeth or broke their ribs or vertebrae. As patients convulsed, they involuntarily defecated, urinated, and ejaculated. Patients were given ECT dozens of times until they seemed more coherent, less manic, and more manageable. All patients reported memory loss; some noted they lost not days but years.[5]

The treatment declined in the 1960s and 1970s as drug treatments such as phenothiazine antipsychotics, monoamine oxidase inhibitors, tricyclic antidepressants, and selective serotonin reuptake inhibitors displaced it. Writings by critics of psychiatry such as Thomas Szasz, Erving Goffman, and later Peter Breggin challenged the acceptance of the treatment and raised concerns about its abuse, citing it as one means of social control or patient management and not an effective therapy. Patient advocacy groups raised concerns about the side effects, especially memory loss. Civil rights organizations called for patient rights and demanded informed consent and a right to refuse treatment.[6]

The claim that ECT was abused and utilized to punish and control patients is not entirely unfounded. Joel Braslow's study of ECT indicates that electroshock was used for behavioral control and implicitly served as a punishment. These behaviors included being noisy, uncooperative, and stubborn. "Recalcitrant" patients at California's Stockton State Hospital were prescribed ECT on a PRN (*pro re nata*, or as-needed) basis. Psychiatric notes indicated that after electroshock, patients were easier to manage and more cooperative. It is conceivable that patients saw the treatment as a punishment and modified their behavior to avoid it. Andrew Scull found similar patterns in studies of hospitals in Georgia, Michigan, and Texas.[7]

Despite the potential abuse, the treatment was never abandoned. Advocates for electroshock, including Max Hamilton, Max Fink, Richard Weiner, Harold Sackheim, Charles Kellner, and more recently Sarah Lisanby, continued using the procedure and encouraged their psychiatric peers to reexamine it. Advocates established new professional journals such as *The Journal of ECT*. Proponents encouraged the American Psychiatric Association (APA) to review electroconvulsive therapy; the APA declared ECT safe and effective. Proponents cited controlled experimental studies of ECT, showing it was efficacious.[8]

Since the 1960s, the treatment has been modified to ameliorate the stress on the body and reduce the effects of memory loss. Electroshock machines now measure the body's electrical resistance and deliver less electricity in a more targeted manner than earlier devices. Patients are given anesthesia to sleep through the procedure, given a drug to dry up secretions, and provided with a muscle relaxant to eliminate the violent thrashing seen in earlier treatment use. Rather than send electricity through both sides of the brain, psychiatrists use unilateral ECT, in which the electricity is sent through only one side. Patients receive far fewer treatments than in the 1940s. Rather than dreading it, many patients have a regular course of maintenance ECT to keep their symptoms from returning. One such patient, Kitty Dukakis, the wife of 1988 presidential candidate Michael Dukakis, was a vocal advocate for ECT.[9]

ECT increased in use because of an increasing number of patients who did not respond to drug treatment or crossed a threshold beyond which drugs were ineffective.[10] Other candidates for electroshock included elderly patients for whom drug interactions were dangerous and pregnant women unable to take medication.[11] By the new millennium, ECT was growing in use, promoted by patient advocacy groups like the National Alliance on Mental Illness, supported by the American Psychiatric Association, and celebrated in hundreds of articles in professional publications and in newspapers such as the *New York Times* and *Washington Post* and famous memoirs by the likes of Norman Endler and Martha Manning.[12]

Despite the rising popularity of ECT among psychiatrists and patients, the treatment remains controversial. A meta-study of studies has found flaws in the data, and there are calls for its ban in the United Kingdom due to its trauma to the brain.[13]

Cinematic Electroshock

A review of key films over the last 75 years reveals Hollywood's use of electroshock to enhance the genres of noir, horror, and social commentary on psychiatry. In dozens of films, ECT has appeared as a tool of social control, punishment, and torture. A few of these movies and their stars have gone on to win Hollywood's highest accolade, the Academy Award, perhaps because they capture American fears of authority, loss of individual autonomy, and foreboding about psychiatry. To a lesser degree, they provide a distorted view of the reality of this treatment.[14] Films remain a flashpoint for advocates who, in numerous journal articles and interviews, disparage Hollywood's depiction of the treatment, which they believe has been detrimental to the public.[15]

In the era before psychopharmacology was available, films utilizing ECT did not necessarily condemn it but sometimes credited it for assisting patients with recovery from mental illness. The first motion picture to include ECT was the Academy Award–winning film *The Snake Pit* (1948), based on the 1946 book of the same name by Mary Jane Ward. Filmed at a time when ECT was in the ascendant, the movie is ambivalent about the treatment and grudgingly treats it as an adjunct to psychotherapy. The movie stars Olivia de Havilland as the mentally troubled protagonist Virginia Cunningham. De Havilland was already a star due to her performance in *Gone with the Wind* in 1939, and she garnered another nomination for her portrayal of the middle-aged writer whose depression leads to psychoses and institutionalization.

Once hospitalized, Virginia is treated by the sympathetic Dr. Kik, who at one point prescribes a course of ECT to close the gap between Virginia's fantasy and reality.

The scene in which Virginia is given ECT draws on the genres of horror and film noir to create a scene of violence and terror that focuses not on the patient but on the electroshock machine. As Virginia is brought into the room, her eyes turn to the machine. Director Anatole Litvak has the camera lingering over the dark and foreboding dials. The device is not benign, and its brutal intent is shown when Dr. Kik pushes a button on the machine. Suddenly, the camera angle becomes lopsided, the shadows grow noir style, and stabbing music stimulates the convulsion, which is not shown on screen. In some ways, this suggested to audiences the horrific nature of the treatment, so difficult to watch that the camera turned away. Dr. Kik orders a course of four electroshock treatments. In a film montage, we see him note a slight improvement as each treatment slowly brings her to reality, allowing her to begin her psychoanalysis and eventually reach a cathartic breakthrough, leading to her recovery.[16]

Perhaps due to its success, *The Snake Pit* lays down patterns that will be seen again: dramatic music, distorted camera angles, elements of horror, and glimpses of the foreboding machine accompany the use of ECT. However, unlike many later movies, the film suggests that ECT is a useful tool of psychiatry and aids in Virginia's recovery. The 1957 movie *Fear Strikes Out* parallels this idea. It tells the story of Boston Red Sox baseball legend Jimmy Piersall, who suffered a breakdown in the 1950s. In the film, Anthony Perkins, three years before his memorable performance as the insane Norman Bates in *Psycho*, receives electroshock off-screen. Rather than showing audiences the procedure, director Robert Mulligan angled the camera on the doorway to the treatment room, creating a sense that something dramatic with electricity was occurring, but leaving it up to the viewer's imagination as to what. The use of ECT is incidental, as Jimmy's eventual recovery comes about only when he gains insight into his relationship with his father.[17]

The Horror of ECT

After 1960, Hollywood vilified the use of ECT, depicting it as a tool of behavioral control, punishment, and torture by sinister and uncaring healthcare professionals. In such movies, the physicians and staff are often less sane than the unfortunate inmates. Rather than look away, directors enhanced the sense of horror and violence by focusing the camera on the patients as they were strapped to a gurney, helplessly brought into a room surrounded by people in white. Electricity raced through their brains at the push of a button, making them shake uncontrollably.

ECT is used as a means of behavior control and punishment in *The Caretakers* (1963), an earnest social commentary on mental health in America. The film was first screened in the United States Senate and is "Dedicated to the caretakers who research and sacrifice to discover the truth." Robert Stack stars as Dr. MacLeod, a modern-day Philippe Pinel who seeks to unchain and bring light to the mentally ill. But his ideas run afoul of Nurse Terry, the old-school head of nursing, played by Joan Crawford. Nurse Terry despises the new doctor and fumes that nurses control their patients at all times. In the battle between control and care lies Lorna Melford, a middle-aged woman sent to the institution following a bout of hysteria in a movie theater.

When Lorna defends a fellow patient from one of the brutish nurses under Terry's command, she inadvertently hurts the nurse, which leads to her treatment with ECT. The implication is clear that this is punishment, not therapy. In the electroshock scene, Lorna, played by Polly Bergen, is wheeled in on a gurney. As she lies helpless and restrained, nurses put a strap around her head and a mouth guard between her teeth. Three nurses hold her down while dramatic music plays, reaching a crescendo as Lorna's body writhes and she struggles to breathe.

A young nurse watching the scene is appalled and leaves the room. Afterward, she tells a fellow nurse that ECT is barbaric. Echoing Nurse Terry, the peer remarks, "It's worth it if it brings them out of depression." Viewers knew that the nurse was wrong; ECT made Lorna more docile but not healthier, and her restoration to sanity

In Samuel Fuller's *Shock Corridor* (1963), Stuart (James Best) is seated to the left, as he raises his arm and flanks reporter Johnny Barrett (Peter Breck), who got himself admitted to a psychiatric ward so he can solve a murder committed in the hospital, but then matters go awry and the reporter is straitjacketed and subjected to ECT. Crouching to the right is an African American patient, Trent (Hari Rhodes), whose psychotic-sounding racist poster reads, "Integration and Democracy Don't Mix."

will only come about, as in *The Snake Pit*, because of the caring and kindness of her male doctor.[18]

Two other movies in the 1960s featured ECT in film noir and were marketed with lurid movie posters.[19] These black-and-white movies share a similar plot device: a sane man goes undercover in an institution to solve a mystery. Once inside and labeled insane, no one believes his claims that the staff are using this therapy to torture patients or to drive them insane.

Shock Corridor (1963) tells the tale of a newspaper reporter who goes into an institution to solve a murder committed there. With the help of his girlfriend, who agrees to play his sister, and of a friendly psychiatrist, he mimics insanity. Once hospitalized, he discovers that the murderer is an orderly at the hospital. Unfortunately for the reporter, the orderly figures out his game and begins a series of torments that will cause a breakdown. The orderly locks him in a ward of nymphomaniacs, who attack and sexually assault him. Then he stirs up a violent race riot that nearly kills the reporter. The orderly also overdoses him with drugs that make him catatonic.

Observing his deterioration, his "sister" consents to a course of electroshock, which is more torment. The scene shows Johnny in restraints, a towel shoved into his mouth, and an electric belt wound tightly across his temples. His eyes plead with the audience just before the electricity shakes him violently to the sound of jarring jazz music in the background. As the scene plays out, images of the horrors Johnny has endured in the hospital dance across the screen. Rather than helping him, ECT drives him to insanity. Although he identifies the murderer, the treatments have destroyed his sanity, and he remains in the hospital.[20] The conclusion is clear that in the wrong hands, the tools of psychiatry, as well as the hospitals that offer such treatments, are harmful.

A similar plot transpires in the film *Shock Treatment* (1964). In this film, an actor, Dale Nelson, played by Stuart Whitman, is hired to go undercover in a mental hospital to locate a missing million dollars. Dale persuades the authorities that he is unfit, but his acting does not convince the head of the institution, Dr. Beighley, played by Lauren Bacall. It turns out she is also seeking the missing cash, and to eliminate her competition, she begins to torture Dale to drive him into insanity. She drugs him and prescribes electroshock. In the ECT scene, his helplessness is evident. He awakens, strapped to a gurney and dizzy from the narcotic Dr. Beighley ordered for him. He looks around as he is wheeled into a room that looks more like a prison than a treatment room. Before he can speak, a rubber mouth guard is forced into his mouth, and an electric belt is strapped across his temples. Dr. Beighley, looking sinister in the lighting, stands in front of the electroshock machine, which looks more like the equipment found in *Frankenstein* than an actual ECT machine. Meanwhile, edgy music plays in the background as she orders a painful shock through Dale's brain, which fails to reach a convulsive threshold. The camera pans high as she orders the highest dosage, which leads to a violent convulsion.

When Dale character awakens, ECT has left his mind numb and impaired and teetering on the brink of insanity. He escapes with the help of his love interest, who is a fellow patient. Together they prove the sinister motives of the doctor. In a plot twist, the movie ends with Dale and his love interest leaving the asylum and the doctor, having lost her mind, now a patient there.[21] This film has several sexist overtones, as Bacall is emblematic of strong women who seek to destroy men and is, simultaneously, one step away from hysteria. Perhaps this is why she intensely disliked the movie and thought it her worst film.[22] Audiences watching the movie may have concluded that electroshock was not good for the brain and that psychiatric wards themselves were potentially dangerous places, because of staff rather than patients.

The films of the 1960s were influenced by earlier movies but also evince themes found in Ken Kesey's novel *One Flew Over the Cuckoo's Nest* (1962). In this book, ECT appears as part of a regime of terror used in the mechanized, machine-centered, emotionless ward at a state mental hospital ruled by Nurse Ratched, who is very much in the mold of the controlling Nurse Terry in *The Caregivers* and the villainous head of psychiatry in *Shock Treatment*. In the novel, patients are described as "machines with flaws inside," and Nurse Ratched carries around a bag shaped like a toolbox that contains "tiny pills that gleam like porcelain, needles, forceps, watchmaker's pliers, rolls of copper wire." The non-conformist Randle McMurphy goes into the institution not to solve a mystery but to shirk working on a prison farm, but he quickly runs afoul of Nurse Ratched and is taken to the "shock shop," where he is told he will be "jointly administered therapy and punishment for your 'hostile go-to-hell behavior.'"[23]

Although a powerful novel, it was the film version that struck a nerve in the American psyche.

No movie has surpassed 1975's *One Flew Over the Cuckoo's Nest* in the public understanding of electroshock, and no history of ECT has failed to mention the film.[24] The film was a big-budget production of the book and drew on the idea of a man trapped in a mental hospital, as seen in *Shock Corridor* and *Shock Treatment*, and also shaped future cinematic interpretations of ECT in movies like The *Fifth Floor* (1978) and *Frances* (1982).

Cuckoo's Nest stars Jack Nicholson as the antiauthoritarian Randle McMurphy, who, after being arrested for antisocial behavior, discovers he can avoid work on a prison farm by feigning mental illness. Sent to the mental hospital, he finds himself trapped under the dictatorial rule of the head nurse, Ms. Ratched, played by Louise Fletcher. Nurse Ratched has all the emotional range of a machine, and her one purpose is to keep order and control over the inmates in her ward. As in the book, McMurphy stages a rebellion against Big Nurse, as she is called by inmates of the hospital, and for this transgression, he is given electroshock treatments. When ECT fails to pacify him, he is subjected to a double lobotomy. In the final scene of the movie, pitying the once vital McMurphy, who is now in a vegetative state, his friend and fellow inmate Chief Bromden suffocates McMurphy with a pillow and then escapes.[25]

The film is a social commentary on the dehumanization of individuals at the hands of authority figures, and it was released at a time when Americans were distrustful of institutions and leaders, having been lied to about Vietnam, experienced the Watergate scandal, and feeling that those in positions of power neglected the needs of individuals.[26] *One Flew Over the Cuckoo's Nest* won top Oscars for the director Miloš Forman, actor Jack Nicholson, and actress Louise Fletcher; it also won Best Picture and writing awards. Not since 1934's *It Happened One Night* had a film achieved such critical acclaim. It was filmed in an actual mental hospital, the Oregon State Mental Hospital. Its director, Dean Brooks, was criticized by other mental professionals for allowing the hospital to be used for filming and its inmates to serve as extras, but Dr. Brooks, who appears in the movie himself, responded that he hoped audiences would see the movie as an allegory of how a man caught in the system could be given electroshock and lobotomized. He also asked filmmakers to add a disclaimer that the movie was not an authentic depiction of a mental hospital.[27]

Unlike electroshock in other films, the depiction is denuded of the elements of horror and has the look and feel of a documentary. No music plays in the background, nor are there any special effects during the seizure. The scene unfolds with McMurphy awaiting his treatment in a hallway. Another inmate, Cheswick, is brought out from the ECT room unconscious. A young nurse calls his name, and McMurphy stands and gives Chief Bromden, played by Will Sampson, a thumbs-up and his wicked grin. Two orderlies escort McMurphy into the room, where his smile leaves as he sees a team of doctors and nurses awaiting him. He is gently laid on the table and told by the doctor, "This won't hurt it, will be over in a moment." The nurse applies a conductant gel to his temples and places the rubber mouthguard between his teeth to prevent him from biting his tongue. The calipers are placed on his temples. The psychiatrist asks, "Are you ready?" as the camera shows him turning the dial on the electroconvulsive shock machine. The machine is not a horror movie prop but an actual circa-1958 Medcraft Model B-24.[28] The camera shifts to focus on McMurphy's face as he begins the convulsions and pans out to show the staff holding down his shaking body, then back to his face as he goes through the seizure and falls unconscious.[29] The audience knows that McMurphy is faking his mental illness, making the perfunctory and bureaucratic administration of ECT is more horrific than the overly dramatized version in earlier films. The thought that anyone labeled mentally ill could be given electroshock without consent resonated with the public and stigmatized electroshock for decades thereafter.

The impact of *One Flew Over the Cuckoo's Nest* is measured in its ubiquity in the discussion of ECT. You would be hard-pressed to find any newspaper or journal article on the subject that does not at least mention the movie.[30] It is not only the popular press but professionals who feel the movie has done a grave disservice to the treatment. Dr. Max Fink, a vocal proponent of ECT, wrote, "A graphic example of abuse is depicted in Ken Kesey's book 'One Flew Over the Cuckoo's Nest,' and in the 1975 film based on the novel.... The unavoidable message is that Electroshock and lobotomies are cruelties."[31] Edward Shorter and Dr. David Healy wrote, "There is no doubt that in its fantastical depictions of ECT, the movie industry played a capital role in stigmatizing the procedure and a terribly irresponsible one from the point of view of the public."[32] Historian Jonathan Sadowsky, sympathetic to the value of electroshock therapy, wrote, "Public fears have been dramatized in numerous novels and films, including the most influential, *One Flew Over the Cuckoo's Nest*, which remains the most vivid association for possible patients. ECT has become a symbol not only of coercion in psychiatry, but for arbitrary authority generally, even as many psychiatric patients view ECT as lifesaving."[33] Experts blamed *One Flew Over the Cuckoo's Nest* for undermining patient confidence in the treatment. Curiously, the descriptions offered by their patients, such as Jack Nicholson "screaming" or his body "flailing," fail to match the actual scene, which suggests that the fear of ECT is being justified by a misremembered film. I would even go as far as to speculate that many of these patients never even saw the movie, which makes professional concerns about *One Flew Over the Cuckoo's Nest* worthy of a study of their own.

After *Cuckoo's Nest*, films dealing with electroshock follow the template of earlier movies. They situate individuals trapped in an institution and forced to undergo ECT as a means of behavioral control, punishment, torture, and murder. This plays to audience fears tied to the stigma associated with mental illness. Perhaps the chief fear is that once labeled mentally ill, your credibility is destroyed. Thus, any claims of abuse at the hands of staff are one more sign that you are paranoid and a confirmation you are ill. To add to the drama, in many movies, patients are women or children, making them even more vulnerable to control by their male doctors.

Although used on male inmates in *Shock Corridor*, *Shock Treatment*, and *Cuckoo's Nest*, since the mid–1970s, ECT is more often seen as an antifeminist weapon intent on the destruction of vibrant women. This may reflect the reality that women are more likely to be given ECT than men. It also reflects the reality that casting female leads in big-budget movies produced by established studies nearly guarantees Academy Award nominations for the actresses.

Such is the case with *Frances* (1982), starring Jessica Lange and Sam Shepard, based on the life of actress Frances Farmer. The film opens with Frances, played by Lange, as a bright young teen in New England, questioning orthodoxy and becoming friends with the local outcast Harry, played by Shepard. Frances becomes a famous actress but rejects the Hollywood system and is arrested for assault and sent to a private mental hospital. She remains obstreperous. With the help of Harry, Frances escapes, but when she announces she will no longer act, her greedy mother commits her to a state mental hospital, an institution from hell. Here she is subjected to a series of torments aimed at breaking her spirit and making her more docile. She is straitjacketed, given ECT, and ultimately lobotomized (in the film, but not in real life). Like the antihero Randle McMurphy, she challenges the system and is severely punished. The movie ends with a broken and hollowed-out Frances pathetically shuffling out to appear on the popular television show *This is Your Life*.[34]

In *Girl, Interrupted* (1999), costar Angelina Jolie's character, Lisa, is prescribed ECT to control her antisocial behavior but like McMurphy, ECT is ineffectual. In this case, ECT becomes a metaphor for patriarchy and the status quo, those who threaten it, especially women, will be punished. Unsurprisingly, Lange received a nomination for Best Actress for her turn as Frances, and Jolie won Best Supporting Actress for her role as Lisa.

In clinical settings, ECT is often used on older women when other treatments fail. In movies, this reality is echoed in its use on middle-aged women, whose angst and suffering derive from their social situation and not biology. In *A Woman Under the Influence* (1974), Gena Rowlands stars as a middle-aged woman whose behavior leads her husband, played by Peter Falk, to have her institutionalized, where she receives a series of treatments, including ECT. There is no question as to whether she is unwell, but the movie suggests it is the stress of her family that is making her ill, not some biological problem. When she returns to her old life, once again, she struggles with despair. The final scene is of Rowlands and her husband cleaning up the mess made by her homecoming party and perhaps cleaning up the mess that is their lives. The director, John Cassavetes, allows the audience to determine what happens next. For her work, Rowlands was nominated for Best Actress.[35]

Requiem for a Dream (2000) stars Ellen Burstyn as Sara, who becomes addicted to amphetamines while attempting weight loss; in addition to her own addiction, she is distraught because her son and daughter-in-law are heroin addicts. Resistant to other therapies, she is prescribed ECT. She manages to sign a consent form and is given a shot but remains awake in a wordless scene during which she is given a mouthguard, and a bilateral set of electrodes is placed on her head to administer the shock. As she is convulsed, the scene is shot with shaky camera footage and flashes from other parts of the film, all accompanied by dramatic and jarring music. When Sara is finally released from the hospital, she is worse off than when she entered. Burstyn received an Academy Award nomination for her role. At best, the film indicates that the mental health profession has failed in its duty of care.[36]

Cinematic views of ECT also use it as a metaphor for sexual assault. The victimization of women by powerful men reflects the fears and sad reality of much of U.S. history. That ECT should be an extension of this is not surprising. One example is *Caged Heat* (1974), a schlock film about female prisoners in which the treatment is meted out to punish them, but once drugged and shocked, the inert women are subject to the sexual desires of the male doctor.[37] *The Fifth Floor* (1978) is the "true" story of a college girl's confinement in a mental hospital. Poisoned with strychnine, the girl is declared suicidal by a male doctor and committed. Once inside, she is trapped, unable to convince authorities she is well, and she is sexually assaulted by Carl, a creepy male orderly played with sociopathic ease by Bo Hopkins. Carl deploys ECT to break down her resistance, to fry her brain until she becomes his sex toy.[38] In *Unsane* (2018), Claire Foy appears as Sawyer, a mental patient stalked by an obsessive orderly. The orderly uses a stolen ECT machine to torture and kill a male patient he deems a potential rival for Sawyer's affection. Although freed, Sawyer is broken by her experience and finds herself wary and fearful of men.[39]

Another thematic use of ECT in movies is to threaten youth and innocence. In movies such as *Return to Oz* (1985), the dark sequel to *The Wizard of Oz* (1939), a very young and fragile-looking Dorothy is slated for a primitive ECT aimed at destroying her dreams of Oz and making her more docile. Fortunately, she is rescued in the nick of time and returns to Oz to fight oppression.[40] In *Moonrise Kingdom* (2012), Wes Anderson has an officious social services employee indicate that young Sam, accused of but not guilty of violence, will be institutionalized and subjected to electroshock. Even when informed by the authorities that Sam is innocent, her response suggests that once returned to state care, Sam will get ECT whether he needs it or not. Once again, ECT looms over officialdom and represents the fear that once in the clutches of the bureaucracy, an individual's freedom to dream or aspire to better things will be eliminated.

Finally, electroshock is a stock item in horror movies. Drawing on the memory losses reported by those receiving ECT, the treatment becomes a tool to erase memories in films such as *Constantine* (2005), *The Manchurian Candidate* (2004), and *Amnesiac* (2014). Drawing on its history of controlling behavior, filmmakers have used it as a means of control in *Lies* (1983) and *Revolutionary Road* (2008). Drawing on patient fears, electroshock is used as torture in films such as *Chattahoochee* (1989), *Asylum* (2008), and *Suicide Squad* (2016). Reflecting fears of personality annihilation, ECT is a murder weapon in *Death Wish II* (1982), *Child's Play* (1988), and *The Ward* (2010).[41]

Finally, we find that the treatment, perhaps as a stand-in for psychiatry itself, is mocked in comedies such as *Hot Shots!* (1986), *The Beverly Hillbillies* (1993), *Running with Scissors* (2006), *and Dark Shadows* (2017).

Curiously, all the examples of ECT cited above occur in mental hospitals or asylums, confirming that the institution itself is as scary—or at least as important—as the treatments meted out in those institutions. There are no mentions of office-based "ECT" (which had its proponents in Brooklyn in the 1970s) or of outpatient ECT, which became more the norm than the exception after managed care limited inpatient hospital stays previously required for ECT. Apparently, arriving at the outpatient clinic in an Access-A-Ride cannot capture spectators' attention in the same way that screaming ambulance sirens, heading into hospitals, can.

Notes

1. Cynthia J. Tsay, "Julius Wagner-Jauregg and the Legacy of Malarial Therapy for the Treatment of General Paresis of the Insane," *Yale Journal of Biology and Medicine* 86, no. 2 (June 13, 2013): 245–54, PMID: 23766744; Timothy W. Kneeland and Carol A.B. Warren, *Pushbutton Psychiatry: A Cultural History of Electroshock in America* (Routledge, 2008), 46.

2. Insulin shock therapy was featured in the film *A Beautiful Mind* based on the life of John Nash who suffered from schizophrenia; see Ron Howard, *A Beautiful Mind* (Universal Pictures, 2001).

3. Initially, Meduna used camphor but replaced this with metrazol. Kneeland and Warren, *Pushbutton Psychiatry*, 46, 68–69; Joel T. Braslow, *Mental Ills and Bodily Cures: Psychiatry in the First Half of the Twentieth Century* (University of California Press, 1997), 97.

4. *Ibid.*

5. See Kneeland and Warren, "The Birth and Triumph of Pushbutton Psychiatry, Electroshock, 1938–1965," in Kneeland and Warren, *Pushbutton Psychiatry*.

6. See Kneeland and Warren, "Rage Against the Machine: The Decline of Electroshock, 1966–1980," in

Pushbutton Psychiatry; Thomas Szasz, *The Myth of Mental Illness* (Hoeber-Harper, 1961); Erving Goffman, *Asylums: Essays on the Social Situation of Mental Patients and Other Inmates* (Doubleday, 1961); Peter Breggin, *Electroshock: Its Brain Disabling Effects* (Springer, 1979).

7. Braslow, *Mental Ills and Bodily Cures*, 96–109; Andrew Scull, *Desperate Remedies: Psychiatry's Turbulent Quest to Cure Mental Illness* (Belknap Press, 2022), 122–123.

8. For a meta review of studies on the efficacy of electroshock, see Ian M. Anderson, "Electroconvulsive Therapy (ECT) versus Sham ECT for Depression: Do Study Limitations Invalidate the Evidence (and Mean We Should Stop Using ECT)?" *British Journal of Psychiatric Advances* 27, no. 5 (2021): 285–91, doi:10.1192/bja.2021.23.

9. Katharine Q. Seelye, "Kitty Dukakis, a Beneficiary of Electroshock Therapy, Emerges as Its Evangelist," *New York Times*, December 31, 2016, https://www.nytimes.com/2016/12/31/us/kitty-dukakis-electroshock-therapy-evangelist.html.

10. Sarah E. Byrne and Anthony J. Rothschild, "Loss of Antidepressant Efficacy During Maintenance Therapy: Possible Mechanisms and Treatments," *Journal of Clinical Psychiatry* 59, no. 6 (1998): 279–288.

11. Emma T. Geduldig and Charles H. Kellner, "Electroconvulsive Therapy in the Elderly: New Findings in Geriatric Depression," *Current Psychiatry Reports* 18, no. 40 (2016), https://doiorg.ezproxy.naz.edu/10.1007/s11920-016-0674-5.

12. During the pandemic the American Psychiatric Association called ECT an "essential procedure"; see "Electroconvulsive Therapy as an Essential Procedure" (2020); National Alliance on Mental Illness, "ECT, TMS, and Other Brain Stimulation Therapies," https://www.nami.org/About-Mental-Illness/Treatments/ECT-TMS-and-Other-BrainStimulation-Therapies; Norman S Endler, *Holiday of Darkness: A Psychologist's Personal Journey Out of His Depression, Rev.* (Wall & Thompson, 1990); Martha Manning, *Undercurrents: A Therapist's Reckoning with Her Own Depression* (Harper, 1994).

13. Anderson, "Electroconvulsive Therapy (ECT) versus Sham ECT for Depression"; The controversy is traced in Jonathan Sadowsky, *Electroconvulsive Therapy in America: The Anatomy of a Medical Controversy* (Routledge, 2016); more recently electroshock use has come under scrutiny in the UK; see Robin McKie, "Brain Damage Claim Leads to New Row over Electroshock Therapy," *The Guardian*, June 26, 2022, https://www.theguardian.com/society/2022/jun/26/brain-damage-claim-leads-to-new-row-over electroshock-therapy.

14. Gabbard and Gabbard, "Typology, Mythology, Ideology," *Psychiatry and the Cinema* (American Psychiatric Press, 1999).

15. I searched the Internet Movie Database for "Electroconvulsive Therapy" and "Electroshock Therapy" https://www.imdb.com/search/keyword/?keywords=electroconvulsivetherapy&ref_=fn_kw_kw_1 excluding all documentaries, films made outside of the United States, made-for-television movies, and direct-to-video films. For television programs see Stenaert Pascal, "Based on a True Story? The portrayal of ECT in International Movies and Television Programs," *Brain Stimulation* 96, no. 6 (2016): 882–891; Avery Madeleine Mathews, Peter B. Rosenquist, and William Vaughn McCall, "Representations of ECT in English Language Film and Television in the New Millennium," *Journal of ECT* 32, no. 3 (September 2016): 187–191; for its use in *Batman* universe, see Timothy W. Kneeland, "ECT in Arkham Asylum: Pacification, Assassination, and Electrocution," in Sharon Packer and Daniel R. Frederick, *Welcome to Arkham Asylum: Essays on Psychiatry and the Gotham City Institution* (McFarland, 2020).

16. Kneeland and Warren, *Pushbutton Psychiatry*, 53, 56; Christina Newland, "New Releases: The Snake Pit," *Sight and Sound* (June 2019): 86; Leslie Fishbein, "*The Snake Pit* (1948): The Sexist Nature of Sanity," *American Quarterly* 31, no. 5 (1979): 641–665.

17. Robert Mulligan, *Fear Strikes Out* (1957); Krin Gabbard and Glen O. Gabbard, *Psychiatry and Cinema* (University of Chicago Press, 1987), 42.

18. Hal Barlett, *The Caretakers* (United Artists, 1963).

19. *Shock Corridor* movie poster at Internet Movie Database (IMDB), https://www.imdb.com/title/tt0057495/; *Shock Treatment* movie poster at IMDB, https://www.imdb.com/title/tt0058585/.

20. Samuel Fuller, *Shock Corridor* (Allied Artists, 1963).

21. Denis Sanders, *Shock Treatment* (Twentieth Century, 1964).

22. David Cairns, "The Forgotten: We're All Mad Here," https://mubi.com/notebook/posts/theforgotten-we-re-all-mad-here.

23. Ken Kesey, *One Flew Over the Cuckoo's Nest* (Viking Press, 1962), 19, 64–65.

24. Max Fink, *Electroshock: Restoring the Mind* (Oxford University Press, 1999), 93; Kneeland and Warren, *Pushbutton Psychiatry*, 64–65; David Shorter and Edward Healy, *Shock Therapy: A History of Electroconvulsive Treatment in Mental Illness* (Rutgers University Press, 2007); Sadowsky, *Electroconvulsive Therapy in America*, 2.

25. Miloš Forman, *One Flew Over the Cuckoo's Nest* (United Artists, 1975).

26. Thomas Borstelmann, *The 1970s: A New Global History from Civil Rights to Economic Inequality* (Princeton University Press, 2011).

27. Richard Levine, "A Real Mental Aid Becomes Movie 'Cuckoo's Nest,'" *The New York Times*, April 13, 1975.

28. See https://www.flickr.com/photos/niftyniall/17466731768.
29. Miloš Forman, *One Flew Over the Cuckoo's Nest* (United Artists, 1975).
30. Mentions of *One Flew Over the Cuckoo's Nest* have appeared in popular newspaper and journal articles such as Jean Deitz, "Shock Therapy: Advocates Give Jolt to Villainous Hollywood Image," *Chicago Tribune*, January 21, 1985, 5; Garry B. Walter, "About To Have ECT? Fine, but Don't Watch It in the Movies: The Sorry Portrayal of ECT in Film," *Psychiatric Times* 21, no. 7 (2004), https://www.psychiatrictimes.com/view/about-have-ect-fine-dont-watchit-movies-sorry-portrayal-ect-film; Kate Golembiewski, "How Electroconvulsive Therapy Saves Lives," *Discover*, December 15, 2022, https://www.discovermagazine.com/health/howelectroconvulsive-therapy-saves-lives. You would be hard-pressed to find any mention of electroshock in newspaper stories, journal articles, or professional publications that do not address *One Flew Over the Cuckoo's Nest.*
31. Fink, *Electroshock*, 93.
32. Shorter and Healy, *Shock Therapy*, 153.
33. Jonathan Hal Sadowsky, *Electroconvulsive Therapy in America: The Anatomy of a Medical Controversy* (Routledge, 2019).
34. Graeme Clifford, *Frances* (EMI Films, 1982). Note that as the credits roll a disclaimer indicates that what happened to Frances is not indicative of mental health treatment in the 1980s.
35. John Cassevetes, *Women Under the Influence* (Open Face International, 1974).
36. Darren Aronofsky, *Requiem for a Dream* (Artisan Entertainment, 2000).
37. Jonathan Demme, *Caged Heat* (New World Pictures, 1974). Demme also used ECT as a trope in *The Manchurian Candidate* (Paramount, 2004).
38. Howard Avedis, *The Fifth Floor* (Film Ventures International, 1978). The production company was known for producing movies that were cut-and-paste imitations of blockbuster movies and perhaps it was meant to be a female-centric *Cuckoo's Nest.*
39. Steven Soderbergh, *Unsane* (Regency, 2018). This film echoes his 2013 *Side Effects*, which also featured involuntary commitment (Open Road Films, 2013).
40. Walter Murch, *Return to Oz* (Walt Disney Pictures, 1985).
41. Francis Lawrence, *Constantine* (Warner Bros., 2005); Jonathan Demme, *Manchurian Candidate*; Michael Polish, *Amnesiac* (XLrator Media, 2014); Jim and Ken Wheat, *Lies* (United States, 1983); *Revolutionary Road* (Paramount Vantage, 2008); Mick Jackson, *Chatahootchie* (Hemdale Film Corporation, 1989); David R. Ellis, *Asylum* (Hyde Park Films, 2008); David Ayer, *Suicide Squad* (Warner Bros., 2016); Don Mancini, *Cult of Chucky* (Universal Pictures, 2017); Michael Winner, *Death Wish II* (Columbia Pictures, 1982); Tom Holland, *Child's Play* (United Artists, 1988); John Carpenter, *The Ward* (XLrator Media, 2010). It has been used for comedic effect in *Hot Shots*! (1986) *The Beverly Hillbillies* (1993), *Running With Scissors* (2006), and *Dark Shadows* (2017).

5

The Historical Horrors of Val Lewton's *Bedlam*

Bryan Senn

bedlam (ˊbed-lam), *n.* 1. a scene or state of wild uproar and confusion. 2. *Archaic.* an insane asylum or madhouse.—*Webster's*[1]

One could also add to the above: "3. a superior horror film produced by Val Lewton in 1946."

Mental illness is an uncomfortable topic for many even today, regardless of the progress in treatment and curatives over the last 50 years. So it is remarkable to see a film from the middle of the last century that addresses the issue in such a compassionate, thought-provoking manner—and in the guise of a horror movie, no less. "The shocking truth about 18th Century London's ill-famed House of Horrors," proclaimed a *Bedlam* tagline, "where only death could free its hopeless inmates from the foul and fancy tortures of a master in monstrousness!"

While the "foul and fancy tortures" disguised as treatments in this "ill-famed House of Horrors" remain largely implied (apart from one poor soul claustrophobically encased in form-fitting medieval gibbet-like irons), the cringing fear of its mistreated inmates creates a palpable atmosphere of terror. More dungeon than hospital—all dank stone walls, iron bars, and filthy straw—the shadowy, oppressive surroundings add an air of despair and dread. This, then, is Bedlam, the infamous London madhouse, as portrayed by the 1946 film *Bedlam*.

Inspired by a set of engravings by artist William Hogarth (specifically Plate Eight of his *The Rake's Progress* series), and joining the ranks of the postwar "message" pictures dealing with mental illness (led by the likes of Alfred Hitchcock's *Spellbound* [1945], John Brahm's *The Locket* [1946], Fritz Lang's *Secret Beyond the Door* [1947], and Anatole Litvak's *The Snake Pit* [1948]), *Bedlam*, set in London in 1761, stars Boris Karloff as Master Sims, the sadistic keeper of the Bethlehem lunatic asylum, commonly referred to as "Bedlam." When an intelligent and independent young woman, Nell Bowen (Anna Lee), scorns him and his aristocratic master, Lord Mortimer (Billy House), Sims has her put away in his horrid madhouse. But with the aid of a young Quaker (Richard Fraser), and her courage and kindness shown toward "the loonies in their cages," she gains her freedom while Sims meets his inadvertent-yet-deserved fate (shades of Edgar Allan Poe's "The Cask of Amontillado") at the hands of his own inmates.

St. Mary Bethlehem Hospital, or "Bedlam," was founded in 1247 in London as a monastery which took in the homeless, sick, and destitute. By the late 14th century, Bethlem (as it became known) specialized in the care and incarceration of the mentally ill, becoming England's first so-called insane asylum. Accepting the medieval notion of insanity as a sickness of the body rather than the mind (with "purging" being the primary curative), starving, beatings, ice baths, bloodletting, and "rotation therapy" (in which patients were strapped to a chair hung from the ceiling and spun until they vomited) were the order of the day. Such torturous "treatments," coupled with the squalid conditions and general corruption and chaos of the institute, gave rise to the sobriquet "Bedlam," a nickname co-opted by the 1600s into a colloquial term for madness and mayhem. Open to the public during the 17th and 18th centuries, Bedlam's ... er, Bethlem's mentally ill patients and their horrific treatments became a spectacle for paying visitors—reportedly tens of thousands each year by the mid–1700s, making it London's most popular tourist attraction after St. Paul's Cathedral. (When Nell Bowen first visits the asylum in the film, Master Sims explains, "Our hospital is ancient and well-known, much written of; I daresay no man or woman comes to London from the country who does not pay his tuppence" and extends his hand for the coin.)

Among the real Bethlem's visitors was artist William Hogarth (1697–1764), whose series of engravings prompted sensitive writer-producer Val Lewton to pen one of his most probing screenplays. (Lewton and director Mark Robson utilized Hogarth's illustrations throughout the film as backdrops to the credits, visual framing models, and scene transitions.) "We virtually used Hogarth as our art director," Robson confessed.[2]

Vladimir Ivan (Val) Lewton was no ordinary movie producer, and much of *Bedlam*'s literate quality can be put down to him. Eyeing the profits made by Universal with their relatively inexpensive horror productions, RKO hired away David O. Selznick's personal assistant/researcher/story editor Lewton in March 1942 and put him in charge of a B-picture unit that was to make horror movies on budgets of around $150,000, based on pretested titles provided by the studio (the first being *Cat People*). This proved to be the best $250 a week (Lewton's paltry salary) RKO ever spent. More than any other Hollywood producer, Lewton proved a hands-on supervisor whose touch pervaded every aspect of his productions (he nearly always rewrote scripts, for instance, without taking credit). Lewton's RKO "horror unit" operated for three years (1942 to 1945) and generated nine low-budget terror films, many of them—such as *I Walked with a Zombie* (1943), *The Body Snatcher* (1945), and this feature—the very best of the decade. Lewton, a well-read man of letters who had authored several published novels, circumvented his bosses' wishes and eschewed the more obvious terrors of Universal's fright factory to produce instead a series of thinking man's horrors—intelligent, suggestive thrillers whose scripts plumbed the depths of the human psyche more than the outer reaches of the preternatural (though the two sometimes crossed paths). What resulted were nine of the finest horror films of the 1940s. Boris Karloff, whose horror pictures of that time consisted mainly of repetitious mad-doctor roles or juvenile entries like *The Ape* and *House of Frankenstein*, starred in three of the producer's more literate pictures and dubbed Lewton "the man who rescued me from the living dead and restored my soul."

The final Val Lewton–produced film for RKO's B-picture horror unit, *Bedlam* is also one of the best of that well-respected subset—despite its not really being a horror film at all (at least according to the movie's star). "Boris [Karloff] used to get quite annoyed when people referred to *Bedlam* as a horror picture," recounted costar Anna Lee. "He said, 'It's not a horror picture, it's a historical picture.'"[3] Karloff himself noted,

"We have here a quality film, based on the stirring events and personages of a remarkable period in English history. So I hope at least it keeps out of those theaters which specialize in chiller-dillers."[4] (The film's director, Mark Robson, jumped on the not-a-horror-picture bandwagon by labeling *Bedlam* a "historical suspense film.")[5] Even so, *Bedlam* still offers an atmosphere rife with terror (with the frightened heroine trapped amid the human "animals" in the asylum) and several moments of true *frisson*, including a walk down a darkened, cage-lined corridor, from whose blackness arms suddenly thrust forth to claw at the protagonist. (The project even carried a preproduction title of *Chamber of Horrors: A Tale of Bedlam* to underscore its intent.)

In this movie poster for Val Lewton's *Bedlam* (1946), directed by Mark Robson and based on the British institution St. Mary Bethlehem Hospital (founded in 1247), actress Anna Lee appears as an inappropriately incarcerated victim-turned-heroine, alongside the sinister Master Sims, played by Boris Karloff, an actor renowned for his horror roles but who insisted that this movie was historical and not horror.

RKO wanted Jane Greer to play the clever heroine whose witty cynicism melts into genuine compassion upon exposure to the Bedlamites, but Lewton insisted on Anna Lee. His persistence paid off, for she brings her shrewd, forthright, and ultimately empathetic character to full-blooded life. Nell becomes the audience identification figure, and her transformation from acerbic narcissist to gentle caregiver is both affecting and gratifying. When she first meets the Quaker outside the asylum, she covers up a momentary sympathy for the hapless lunatics with the comment, "My heart is flint, sir; it may strike sparks but they're not warm enough to burn." But such is not the case, and ultimately her heart—and the heart of the viewer—burns alternately with pity, indignation, fear, and finally triumph.

Engrossing (and even frightening) as it is, *Bedlam* offers more than just an emotionally involving historical story of the mistreatment of the mentally ill. While writing the screenplay, Lewton (employing his penname of Carlos Keith) and director/co-scripter Mark Robson consulted the memoirs and letters of such 18th-century luminaries as Boswell, Lord Chesterfield, and Benjamin Franklin to add authenticity to the characters' dialogue and mannerisms. (Lewton rarely received screen credit for his writing efforts, and when forced to, he employed a pseudonym. "The reason I do not ordinarily take credit for my very considerable work on my own scripts is that I have a theory that if I take credit, whenever I rewrite another writer's work, I can very properly be suspected of rewriting merely to get such credit.")[6] Evocative settings, well-drawn characters, unnerving set pieces, involving acting (particularly from Karloff's cruel toady and Lee's awakening humanist), and some clever irony (especially in its chilling ending) make *Bedlam* a superior specimen of 1940s cinema. It also presents a moral lesson: how treating human beings—no matter how imperfect—*as* human beings brings to the fore man's inherent humanity. One even sympathizes with the despicable Sims by film's end. A perceptive man of letters (he even writes poetry), Sims has done what he has out of fear. When the inmates finally have their tormentor at their mercy and ask him why he mistreats them, he blurts, "I was frightened." It was "fear of the great world" that caused him to turn brutal, "the great world of this Age that gave me my place, the comforts and the authority, what little I have of riches. What that world thinks, *I* must think; what they do, *I* must do." The vicious master of Bedlam is nothing but a frightened little man reflecting the status quo—and one to be pitied. As the Quaker asks, "Has not Sims a madness that thee can pity?"

As Bedlam's master, Boris Karloff creates another superb portrayal (his third—and last—for Lewton, the others being *The Body Snatcher* and the fearful general lording over the *Isle of the Dead*). "All the famous men of that age had to have sponsors," explained the actor, who obviously put much thought into his characterization. "They couldn't make a living in the arts. Therefore, there were toadies, foot-kissers, and all-around scoundrels and hypocrites—like this chap I'm playing—a poet who has charge of that notorious insane asylum. There he takes his spleen out on the loonies in his charge, in sadistic cruelties and graft at their expense."[7]

For the illustrative scene in which Karloff's Master Sims stages a comedy masque starring his "loonies" for the entertainment of his patron, Lord Mortimer, Sims has a young inmate painted gold and taught to recite a few lines as "The Age of Reason." But, to the amusement of Sims, Mortimer, and his aristocratic guests, the lad collapses. At this, Nell shows concern for the boy. "If I understand you properly," retorts Sims, "this boy is dying"—here Karloff pauses, glances at the prone figure, then continues on without altering his unctuous tone—"this boy is dead because his pores are clogged by the gilt. Well, sweet Mistress Bowen, since you are such a stickler for the correct definition, you will grant me the fact that this boy died by his *own exhalation*." Karloff's mocking voice, tinged with a flinty mirth, reveals the callous cruelty of the man, and he finishes (after soaking in the chuckles his little "joke" elicits from his audience) with "You might say, he poisoned himself." But Karloff's was not a one-note portrayal of cold evil (despite his occasional wicked half-smile), as he brings a complicated depth to this vile character, who, after all, is shaped as much by circumstance as by inherent evil.

Toward the end of the film, during the inmates' mock trial of their hated keeper (which concludes when they find Sims "sane"), the asylum master pleads for his life. "I've had to fawn and toady and make a mock of myself 'til all I could hear was the world *laughing* at me!" he justifies, Karloff's voice and face tinged with bitter anger. "But once I had what I wanted," he continues, looking around, "*this*, my *place*"—his voice lowering and his eyes turning inwards with self-satisfaction at the thought—"I had to please those to whose favor I owed everything." Intent, and desperate to make his captors understand, he almost whispers, "I was afraid." Karloff's multilayered performance transforms Sims's sadistic boogeyman into a complex human being.

"I thought that Boris gave one of his very finest performances in *Bedlam*," enthused costar Anna Lee, who had acted with the horror star nine years earlier in the 1936 British chiller *The Man Who Changed His Mind* (released as *The Man Who Lived Again* in America). "He was so sadistic and so unpleasant, but at the very end he became so pathetic and pitiful when he was pleading for his life and trying to explain what had caused him to be so cruel that one was almost sad to see him walled up!"[8] Lee was overjoyed to be paired with Karloff once again, recalling that "we'd recite poetry to each other for hours," and that "the reunion with Boris was wonderful, as was the atmosphere on the set of *Bedlam*—because Boris had a great sense of humor, and he used to laugh about everything."[9]

Bedlam was the fifth Lewton film directed by Mark Robson. After Robson served as editor on the producer's first three efforts (*Cat People*, *I Walked with a Zombie*, and *The Leopard Man*), Lewton promoted Robson to director on *The Seventh Victim*. Pleased with the result, Lewton sat him in the director's chair four more times—for *The Ghost Ship*, *Youth Runs Wild*, *Isle of the Dead*, and of course *Bedlam*. Robson went on to helm 28 more features over the course of his impressive directorial career, a career launched by Lewton, which saw Robson nominated twice for Best Director by the Academy of Motion Picture Arts and Sciences (for *Peyton Place* and *The Inn of the Sixth Happiness*). While much of what makes *Bedlam* memorable is its witty, insightful, and thought-provoking dialogue, Robson's direction, augmented by cinematographer Nicholas Musuraca's chiaroscuro lighting, makes the film anything but static. (Musuraca not only photographed four other Lewton horrors—*Cat People*, *The Seventh Victim*, *The Ghost Ship*, and *The Curse of the Cat People*—but several film noir classics as well, including *Stranger on the Third Floor*, *Out of the Past*, and *Clash by Night*.) Utilizing varied angles and clever camera movement, Robson takes the viewer inside not only the dreaded asylum itself but the life—and fears—of its unfortunate occupants. For our first look into their terrifying, claustrophobic, squalid existence, the camera watches as Nell steps toward us through the heavy wooden door into the dungeon-like hell of the asylum ward. Her self-assured expression transforms into a look of alarm as she hesitates, and (accompanied by a cacophony of murmurs, mutterings, and cries on the soundtrack) the camera steadily draws back from her to fully reveal the crowded, chaotic, frightening space, exposing her (and us) to the full madness of Bedlam.

Budgeted at $350,000 (the same amount Universal spent on the previous year's *House of Frankenstein*, also starring Karloff), and filmed over four weeks in the summer of 1945, *Bedlam* was the most expensive of Lewton's efforts (*The Body Snatcher* came in a distant second at $246,000). This was still a relatively low-budget (but high-*brow*) production, however, and Lewton cut costs wherever he could. In a bit of upscale economizing, for instance, Anna Lee wears Vivien Leigh's curtain-made dress from *Gone with the Wind* (1939) and Hedy Lamarr's ball gown from *Experiment Perilous* ("I wore all hand-me-downs from various actresses," laughed Lee[10]). The asylum itself was the converted church set from the 1945 Bing Crosby vehicle *The Bells of St. Mary's*. ("I learned a great secret about film producing from Val," noted producer-director-writer Tom Gries. "He always told me not to spread a small budget over five or six sets—instead, pick the location where most of the action will be played and make that a real showpiece. Then make do with the rest of the scenes. One elaborate set makes a film look much richer than it deserves to look. Val was a very careful man; he knew how to spend money and how to put it on the screen."[11]) As Lee opined, "*Bedlam* was done on a very low budget, but I don't think it ever really showed because it was, *I* thought, so beautifully done."[12] Indeed it was—intellectually, emotionally, *and* cinematically. Unfortunately, the paying public did not think so, at least in sufficient numbers, as a total of $257,000 in domestic rentals plus $98,000 in foreign territories saw the picture end up on the wrong side of the fiscal ledger to the tune of a $40,000 loss. Sadly, Lewton went out with a whimper rather than a bang where it counted most—at the box office. Still, *Bedlam* generally fared well with the critics (no doubt boosted by its "social message" status), certainly better than the typical "horror hokum" at which so many looked down their noses. The *New York Times* labeled it a "production several cuts above the average run of so-called horror films" and "a generally straight-forward and imaginative estimate of a two-century-old sociological theme," while *Variety* opined, "Bedlam is a suspenseful exploitation picture from which RKO may expect heavy grosses. … The film has been directed forcefully by Mark Robson, with many a sock dramatic moment." *Time* noted, "Producer Val Lewton and writer-director Mark Robson wring some effective moments of pity and horror out of the assorted lunatics and … attack the more callous self-delusions of the Age of Reason." "It is not easy to categorize the attraction, since nothing quite like it has been seen," concluded the *Motion Picture Herald*, "[but] under whatever billing, it will make itself remembered as a powerful use of the camera to tell a story of importance." The *Los Angeles Daily News* offered, "Done realistically and with a sense of responsibility to its subject, *Bedlam* reaffirms the conviction that a problem drama can combine thoughtfulness with traditional entertainment elements." And following its New York premiere on April 19, 1946, *Cue* crowed, "*Bedlam* is actually far less horrible than most of the Rialto's film offerings, and is considerably more intelligent in writing, production, direction and performance." Despite such plaudits, British censors banned the film outright (perhaps feeling it hit too close to home?), so that it remained largely unseen in the U.K. for over half a century.

"Val [Lewton] was a great workaholic," concluded Anna Lee. "I don't think he ever stopped working on any project he was doing. … He had a great imagination and was very erudite in everything he did. But it had never dawned on me, in those days, that Val was driving himself that way to death."[13] After finishing *Bedlam* and departing RKO for brief stints at Paramount, MGM, and Universal, Lewton produced only three more pictures before dying of a heart attack in 1951 at the young age of 46. He left behind a lauded cinematic legacy, of which *Bedlam* proved a fitting coda.

In 1814, inspectors came away appalled by what they found at Bethlem Hospital, noting that it had more "the appearance of a dog kennel" than a hospital.[14] This led to reforms that transformed the fearful madhouse into a true healing institution, so that by the mid-19th century, Bedlam was finally transformed into a genuine infirmary devoted to the care—rather than punishment—of the mentally ill. (Though the film ends with a written coda claiming that "reforms were begun in 1773," this was more wishful thinking than historical fact, as it took a bit longer for "Bedlam—once a by-word for terror and mistreatment—[to] lead the way to enlightened and sensible treatment of the mentally ill.") Having occupied four different locations over the centuries, Bethlem Royal Hospital, as it is known today, now humanely serves patients in the London borough of Bromley.

Bedlam (RKO, 1946); 79 minutes; director: Mark Robson; producer: Val Lewton; screenplay: Val Lewton (as Carlos Keith), Mark Robson; cinematographer: Nicholas Musuraca. Cast: Boris Karloff, Anna Lee, Billy House, Richard Fraser, Glenn Vernon, Ian Wolfe, Jason Robards Sr., Leland Hodgson, Joan Newton, Elizabeth Russell.

Notes

1. *Webster's Encyclopedic Unabridged Dictionary of the English Language* (Gramercy Books, 1996).
2. Gregory William Mank, *Hollywood Cauldron: Thirteen Horror Films from the Genre's Golden Age* (McFarland, 1994).
3. Tom Weaver, *Science Fiction Stars and Horror Heroes: Interviews with Actors, Directors, Producers and Writers of the 1940s Through 1960s* (McFarland, 1991).
4. Victor Gunson, "Frankenstein's Monster Rebels! Film Boogey Man Tired of Scaring Folks," *Winnipeg Evening Tribune*, December 10, 1945.
5. Stephen Jacobs, *Boris Karloff: More Than a Monster* (Tomahawk Press, 2011).
6. Joel E. Siegel, *Val Lewton: The Reality of Terror* (Viking Press, 1973).
7. Gunson.
8. Scott Allen Nollen, *Boris Karloff: A Gentleman's Life* (Midnight Marquee Press, 1999).
9. Mank.
10. Weaver.
11. Siegel.
12. Weaver.
13. Paul Chambers, *Bedlam: London's Hospital for the Mad* (Ian Allan Publishing, 2009).
14. Chambers.

SECTION III

Darkest Depictions

6

John Carpenter's Career

From Halloween *to Lovecraft*

JEFFREY BULLINS

The asylum or "madhouse" has been a staple setting in the horror genre since the days of silent film. Still discussed as one of the most influential films that birthed the genre, the titular antagonist of *The Cabinet of Dr. Caligari* is a director of an asylum for the mentally ill. Robert Cumbow cites *Caligari* as "the first horror film,"[1] and the image of the mad doctor and the deteriorated asylum causing more harm than good have been recurring themes in horror films for the past century. Goodwin notes the horror film as particularly guilty of negative depictions of mental illness and mental health care environments. He states most horror films feature "inaccurate definitions [that] are commonly presented as 'truths,' while outdated MHCEs are frequently presented as representative of the current standard for treatment."[2] With this statement made in 2013, it seems little progress has been achieved in representations of mental illness since *Caligari.* However, while most presentations remain negative, changes in depictions of asylums and mental illness have occurred in the horror genre. Particularly, this can be seen in the past 60 years, since the release of *Psycho* in 1960, one of the genre's most influential films.

The adjustments in asylum depictions are at times cyclical and move from the institution as containment to questions of its efficacy and necessity. Further, these changes coincide with Charles Derry's observations of specific horror threats, namely of "personality," "Armageddon," and "the Demonic,"[3] which are more prevalent during certain times. To illustrate differing depictions of asylums and mental illness, this essay will examine differences in the presentation of asylums by focusing on three films directed by John Carpenter. Though his oeuvre spans various genres, he is consistently recognized as a "master of horror" (after all, he contributed two entries to the Showtime television series named such). The films examined are spaced evenly through his career. Beginning with *Halloween* (1978), the asylum is depicted as a place to house a villain of "pure evil." Sixteen years later, *In the Mouth of Madness* (1994) opens with the incarceration of a character who may be the only one who knows the "truth" of reality. Thirty-two years after *Halloween*, we encounter *The Ward* (2010), which was shot in Eastern State Hospital in Spokane, Washington, and follows the story of a committed young woman whose fears are dismissed.

The asylum has certainly been a longtime object of fascination and interest in popular culture. By the 17th century, "the mental hospital had become a fixed part of

Charlatan psychiatrist and sideshow performer Dr. Caligari, played by Werner Krauss, meanders through out-of-kilter streets in *The Cabinet of Dr. Caligari* (1919–20), a post–World War I film whose name became synonymous with German Expressionism and was used to signify this emerging artistic style at a time when Europeans avoided associations with their recently defeated Germanic enemy.

European society," in part due to the belief that mental illness should be treated similarly to other contagious diseases.[4] As such, isolation and confinement were common methods of treatment. With fear of the unknown being at the heart of any good horror story, the secluded, mysterious asylum was primed to be an affective generic image. Since the goal of the horror genre is to frighten, such unknowns are always exploited. A sunny garden in which patients peacefully walk and smell flowers does not necessarily evoke feelings of terror. With a negative representation established, though, the 19th century saw activists working against it. "Beginning with Philippe Pinel in France (1745–1826) and including such others as the American Dorothea Dix, Benjamin Rush, and Clifford Beers, these reformers believed that the mad should be treated, not simply rejected as pariahs of society."[5] Pérez-Fernández and López-Muñoz, in their discussion of Thomas Kirkbride's influence on hospital architecture, note that modernization and population growth at the turn of the 19th century necessitated an increase in care facilities.[6] The authors go on to discuss ideas of "moral treatment" that emerged in the early 19th century. New attitudes regarding mental illness moved away from long-term confinement to creating paths toward meaningful treatment and cure. While some extreme treatments persisted, such as cages and isolation, doctors such as Kirkbride hoped to create a more moral, compassionate way of approaching mental illness.[7]

The early 19th century was a comparatively progressive time for mental health care facilities, and asylums at this time often featured beautiful grounds in addition to better lit and ventilated indoor spaces. The public was allowed more access, but with dubious motives. Benjamin Reiss notes, "Asylum tourism also allowed visitors to indulge in some of the spectatorial pleasures that they might be too ashamed to pursue in public, at the popular freak shows of the day."[8] As such, is it that different for cinemagoers to gawk at asylum inmates? While positive advances were occurring, public opinion regarding asylums seemed to remain rooted in the past. Reiss observes the popularization of the asylum "captivity" narrative occurring "virtually coincident with the rise of the asylum movement in the nineteenth century."[9] In such stories a protagonist is wrongfully held, persecuted, and when released exposes the unjust asylum and its doctors. Built upon actual experiences such as that of Nellie Bly, these sensational stories captured the imagination of a public still largely ignorant of how mental hospitals operated. A lack of resources following the Civil War resulted in more such tales, both real and contrived. As such, the image of the mysterious asylum that both contained dangerous individuals and could potentially confine any "normal" person persisted. In Hollywood, *The Snake Pit* (1948) directly explored the latter. It contributed, along with films such as *Gaslight* (1944) and *The Spiral Staircase* (1945), to the "paranoid woman's film," which blended at the time with horror and noir.[10] By the 1960s, the moral treatment methods of the previous century seem all but forgotten. Reiss states that even when remembered, any potential positives in asylum reform were seen as "elaborate ruse[s] for the confinement of women, the punishment of deviants, the gratification of unscrupulous relatives (usually husbands), and the sadistic pleasures of doctors and their attendants."[11]

Such images and stories faded in the genre, and horror films in the 1950s are often discussed regarding their blending with science fiction. Perhaps due to postwar atomic anxieties, Derry sees the "pseudoscientific basis" as supplanting other reasons for horror film antagonists, but with the success of *Psycho*, the psychological explanation and the "horror of personality" became most popular.[12] This is something of a return to anxieties about asylums explored in the previously mentioned films of the 1940s. However, the focus has shifted from the unfairly incarcerated protagonist to a psychotic antagonist who needs to be contained. Though *Psycho* deals with a mentally unstable character, an asylum is not shown until the end of the film after Norman is arrested, when a doctor explains the psychological disorder that caused him to murder (de rigueur in these types of movies). Such rationale may have been reassuring to some audiences, but it is unlikely that many of these killers will be rehabilitated. Thus, the image of the asylum as a container for dangerous psychopaths is affirmed. By the release of *Halloween* in 1978, an explanation as to why Michael Myers kills is gone. He is described by psychiatrist Dr. Loomis as "pure evil," and as such must be incarcerated indefinitely. Though an explanation (pseudoscientific or otherwise) is absent in the film, Derry notes that "*Psycho*, of course, was the key influence on *Halloween*."[13] The villain is not a supernatural monster or radioactive ant, but a human being. How could a person commit such terrible acts? We do not know, but they definitely need to be locked up!

Examining spaces in John Carpenter's films, Robert Ziegler refers to places "meant to quarantine evil and circumscribe the unknown. Law-abiding, normal citizens rest easier when deviants and madmen are known to be confined to asylums or to jails."[14] In the opening scene of *Halloween*, six-year-old Michael kills his sister without explanation. The film proper unfolds 15 years later, with Michael having been held during that time at Smith's Grove Sanitarium. That Michael has not spoken a single word during this time leans into the genre trope of inadequate or incompetent treatment. Further, his silence prevents any insight into why he killed. Such lack of detail is a strength of the film, giving the story an accessible simplicity free of psychobabble. Yet in doing so, images such as gown-wearing patients wandering aimlessly outside the sanitarium reinforce genre tropes of contagious insanity spilling out of asylums. The interior of Smith's Grove is not seen, but as Murray Leeder notes, Dr. Loomis's description of Michael's silent isolation provides a compelling image. Further, Loomis can also be seen as somewhat unhinged himself after spending so long trying to connect in some way with Michael.[15]

Halloween began a cycle of films featuring insane, knife-wielding killers, and its enormous box office success (compared to its budget) resulted in plenty of imitators. Sequels within the franchise move toward a focus on Michael as an unstoppable, unkillable threat rather than revisiting asylums or psychological explanations. Smith's Grove does feature much more prominently in Rob Zombie's 2007 remake and David Gordon Green's 2018 sequel/reboot, *Halloween*. In the former, Michael's traumatic childhood is explored and presented as a potential reason for his behavior. Plenty of time is spent with him in Smith's Grove as he remains silent and obsessively makes papier-mâché masks. In the latter, podcasters visit Michael, who is seen restricted to a spot in an outside area of the hospital. Again, the solution for him is simply containment, but at least in this one he gets some fresh air. Overall, the depictions of asylums in these newer films are somewhat more positive, in that they are not sunless dungeons. Carpenter's original *Halloween*, in not showing the interior of the asylum, allows the audience to imagine any type of space, horrific or otherwise. As such, it played more strongly to established tropes within popular culture at the time.

With *Halloween* following *Psycho* and a subgeneric cycle of masked killers in the 1980s, horror films maintained the image of the asylum as containment for dangerous psychotics. By the mid–'90s and with Carpenter's Lovecraftian homage *In the Mouth of Madness* (1994), one can see a return to mid-century depictions of wrongful incarceration à la *Snake Pit*. Or at least to the idea that patients are not inherently dangerous and may indeed have some sort of insight that "sane" characters do not. Cumbow notes Carpenter's themes, recurrences of "neurosis, psychosis, or some other mental aberration, recognizing ... that the truly mad do not suffer from a jumbled confused view of the world around them, but from a tendency to see things all too simply and clearly."[16] In this sense, those who know "the truth" are contained within the asylum through either sinister purposefulness or dismissal. *Mouth of Madness* has obvious ties to Lovecraft with the epic threat of unfathomable, tentacled creatures breaking into our reality from some cosmic abyss. Protagonist John Trent is aware of the ushering of these creatures through horror author Sutter Cane's supernatural prose. As such, the opening scene of the film has Trent admitted to a mental hospital. The film is mostly told in flashbacks as Trent talks with a psychiatrist.

Though Trent violently resists being admitted to the hospital, he appears more of a victim than a threat; someone who has seen something incomprehensible and is forever changed. This is in line with Lovecraftian themes. His novella *The Case of Charles Dexter Ward* (1927) can be seen as a particular influence on *Mouth of Madness*. In the story, the title character claims "in his madness" that "he had discovered or rediscovered something whose effect on human thought was likely to be marvelous and profound."[17] Such a claim follows the idea that those deemed "mad" may in fact be more in touch with unseen truths in the universe. Further, Trent calls into question the nature of reality, claiming it "is just what we tell each other it is. Sane and insane could easily change places." For the purposes of the story, Trent's unreliability produces intrigue. For the depiction of the asylum, it challenges *Halloween*'s concept of containing evil. In *Halloween*, the threat of an escaped murderer follows Derry's concept of "horror of personality." In *Mouth of Madness*, we see his second category, the "horror of Armageddon."[18] The world is going to be overtaken by hideous monsters, but the only person who knows that is locked up in a padded cell. While this is the case, *Mouth of Madness* moves between moments of believing and doubting Trent. How closely the audience identifies with him and follows his actions directly impacts his credibility. When distanced from him, he is likely to be viewed as insane, but "the more we see things with his eyes, the more we identify with him, the more likely we are to see him as the only sane one left."[19]

In his detailed examination of the film, Michael Blyth notes that *In the Mouth of Madness* blurs "the lines between fantasy and reality, and in turn, the lines between sanity and madness."[20] This is key for generating uncertainty, fear, and anxiety in the film. Following Trent closely, the audience experiences shocking revelations about the fabric of reality. Stepping back to a more objective perspective, such as that of the psychiatrist or Trent's coworker, perhaps he is completely delusional. This ambiguity differs from aforementioned paranoid woman's films of the 1940s in which it was clearly understood that characters did not belong in an asylum. This is a strength of the film, increasing tension as both Trent and the audience are constantly questioning what they see. The film becomes self-reflexive (common to the genre in the late '90s). Blyth observes that Trent's discussion with the psychiatrist in his padded cell seems particularly unreal and that Trent is aware "of the constructed performance of insanity."[21] So, layers of un/reality and in/sanity are present inside and out of the film's diegesis. At the end of the film, all of this breaks down when Cane's cosmic terrors do enter our world. Trent emerges from the demolished hospital and wanders into town. The insanity spread through Cane's books has expanded to a movie, *In the Mouth of Madness*. Trent sees his picture on a poster for the film and when he enters a cinema, the movie we have just seen is playing. It is impossible to discern reality from fantasy. In addition to challenging narrative expectations, *Mouth of Madness* questions the efficacy of the asylum in the face of widespread madness. Trent knows the truth about what is happening: rather than madness spreading out of the asylum, it spreads throughout the population. Since the audience's perspective is almost always that of Trent, we believe and side with him.

This connection with a questionably sane protagonist is also at the heart of Carpenter's 2010 film *The Ward*, which opens with shots of the Coos Bay Psychiatric Hospital. Flashes of lightning briefly illuminate darkened corridors while layers of sound effects create a spooky atmosphere. In this sequence, patient Tammy is killed in her room by an unseen assailant. This scene transitions to opening credits featuring fracturing glass and images of psychiatric treatments throughout history. Drawings of medieval tortures give way to photographs of lobotomies and electroconvulsive therapy. In a commentary track for the film, Carpenter notes that some photos are real, others staged, but they "give you an idea of some of the crazy things they did for treatment."[22] Thus, the clear message from the start of the film is the questionable nature of psychiatric treatment. Forcén succinctly states that "psychiatry's obsolete treatments provide a perfect setting for a horror film."[23] Likewise, the presentation of the asylum checks many of Goodwin's trope boxes such as isolation, flickering light, and danger.[24] Interestingly and ironically, Carpenter noted in an interview that the campus of the hospital was beautiful, echoing sentiments about the appealing grounds of 19th-century asylums.[25] The opening credits focus on the pained expressions of patients and associate treatment with torture. Instead of a psychotic masked killer, here the asylum patients are victims. Though this is an evolution in the depiction and function of the asylum, from needed containment to unnecessary prison, such themes are cyclical and somewhat incongruent. In popular culture, the asylum is simultaneously keeping us from danger and oppressing the innocent.

Following the opening, a young woman, Kristen, runs through the woods before arriving at a farmhouse and setting it on fire. She is subsequently arrested and taken to Coos Bay Hospital. She is quickly and roughly processed with little discussion of why, although hospital head Dr. Stringer does appear altruistic rather than sinister. As Kristen is led through the hospital, she anxiously glances around at other patients, who appear to be suffering from greater degrees of mental illness than she. The supposition here is that though Kristen may have committed arson, she does not belong in an asylum. Carpenter noted of the 1966 setting for *The Ward* that the '60s was chosen because reform laws in the 1970s prevented institutionalizing someone for an indefinite amount of time.[26] Though *The Ward* takes place in a more modern setting, this recalls the stories of unwarranted incarceration or inhumane treatment exposed by journalists such as Nellie Bly.

Bly's *Ten Days in a Mad-House* (1887) was published 80 years prior to the setting of *The Ward* and well over a century prior to the release of the film, but such asylum depictions remain the standard in popular culture. Indeed, concerns about trust in MHCEs persist, and in 2022 Merriam-Webster chose "gaslighting" as their word of the year.[27] Intentionally convincing someone that what they think is false is at the core of concerns about unwarranted asylum incarceration. Interestingly, gaslighting was also included on Lake Superior State University's 2022 list of words that should be banished due to incorrect usage or overuse.[28]

In the film's setting, there are no laws preventing Kristen from being kept in the hospital indefinitely, and since the audience experiences almost the entire story through her perspective, we are by extension trapped there as well. As with Trent, our closeness and identification with Kristen directly determines believability. While that fluctuates in *Mouth of Madness*, *The Ward* ties the audience closely to Kristen all the way to a twist ending. In an examination of 20th-century horror films featuring mental illness, in which *The Ward* was included, Goodwin found that just under 20 percent featured patients "telling the truth; that is, they were not psychotic."[29] The vast majority still featured homicidal maniacs. By presenting the (questionably) mentally ill as protagonists and victims, *The Ward* is a departure from stereotypes instigated by Carpenter 30 years prior.

As the film progresses, expectedly, strange things begin to happen at night in the hospital as Kristen and her fellow patients are menaced by the disfigured ghost of Alice. It is revealed that Alice had been killed by the other girls because of her cruelty and malice. In introducing a supernatural antagonist, *The Ward* exhibits Derry's third type of horror, that of the demonic. He includes ghosts and other supernatural evils in this category, not just the devil and witchcraft.[30]

As such, the film continues as a typical ghost story with the girls dodging or being dispatched by Alice, and Kristen planning an escape. Besides the element of confinement, it does not seem particularly necessary that the story take place in an asylum. Indeed, Carpenter noted on the film's commentary track that "it was an empty building for us." However, the choice of an asylum has built-in, effective horror tropes. The patients are killed via ECT, scalpels, and sharp lobotomy picks. So, the location is of major importance even if the general narrative need not be specifically tied to it. Actor Jared Harris commented that he felt bad during scenes involving ECT, as if he were torturing the actor. Carpenter responded that actual ECT footage he had seen was "very hard to watch and disturbing."[31] Such images and tropes are so embedded in popular culture's depictions of asylums that they trigger strong reactions in both the audience and filmmakers alike. *The Ward* utilizes these spooky stereotypes without regard or commentary. To push against them would undermine the inherent creepiness of the asylum.

The girls continue to be chased through the darkened hospital corridors, with Kristen eventually attacking Alice and defeating her. Looking at Alice's file in Dr. Stringer's office, Kristen is confronted by the doctor, who is successful in initiating a breakthrough. A twist ending reveals that Kristen is Alice, and all the other patients were manifestations of her dissociative identity disorder, referred to by Stringer as multiple personality disorder. It turns out that the gruesome deaths we witnessed were just in Kristen/Alice's head. This twist ending functions as just that, unfortunately subverting the close identification between the audience and Kristen. This revelation perhaps gives some relief to an audience fearful of unwarranted incarceration and positively recalls methodologies from the 19th century. However, it also regresses to the trope heralded by *Psycho* of the learned doctor explaining away everything. This is not surprising according to Derry, who, revisiting concepts in *Dark Dreams* years later, states the horror of personality to be "most vital," with *Psycho* "more influential now than in the sixties or seventies."[32] Following this, he sees the horror of the demonic as "the one most dominated throughout the last thirty years."[33] The ending of *The Ward* ends up blending these modes. The antagonistic ghost and all the carnage of the previous hour and a half is explained away via psychosis. While Kristen/Alice is not a purely evil masked killer like Michael Myers, the need for her institutionalization is clear. In this, *The Ward* merges two seemingly incongruous depictions of the asylum: the necessary container and the unwarranted prison. In 1985, Ziegler observed Carpenter's theme of showing "that the darkest side of one's own conscience wears not a mask but a familiar face."[34] Twenty-five years later, the ending of *The Ward* brings this theme full circle, unites previous films' various depictions of asylums and insanity, and confronts the audience with deep questions about human nature.

Notes

1. Robert C. Cumbow, *Order in the Universe: The Films of John Carpenter* (Scarecrow, 2000), 201.
2. John Goodwin, "The Horror of Stigma: Psychosis and Mental Health Care Environments in Twenty-First-Century Horror Film (Part II)," *Perspectives in Psychiatric Care* 50, no. 4 (2013): 224–234, https://doi.org/10.1111/ppc.12044, 224.
3. Charles Derry and John Russell Taylor, *Dark Dreams 2.0: A Psychological History of the Modern Horror Film from the 1950s to the 21st Century* (McFarland, 2009), 1–2.
4. Michael Fleming and Roger Manvell, *Images of Madness: The Portrayal of Insanity in the Feature Film* (Fairleigh Dickinson University Press, 1985), 44.
5. Fleming and Manvell, 24.
6. Francisco Pérez-Fernández and Francisco López-Muñoz, "The Kirkbride Buildings in Contemporary Culture (1850–2015): From 'Moral Management' to Horror Films," *History of Psychiatry* 30, no. 3 (2019): 336–351, https://doi.org/10.1177/0957154x19839912, 337.

7. Pérez-Fernández and López-Muñoz, 336–351.
8. Benjamin Reiss, *Theaters of Madness: Insane Asylums and Nineteenth-Century American Culture* (University of Chicago Press, 2008), 13.
9. Reiss, 169.
10. Mario DeGiglio-Bellemare, Ellbé Charlie, and Kristopher Woofter, *Recovering 1940s Horror Cinema: Traces of a Lost Decade* (Lexington Books, 2015), 88.
11. Reiss, 180.
12. Derry and Taylor, 23.
13. Cumbow, 147.
14. Robert E. Ziegler, "Killing Space: The Dialectic in John Carpenter's Films," *The Georgia Review* 37, no. 4 (1983): 770–786, 771.
15. Murray Leeder, *Halloween* (Auteur, 2015), 85.
16. Cumbow, 3.
17. Howard Phillips Lovecraft, "The Case of Charles Dexter Ward by H. P. Lovecraft," The H.P. Lovecraft Archive, August 20, 2009, https://www.hplovecraft.com/writings/texts/fiction/cdw.aspx.
18. Derry and Taylor, 59.
19. Cumbow, 208.
20. Michael Blyth, *In the Mouth of Madness* (Auteur, 2018), 11.
21. Blyth, 81.
22. John Carpenter, commentary, *The Ward* (2010).
23. Fernando Espí Forcén, *Monsters, Demons and Psychopaths: Psychiatry and Horror Film* (CRC Press, 2017), 205.
24. Goodwin, 224–234.
25. Chris Eggertsen, "Interview with 'The Ward' Director John Carpenter," Bloody Disgusting, June 3, 2011, https://bloody-disgusting.com/interviews/24827/interview-with-the-warddirector-john-carpenter/.
26. *Ibid.*
27. Joseph Pisani, "'Gaslighting' Is Merriam-Webster's Word of the Year," *Wall Street Journal*, November 28, 2022, https://www.wsj.com/articles/gaslighting-is-merriam-websters-word-of-the-year-11669654788.
28. Becky Sullivan, "An inflection point for GOATs: Please quiet quit these 'banished words' moving forward," NPR, January 1, 2023, https://www.npr.org/2023/01/01/1146517288/goat-gaslighting-banished-words.
29. Goodwin, 224–234.
30. Derry and Taylor, 89.
31. John Carpenter, commentary, *The Ward* (2010).
32. Derry and Taylor, 112.
33. *Ibid.*, 203.
34. Ziegler, 786.

7

Film Noir

Dark Dramas About Insane Asylums

W. Harrison Taylor *and*
David Andrew Harmon

"The world needs a wash and a week's rest."[1] So claimed Quant, a character in W.H. Auden's Pulitzer Prize–winning poem, "The Age of Anxiety." This pithy remark and captivating title seemingly gave voice to the generations between 1914 and 1950. While traumatic and transformative historical events were not exclusive to the early and mid-20th century, those experiences and the resulting influence on American society have helped set the "Age of Anxiety" apart for scholars. The social disruptions of World War I, the Great Depression, World War II, and the budding Cold War (as well as host of other developments and processes) provided the foundation for this age and the corresponding rise in mental health issues such as anxiety and depression.[2]

Within this larger conflicted context, American popular culture saw the rise of film noir, with the 1940s and 1950s heralded as the golden age for the genre. The stories and characters put forward in film noir have proven popular among lay and scholarly audiences alike. This fascination is partly the reason for the embarrassment of riches that is the literature exploring this film genre. While much of that work examines film noir in the context of the tumultuous early 20th century, little attention has been given to the role of asylums, mental hospitals, or sanitariums—the so-called "madhouses"—during this Age of Anxiety.[3] Addressing this lacuna and offering an introduction for further study, this essay examines four films during the golden age of film noir: *Spellbound* (1945), *Shock* (1946), *Possessed* (1947), and *High Wall* (1948). Interestingly, each of these films put forth a new tool for American society to use in their ever-changing world—the legitimate and cutting-edge scientific work of psychiatrists in their sanitariums, asylums, and mental hospitals. These realms of psychiatric health were shown as more than another social bulwark; they were portrayed as *the* safe haven for an increasingly anxious people.

However, institutions for mental health were not new and by the 1940s had established an ominous reputation within popular culture. A herculean task fell to film noir directors and producers to create a compelling counterpoint to popular horrific images of asylums that had become commonplace in America and across the English-speaking world. Lingering stories of Bedlam and personal accounts such as Lydia Smith's *Behind the Scenes* (1878) and Nellie Bly's *Ten Days in a Mad-House* (1887) mingled with fictional depictions in works such as Charles Reade's *Hard Cash* (1863), Wilkie Collins's *Woman in White* (1859), and Bram Stoker's *Dracula* (1897). The resulting image was not one of benevolent care, cutting-edge scientific endeavor, or diligent and tireless efforts of the doctors involved. No, as one scholar has aptly written, the resulting portrait was one of "*Madhouses, Mad-Doctors and Madmen.*"[4] Film noir during the late 1940s worked to clear the cultural slate and turn any idea of a "madhouse" on its head.

Spellbound *(1945)*

The first effort fittingly came on Halloween night, 1945, when theatergoers were first treated to *Spellbound*, a film noir dedicated to reconsidering and reimagining "madhouses" and their place in society.[5] Not coincidentally, *Spellbound* was also one the one of the first films to embrace psychoanalysis as a method of treating mental disorders. Premiering less than two months following the conclusion of World War II, the film was a personal project of David Selznick, whose own positive experience with the treatment prompted him to inform others of the benefits of psychoanalysis. To that end, Dr. May Romm, Selznick's therapist, was enlisted to serve as the film's psychiatric advisor alongside Alfred Hitchcock as the director. With Dr. Romm and Hitchcock in tow, Selznick found the perfect vehicle for his project, the 1927 novel *The House of Edwardes*, written by Hilary St. George Saunders and John Palmer.

The driving impulse for *Spellbound* is evident from the start as Selznick and company employed a scroll-over, a technique he had used in *Gone with the Wind*, to explain the process of psychoanalysis. With Green Manors mental hospital as the backdrop, audiences were informed that "once the complexes that have been disturbing the patient are uncovered and interrupted, the illness and confusion have disappeared ... and the devils of unreason are driven from the human soul." The film made it clear that the work undertaken by the professionals at such institutions was serious and should be seen as a great boon for society. Further to this point was the casting of Ingrid Bergman as the intensely professional psychoanalyst Constance Petersen, and Gregory Peck as the handsome, mysterious Dr. Anthony Edwardes. In the popular hands of Bergman and Peck, *Spellbound* afforded the work of mental hospitals an opportunity to be taken seriously by the American public.

As important as this work was, it had to be challenged and prevail under Hitchcock's direction. *Spellbound* begins with the doctors at Green Manors waiting for the arrival of Dr. Edwardes, who is coming to replace Dr. Murchison as the head of the hospital. Dr. Murchison was forced to retire due to nervous exhaustion. While Dr. Edwardes is known for his recent and well-received book on the guilt complex, no one at the hospital has seen or met him. Among the expectant staff is Dr. Constance Petersen, who, while serving as the only woman on staff, is portrayed as an effective and well-regarded psychoanalyst, even if her older male colleagues see her as emotionally and socially aloof. With this, Hitchcock set the first challenge, as the arrival of the unexpectedly young Dr. Edwardes draws the immediate attraction of the typically reserved Dr. Petersen, to the shock and amusement of her male colleagues.

The two doctors develop a romantic relationship. During their time together, Constance notices that Anthony has a peculiar reaction to some parallel lines that were drawn by a fork on a white tablecloth. He also had a similar reaction to parallel lines in her bathrobe. Sensing something is amiss, her professional instincts push her to investigate, and her findings point conclusively to the fact that the young Dr. Edwardes is an impostor. Dr. Petersen, still romantically drawn to the ersatz Edwardes, confronts him personally instead of exposing him to the others. Similarly moved, Edwardes confesses to Petersen that he murdered the real Edwardes and has taken his place. When Petersen presses for more information, Edwardes also reveals that he has amnesia and cannot recall his name, his past, or why he has taken Edwardes's place. Driven by the dueling interests of romance and professional interest, Dr. Petersen keeps Edwardes's secret and starts the process of uncovering the troubles that beset him. These developments leave audiences unclear whether her emotions will mislead or possibly corrupt her objectivity as a psychiatrist.

Unable to stand the position in which he has put Dr. Petersen, Anthony quietly leaves the hospital. He also leaves a note for Constance informing her that he loves her, but it would be in her best interests not to get involved with him. Again, audiences are presented with the conflicting interests of Dr. Petersen as she tracks the faux Edwardes to his hotel in New York City. She clearly wants to be with him, but she also wants to cure his dissociative amnesia through psychoanalysis. Given her need for help, on multiple levels, she and Edwardes travel to the home of her former mentor in Rochester, New York.

It is here that Edwardes has a vivid and striking dream designed by none other than Salvador Dali. Within this Dali dreamscape, Edwardes is transported from a gambling hall to the roof of a building, and finally to a hill. Throughout the progression of bizarre scenes and activities, Edwardes interacts with two mystery men, one bearded and the other masked. While it was undoubtedly Hitchcock and Selznick's intent to confuse the audience with the Dali-crafted dream sequence, the two psychiatrists are in their element and ready to suss out this clue that is beyond the reach of the non-psychiatric world. It is by analyzing this dream and studying his behavior that Petersen and her mentor help Edwardes recover his memories. This discovery leads the couple to the Gabriel Valley Ski Lodge where, under Dr. Petersen's expert guidance, Edwardes remembers even more. He had been at the resort with the real Dr. Edwardes, who died in a skiing accident. He also remembers that his real name is John Ballantyne, and that as a child he had accidentally killed his brother by knocking him into a spike fence while playing in the snow. The experience of these two deaths, Dr. Petersen concludes, is the root cause of his guilt complex–inspired amnesia.

With the film's central mystery seemingly solved through the persistence and dedication of professional psychiatrists, a new challenge is introduced. After Peterson and Ballantyne tell their story to the police, who have been in pursuit all the while, the body of the real Edwardes is found. Unfortunately for Ballantyne, the cause of death was not an accidental fall; Dr. Edwardes had been shot in the back. In short order Ballantyne is arrested, tried, and convicted for Edwardes's murder. Confused, yet determined to figure out this new mystery, Dr. Petersen returns to Green Manors hospital, where Dr. Murchison has been restored as the head of the hospital. As Dr. Murchison attempts to console Petersen, while suggesting her emotions have misled her professional instincts, he inadvertently reveals that he knew Edwardes prior to his appointment as the new head of Green Manors. Dr. Petersen, the consummate professional, takes note of this admission and reviews her notes of Ballantyne's dream. She concludes that Dr. Murchison was the masked mystery man in the dream and that his actions therein indicated that he was the real culprit behind Dr. Edwardes's murder. Again, her dedication to her profession proves decisive and offers a solution that could be found nowhere else. When Dr. Petersen confronts Murchison, he threatens her with a revolver—the same one used to shoot Edwardes—but she warns him that her death would only guarantee his execution. She leaves his office unscathed, but as she leaves Dr. Murchison commits suicide.

With this last challenge overcome, Dr. Petersen and Ballantyne appear set for a relatively happy future together. Yet, as the curtain fell that Halloween night 1945, *Spellbound* left theatergoers with more than minds racing over another classic Hitchcock narrative; it left them with a clear message concerning the incomparable and heroic work of mental hospitals and the doctors who worked there. Despite the obstacles, intentional and otherwise, psychoanalysis had both cured John Ballantyne of his inner demons and restored his place in the world. The good news was that if a similar fate befell them, they knew whom they could trust.

Shock *(1946)*

As autumn 1945 gave way to winter 1946, film noir was once again used as a vehicle to reexamine "madhouses" for the benefit of an anxious world. When audiences gathered in cinemas on January 10, 1946, to watch Alfred Werker's film, *Shock*, another important milestone was being set that would remind them of the state of instability in their world.[6] Earlier that day in London, the delegates of the General Assembly of the United Nations first met. This international organization, crafted to maintain peace and order for a convalescing world, would prove to be a formidable influence following World War II.[7] As if to supplement that body's work, 20th Century–Fox's *Shock* offered another sort of balm for the troubled world. This low-budget but moderately successful movie, starring Vincent Price and Lynn Bari, gave audiences, via a film noir horror story, a complicated but overall positive view of psychiatry that helped position the field as a complementary boon for postwar Americans.

The film opens with a jarring orchestral piece and an image of a sanitarium in the background. Throughout the opening credits, the centrality and conflict of this "madhouse" is reinforced as lightning flashes and rain pours around it. The institution is run by Dr. Richard Cross, played by a mustacheless Vincent Price. From the beginning of the movie, Dr. Cross and his private sanitarium outside of San Francisco are held in high regard. This is not a horrifying "madhouse," and Dr. Cross is not a diabolical scientist. Even so, this situation does become more complicated as *Shock* progresses.

This complication revolves around Janet Stewart and her husband Lieutenant Paul Stewart. Janet travels to San Francisco to meet Paul, who has just been released as a prisoner of war during World War II. While a worried sick Janet waits for Paul in a hotel room, she sees a mysterious married couple arguing in a nearby room. When the husband eventually strikes and kills the wife with a candlestick, Janet experiences a "shock" which leaves her in a catatonic state. When Paul eventually arrives, he calls the "house doctor" who immediately offers a diagnosis of "shock" and recommends the specialist Dr. Cross, who is "one of the best men in this part of the country." To Paul's surprise, Dr. Cross has a room in the hotel and is quickly summoned. On his arrival, both the house doctor and Paul defer to the preeminent psychiatrist, who confirmed the diagnosis of "shock" or "nervous collapse" and suggests that Janet be moved to his private sanitarium. Paul simply responds, "Okay, you men know best."

In *Shock* (1946), Dr. Cross (Vincent Price), who conveniently owns a private psychiatric sanitarium, hovers over his helpless patient (Anabel Shaw) as she regains consciousness from insulin shock therapy, all the while wondering if she recognizes him as the man who murdered his wife and inadvertently sent this new patient into a state of "shock."

There are no worried glances, no whispers as one might expect if Janet had been referred to Bedlam, or one of its ilk. Yet, it was amid this professional setting that Dr. Cross realizes Janet has in fact seen him kill his wife after she refused to give him a quiet divorce. Conflicted, Dr. Cross tells his nurse and lover, Elaine, about the development. Concerning the murder, Elaine bluntly responds: "You're not sorry, are you?" The ensuing argument only further establishes Dr. Cross as a capable professional torn and tempted by Elaine, the film's relentless femme fatale. After the verbal sparring ends, Cross, the instinctively good doctor, is nevertheless tempted and goaded into bending his medical integrity to address the problem of Janet and her memory. While Elaine argues for keeping Janet in a state of shock, Dr. Cross resists such a blatant breach of his professional standards. Instead, he resorts to hypnosis and suggestion to convince Janet that the memory of the murder was only a dream.

Even while partially giving into the temptations of Elaine, Dr. Cross presents a view of psychiatry and the work of sanitariums that reinforces their usefulness to society at large. When discussing Janet's condition with her husband Paul, he does put the blame on his reported death during World War II, his miraculous return to life after his release, and his delayed return to her. It was not uncommon for such tumult and the resulting shock to be introduced due to the war, but it was only psychiatry that could produce a solution. Dr. Cross makes the point most clearly when he reassures Lieutenant Stewart, "Have faith in yourself, your wife, and me." The solution did not lie within a return to work, or social engagement, or even the church; it lay within the cooperative activity of patient, family, and doctor in a sanitarium.

Another challenge presents itself for Dr. Cross's plan on a stormy night when the thunder and lightning drive a frightened patient, simply called "Mr. Edwards," into Janet's room. Janet is unconscious and unaware of his arrival; however, Elaine finds Mr. Edwards in the room and tries to walk him back to his own room. When the patient struggles with Elaine, the altercation rouses Janet just in time to see him strike Elaine and knock her to the floor. Once Mr. Edwards is safely detained and returned to his room, Elaine sees an opportunity. She wants Janet to tell everybody that she saw Dr. Cross kill his wife. The more Janet tells the story, the more it will appear that she has confused Dr. Cross with Mr. Edwards. Elaine believes this will allow Dr. Cross to diagnose Janet with hallucinations so she can be permanently committed. Again, Dr. Cross succumbs to the wiles of Elaine, this time with less struggle. When Janet continues to accuse Dr. Cross of murdering his wife, he bluntly responds, "Your mind is sick and getting worse. You're losing your mind, Mrs. Stewart."

As law enforcement investigates the death of Dr. Cross's wife, the conflict is once again seen in the inherently good doctor. Cross fully cooperates with the investigation and even states aloud that the guilty must be punished. While he admits nothing at that time, he appears content to let his conflict be resolved through the professional work of the law. Dr. Cross seems almost happy at the thought that a careful scientific pursuit by law enforcement will lead them to the conclusion that he is the murderer. As he discusses the progressing investigation with Elaine, she again works to change his mind. While it initially appears that Elaine is again successful in manipulating Dr. Cross, the doctor has a different mien in his acquiescence. Yes, he agrees to give Janet a deadly overdose of insulin in the process of treating her, but he does not rush. He follows the clearly established protocol set for the procedure and calmly and precisely administers the insulin. While he could have given Janet an overdose during any of the stages of the insulin treatment, he waits for the very last moment to give the killing injection.

Dr. Cross's resignation to being discovered by others dedicated to the scientific process manifests itself in his deliberate work, which is partly an effort to stall for time in order to be stopped. When this does not happen, Dr. Cross stops himself by giving Janet a shot of dextrose to revive her. He could not sever this last thread of his medical integrity. However, before he can give the shot, the ever-determined Elaine tries to stop him, and in the ensuing struggle Dr. Cross kills her. In the end, Dr. Cross cannot bring himself to undermine the great work performed at psychiatric hospitals by killing a patient under his care. Interestingly, this resolution to his craft also sees him willing to kill to preserve its reputation. So, while film noir presents a doctor and his institution approaching the very threshold of the treachery and madness often ascribed to asylums, sanitariums, and mental hospitals, the thoroughly embedded professionalism of the field wins out in the end.

Possessed *(1947)*

The new image of psychiatry was reinforced in July the following year. By that time, it was increasingly clear that the post–World War II world would be dominated by the tense relationship with communist Russia and its allies. July 26, 1947, saw President

Truman sign into law the National Security Act, which called into existence tools to help America succeed (at home and abroad) in this Cold War, such as the National Security Council, the Department of Defense, the Air Force, and the Central Intelligence Agency.[8] Another monument in the Age of Anxiety had been erected, and that very same day, film noir offered a fresh reminder of the restorative care afforded by mental health institutions in the form of the film *Possessed*.[9]

In *Possessed*, director Curtis Bernhardt highlights the role of psychiatric treatment to help a woman afflicted with mental illness resulting from her obsession with an ex-lover. Like the directors before him, Bernhardt enlists well-known movie stars to further the appeal of the film and its message, in this case Joan Crawford as the mentally unstable woman, Raymond Massey as her former employer and husband, and Van Heflin as her ex-lover. Further adding to the legitimacy of the film's portrayal, Joan Crawford, to prepare for her role, visited several mental hospitals and talked to several psychiatrists.[10]

The opening scene of the film focuses on Crawford in a confused state wandering the streets of Los Angeles. To each person she passes, she simply says the name, "David." She collapses in a diner and is eventually admitted to a hospital's psychiatric ward. After giving her some medication, a psychiatrist, Dr. Harvey Willard, elicits her name, Louise Howell. Through a series of flashbacks, coupled with scenes of the doctors carefully treating Louise, she recovers her story through their expert help.

At the start of her tale, she was employed by one Dean Graham as a private nurse for his invalid wife. At this time Louise mentions her love interest, David Sutton, who is Graham's neighbor and a mechanical engineer. The consummate playboy, Sutton does not share her feelings, and he bluntly tells her as much. Heartbroken Louise returns to her duties as caretaker, where she is confronted with further difficulties. Her charge, Graham's invalid wife Pauline, accuses Louise of having an affair with her husband. Shortly after this altercation, Pauline is found drowned in the lake in front of her home, but the how and why of the death are not clear. Graham believes that his wife committed suicide, but his daughter Carol, freshly home from college, confronts Louise, claiming to have letters from her mother in which she states that Louise is attracted to her father. The troubles of Louise are far from over.

As the accusations linger and the tensions mount, Dean Graham asks Louise to accompany him and the family to Washington, D.C., as a babysitter for his son. In this new setting, seemingly far removed from David Sutton, Louise sees him again, now employed by Graham's company as a mechanical engineer. Hopeful that time apart has changed his feelings for her, Louise approaches David, who promptly tells her that he will never love her. Distraught, she makes plans to leave Graham's employment, but when she informs Dean of her decision, he quickly asks her to marry him. Louise agrees, as it is one way in which she can maintain contact with David. This turn of events is followed by Louise's surprising reconciliation with Graham's daughter, Carol. As with Mrs. Graham's mysterious death, the gathering troubles of Louise seem to scatter just as they appear ready to overwhelm her.

However, as Louise's continual treatment in the psychiatric ward indicates, her difficulties have not been overcome. Still, Dr. Willard helps her recover memories of her wedding day, a day when David again makes an entrance. This time, not only does he casually dismiss Louise, but he also brazenly flirts with Carol Graham. Irate, Louise demands that David leave the wedding and any intentions he had for Carol. Later, Carol

Although known for more glamorous roles, Joan Crawford also played mentally disturbed women, as in Curtis Bernhardt's *Possessed* (1947), where multiple mirror images imply that her internal sense of self is similarly fractured and confused, and that her relentless pursuit of her rejecting ex-lover will immobilize her in a catatonic state that lands her in a locked psychiatric ward.

and Louise (as evidence of their budding new friendship) attend a piano recital. Carol sees David at the recital and invites him to come over to their box. Louise becomes distraught because David used to play the piano for her on their dates. She leaves Carol and David at the recital, returning early to her home. Later that night, Louise has a hallucination. She hears people at the front door of her home and when she investigates, she finds Carol and David kissing. After David leaves and Carol is climbing the stairway, Louise confronts her, and in the ensuing row, Louise lets slip that she had in fact killed Carol's mother. When Carol threatens to inform her father, Louise hits her and sends her rolling down the stairs to her death. Yet, at that moment, and indicative of the hallucination that Dr. Willard is teasing out of Louise during her treatments, the real Carol walks through the door. She is very much alive and without an amorous David.

Disturbed by her hallucination, Louise, under a false name, goes to see a doctor. The doctor, reinforcing the validity of psychiatric work, recommends that she see a psychiatrist. Ignoring this advice, she goes home where she promptly asks Dean for a divorce, as his dead wife Pauline hates Louise for killing her. Dean, sensing Louise's mental anguish, takes her to the lake house where his first wife died to help her overcome this problem. Louise does not fare well initially during this lake house intervention. However, after much calming and reasoning, Dean seemingly convinces Louise that she could not have killed Pauline, as it was her day off and she was away in the local village.

Again, director Bernhardt pulls Louise back from being completely overwhelmed, and again it proves a short respite. Returning from the lake house, Louise and Dean decide to go dancing at a local nightclub, where they see Carol and David together. When Louise confronts Carol about her relationship with David, the resulting fight sends Louise spiraling. Desperate and spinning a web of lies to drive a wedge between Carol and David and Dean, Louise is found out. Dean tells her that he is going to get a psychiatrist to examine her, and while she agrees, she is secretly bent on cornering David and forcing some sort of resolution to their story. When she eventually finds David and once again he rejects her love while professing it for Carol, Louise reveals a gun and shoots him.

The great event that led to the film's opening scene has occurred and audiences are once more among the psychiatric doctors working to resolve Louise's mental illness. Dean visits the hospital, and the doctor tells him that Louise has psychosis. Dr. Willard believes that he can restore Louise's mental health, but it will be a difficult process and will take a long time. Still in love with her, Dean tells the doctor that he will support Louise's full recovery. As the curtains fall on another film noir treatment, a happy ending is not in hand, but it is within grasp. Despite the tangled web that Louise has, in part, made for herself, the work of the psychiatrist is consistent. From beginning to end, the psychiatrists in the film are presented as being very compassionate, professional, and having full confidence that their treatment can restore her to full mental health.

High Wall *(1947)*

Director Curtis Bernhardt treated American audiences to another film noir depiction of the stalwart work of asylums on December 17, 1947, with *High Wall*.[11] That theater-going Americans might need this timely reminder was illustrated that same day as Cold War tensions heightened, first through the first successful testing of the Boeing XB-47 Stratojet bomber and second by the treaty between the recently converted Communist countries of Bulgaria and Albania, which allied the countries in opposition to the United Nations' efforts to keep Communism out of Greece.[12] The uncertainties produced by World War II and the subsequent Cold War were not fading quickly into the background, and this reality was clearly addressed in *High Wall*.

Like the previous films discussed, uncertainty permeates the world of *High Wall*. The film opens on one of film's stars, Herbert Marshall, playing an uncomfortable looking man—later identified as Willard Whitcombe—in a nightclub. After a short while, Whitcombe leaves for his office at Brattle Press. There he inquires with a secretary about a manuscript but is told that the assistant sent to retrieve the manuscript from his home has not returned and will likely not return that evening. When pressed for more information, the secretary reveals that the husband of the assistant in question, Helen Kenet, showed up to the office looking to surprise her after a two-year absence. The secretary informed Steven Kenet where he could find his wife and their reunion, she presumed, would delay the arrival of the manuscript that evening. The film moves abruptly to the well-known actor Robert Taylor, driving frantically and then intentionally off a low bridge. Beside him in the car is an unconscious, perhaps dead woman. With little to no clarity the film moves again, this time to police headquarters, where Whitcombe is identifying the body of Helen Kenet and reporting that her husband had come looking for her earlier in the day. Whitcombe is informed that Steven Kenet is there and being questioned. Curiously, Whitcombe is ushered into the interrogation room where Robert Taylor, now shown to be Kenet, is admitting to murdering his wife and attempting to kill himself by driving off the bridge. This quick resolution to the film's many driving questions is just as abruptly derailed. As the assistant district attorney is preparing to whisk Kenet off to jail, a doctor in the surprisingly crowded interrogation room informs him that Kenet must go to "Psycho first."

This new twist that wrenches a quick resolution from the hands of the police only introduces more uncertainty. Instead of being escorted promptly to jail, Steven Kenet is sent to the county psychiatric hospital. According to the doctor, Kenet has had "some head surgery" that requires further investigation. Quick to the task, the doctors of the hospital discover that Kenet was a bomber pilot during the war who suffered injuries that required a series of head surgeries.

Unfortunately, Kenet only received the first surgery, which left him with periodic blackouts. While the district attorney's office works to get Kenet the surgery so he can stand trial as a sane man, Dr. Ann Lorrison, one of the hospital's capable psychiatrists, played by Audrey Totter, takes on the task of discovering the reality of Kenet and his case. Throughout all of the interactions in the psychiatric hospital—though the accommodations are austere, fitting the setting of a facility designed to house potential convicts—there is no hint of anything nefarious. The interactions between Dr. Lorrison and her colleagues (and with Steven) are all professional and in keeping with the previous film noir depictions of asylums and sanitariums. This is the realm of progressive and hard-working detectives of the mind, who are the only people equipped to deal with the damage left in the wake of their tumultuous world.

While the film's psychiatrists are not the villains, the plot does present several challenges for the field. The chief difficulty presented in *High Wall* (as in the other films) is the overwhelming demand for psychiatric care. The county hospital where Kenet is being treated is simply overcrowded; as one doctor comments in passing, there are "2,500 patients and only 12 doctors." Every day brings more people plagued by the troubles of the world, and while the only real safe haven is an asylum, there are not enough doctors. The second challenge, closely linked to the first, comes in the form of pressure applied by the villainous Willard Whitcombe, as well as the pressure applied by the assistant district attorney. Both look to manipulate the overworked men and women of the psychiatric hospital in order to accomplish their own agendas. Whitcombe works to have Kenet take the fall for the murder he has committed, and the assistant district attorney wants Kenet to move through the hospital as quickly as possible to resolve the case with his conviction. Against both obstacles, the doctors maintain their integrity, not without some straining, and are able to provide a more honest resolution to the multiple crises they are presented with.

To be sure, according to the film, most of this work is done by Dr. Lorrison, who tackled the first two challenges as well as a third. *High Wall*, like *Spellbound*, introduces the seemingly inevitable tensions that arise from a woman being in a position of authority. Interestingly, while Ingrid Bergman's character in *Spellbound* is almost immediately and overtly smitten with Gregory Peck's character, *High Wall*'s Dr. Lorrison remains distanced from any romantic entanglement for most of the movie. She is shown as a diligent and devoted psychiatrist working the Kenet case as any other. It is only toward the film's conclusion that another doctor, who has shown interest in Dr. Lorrison, contends that her perseverance is due to her feelings for Kenet. Calling on the commonly held belief that a woman, regardless of position or authority, cannot help but fall for attractive men and succumb to the whims of passion over logic, this accusation threatens to undermine both Dr. Lorrison and the integrity of the field. It is only when Kenet finally clears his name, largely through the invaluable detective work of Dr. Lorrison, that the good doctor is shown overcoming this last challenge. Granted, the film's resolution does immediately lead to Dr. Lorrison and Steven Kenet finally holding hands, embracing, and, in the final shot of the film, kissing. Yet to that point, Dr. Lorrison has remained remarkably focused on her work, sleuthing the clouded troubles of Kenet's past to restore both his mind and his reputation. This is the job, and despite the myriad challenges, film noir presents another example of invaluable service provided by the oft-derided madhouses.

Across a variety of production houses, producers, writers, and directors, the golden age of film noir presented a strikingly uniform depiction of asylums, sanitariums, and mental hospitals as well as the doctors who staffed them. The image of the madhouse operating for the nefarious purposes of mad doctors was gone. In its stead, and placed upon a pedestal, was a portrait of a haven, a respite, a place where modern professionals worked tirelessly to unravel and sort out the mental issues that plagued their society. Across the four films explored here—*Spellbound*, *Shock*, *Possessed*, and *High Wall*—numerous challenges contended with and threatened the integrity of these institutions, yet in each case they prevailed, testifying to their worthiness as social bulwarks in an Age of Anxiety. If, as W.H. Auden wrote, the world needed a bath and a rest, film noir had the perfect place in mind—a redeemed madhouse.

Notes

1. W.H. Auden, "The Age of Anxiety, A Baroque Eclogue" (Random House, 1947).
2. For more, see Modris Eksteins, *Rites Of Spring: The Great War and the Birth of the Modern Age* (Mariner Books, 2000); George L. Mosse, *Fallen Soldiers: Reshaping the Memory of the World Wars* (Oxford University Press, 1991); David M. Kennedy, *Freedom from Fear: The American People in Depression and War, 1929–1945* (Oxford University Press, 1999); and Allan V. Horwitz, "How an Age of Anxiety Became an Age of Depression," *The Milbank Quarterly* 88, no. 1 (March 2010): 112–138.
3. Foster Hirsh, *The Dark Side of the Screen: Film Noir* (Da Capo Press, 2001); William Luhr, *Film Noir* (Wiley Blackwell, 2012); Spenser Shelby, *Dark City: The Film Noir* (McFarland, 1984); Andrew Spicer, *Film Noir* (Routledge, 2016); Mark A. Vieira, *Into the Dark: The Hidden World of Film Noir, 1941-1950* (Running Press, 2016); James Naremore, *More than Night: Film Noir in its Contexts* (University of California Press, 1998); Dennis Broe, *Film Noir, American Workers and Postwar Hollywood* (University Press of Florida, 2009); Mark T. Conard, ed., *Philosophy of Film Noir* (University Press of Kentucky, 2007).
4. Andrew Scull, ed., *Madhouses, Mad-Doctors, and Madmen: The Social History of Psychiatry in the Victorian Era* (University of Pennsylvania Press, 1981). See also Benjamin Reiss, *Theaters of Madness: Insane Asylums and Nineteenth-Century American Culture* (University of Chicago Press, 2008); Gerald N. Grob, *Mental Institutions in America, Social Policy to 1875* (Routledge, 2008); Constance M. McGovern, *Masters of Madness: Social Origins of the American Psychiatric Profession* (University of Vermont Press, 1985); and Walid Fakhoury and Stefan Priebe, "Deinstitutionalization and Reinstitutionalization: Major Changes in the Provision of Mental Healthcare," *Psychiatry* 6, no. 8 (August 2007): 313–316.
5. *Spellbound*, directed by Alfred Hitchcock (United Artists, 1945).
6. *Shock*, directed by Alfred Werker (20th Century Fox, 1946).
7. Stanley Meisler, *United Nations: A History* (Grove Press, 2011).
8. M. Kent Bolton, *The Rise of the American Security State: The National Security Act of 1947 and the Militarization of U.S. Foreign Policy* (Praeger Security International, 2017).
9. *Possessed*, directed by Curtis Bernhardt (Warner Bros., 1947).
10. Vieira, *Into the Dark*, 187–189.
11. *High Wall*, directed by Curtis Bernhardt (Metro-Goldwyn Mayer, 1947).
12. Jan Tegler, *B-47 Stratojet: Boeing's Brilliant Bomber* (McGraw-Hill, 2000); Nikos Maranzidis, "The Greek Civil War (1944–1949) and the International Communist System," *Journal of Cold War Studies* 15, no. 4 (Fall 2013): 25–54.

SECTION IV

Incarceration, Voluntary vs. Involuntary

8

Where Is My Child?

A Weird Welcome to America

Sharon Packer

Involuntary incarceration is such a primal fear—and such a scary historical reality—that this trope surfaces in many madhouse movies. Theoretically, we could take our pick of such movies, but we might need a complete book, rather than a single essay, to cover all relevant entries. So we will focus on one film only, one that may not be well-known to most readers: *Where Is My Child?* (1937).

Before "moving pictures" made their way to the silent screen, when "serial montage" was the closest substitute for cinema, parallel tales appeared in influential 19th-century memoirs. The classic account was written by Elizabeth Jane Cochran, an intrepid young journalist who used the pseudonym Nellie Bly. Many say that *Ten Days in a Mad-House* (1877) is the gold standard of madhouse memoirs, even if the initial hospital admission was orchestrated by the author herself and was not entirely involuntary. Her release from the hospital, however, was not automatic, and required intervention by an attorney.[1]

Ten Days was published as a series of articles in *New York World*, and later in book form by Norman Munro in 1887. This report prompted a grand jury investigation into the inner workings of the "madhouse," and important reform measures followed. Additional public funds were allocated for such asylum care.

Despite the report's social impact, screen adaptations were slow in coming, and none achieved the acclaim of Bly's original reportage. In 2015, Pendragon Pictures released *10 Days in a Mad-House*, a low-budget, independent film version. *Escaping the Madhouse: The Nellie Bly Story* debuted on Lifetime in 2019. The higher profile *American Horror Story: Asylum* (2012) was vaguely based on Bly's memoir. A TV series titled *10 Days in a Mad-House*, featuring Bly, was announced in 2017. Stage adaptations and even operas have surfaced from time to time, as recently as 2023.

Another woman—Elizabeth Packard—deserves mention here as well, but not because of her memoirs, per se. Packard was institutionalized from 1860 to 1863 in Illinois's first psychiatric hospital because she disagreed with her minister husband's approach to child rearing, family finances, and slavery. As a married woman without individual rights, as was the custom at the time, she had to "prove her sanity" before she could be discharged from the facility. Today, the admissions process almost always operates the other way around, where the hospital or admitting psychiatrist must document credible criteria that confirm the need for involuntary hospitalization. However, those established standards may be challenged soon. As reported on April 25, 2025, by Jordyn Jensen in Britain's *The Guardian*, "The United States is witnessing the return of psychiatric imprisonment."[2] The details of Jensen's well-supported allegations are beyond the scope of this essay, but the original article merits review.

As for Packard, she subsequently wrote several books on the subject, but it is her success at social activism that remains most remarkable. Packard was responsible for 34 bills that protected women from unwarranted hospitalization and treatment. In 1867, she founded the "Anti-Insane Asylum Society," which was a thought-provoking but poorly documented proto-anti-psychiatry organization, as per Ashley Barry, Ph.D., who teaches college courses on Mad Studies. As we shall see, Packard's personal experiences bear striking similarities to *Where Is My Child?*

Where Is My Child? (*Vu Iz Mayn Kind?*, 1937)[3] is an American-made Yiddish-language film that enjoyed great success when it premiered in 1937. Most readers will not have seen this film, and I might not have known of it, were it not for the Yiddish film seminar hosted by Hebrew Union College. Clearly, the cars and the clothes in this film are dated, but the scene of the proverbial "men in the white coats" is timeless, and it is curious—yet unsettling—that this movie trope from 1937 mirrors Packard's accounts from 1867, a full 70 years earlier.

Where Is My Child? revolves around "evil institutions" where corrupt staff—and equally evil outside accomplices—conspire to institutionalize, and essentially incarcerate, an unwitting woman for their own gain alone, without concern about harming her. In fact, no one is concerned about whether this woman should be a psychiatric patient at all—until one important individual expresses concern near the film's finale.

The plot of *Where Is My Child?* highlights duplicity and deception—although many reviewers focus only on the family ties portrayed in the initially tragic, but ultimately redemptive storyline. This film exemplifies a fear that strikes a chord for almost all potential patients today, when they themselves are seeking psychiatric care or, worse yet, when others pressure them into starting treatment. Being remanded to a psychiatric ward of a hospital by a court or a custodian is even scarier. The terror that one can be involuntarily locked in a mental institution—whether temporarily or possibly even indefinitely—persists to this day, even though contemporary safeguards prevent the events that drive the plot in *Where Is My Child?* In fact, those stringent safeguards have since been critiqued for being too lax, and for permitting many people who need hospitalization to leave the premises too soon, to their detriment.

This English-subtitled Yiddish-language "talkie" was made in the same year that Disney's original *Snow White and the Seven Dwarfs* (1937) premiered, but that chronological correspondence is the sole similarity between the two feature films. Everything else departs. One might say it was a forerunner of the so-called "paranoid woman's film" genre that came into full force in Hollywood the 1940s, when *The Snake Pit* (1948), *Gaslight* (1944), and *The Spiral Staircase* (1945) merged with horror and noir. But this film falls into still another category.

Despite its American origins, *Where Is My Child?* is a prime example of *shund* films, a once popular genre of Yiddish films. The term *shund* defies exact English translation, but the genre can be compared to low-brow, American-made B-movies. The plot of *Where Is My Child?* goes far beyond the concept of gaslighting, an increasingly popular term that became one of the most often used (and misused) words in 2021, which refers to the malicious act of making someone believe that she has lost touch with consensual reality and is thereby psychotic or delusional—or, to use a more common albeit inaccurate adjective, "insane." As mentioned earlier, "gaslighting" appears in the titles of two famous films, a noirish one made in the U.S. in 1944 by George Cukor, and an earlier U.K. version in 1940. It is also the title of a 1938 play that appeared less than a year after *Where Is My Child.*

The trope of inhospitable psychiatric institutions or deceptive doctors—or even the imagery of the proverbial "men in white" who drag an unwitting victim into an ambulance—all of which are featured in *Where Is My Child?*—are tried and true. However, film reviewers of the late 1930s zeroed in on the mother-child relationship depicted in this film. The allusions to faithful families ruptured by relocation to the New World impressed audiences and critics alike.

Mother-son ties, and familial bonds, whether broken or unbending, were popular Yiddish literary and cinematic themes, both inside and outside of America. However, the American immigrant experience, which occurred far away from Europe's "Old World," presented unique challenges and often inspired dramatic interpretations. Yet, for our purposes, the relevance of the institution reigns supreme, since this book concerns madhouse movies.

Vu Iz Mayn Kind?/Where Is My Child? was made for an immigrant Eastern European Jewish audience that was barely conversant in English but still spoke Yiddish on a day-to-day basis. The scholarly, on the other hand, wrote in Hebrew, the "Holy Language," and dismissed Yiddish as a second-class jargon, suitable mostly for women who were rarely formally schooled in Hebrew. Besides being the language of prayer and devotional texts and Torah studies, Hebrew was also the high-brow literary language, understood by only the educated elite. The next generation shied away from Yiddish, this so-called "mother tongue," which was associated with new arrivals or "greenhorns." To accommodate later generations of non-native Yiddish speakers who could not follow the dialogue, *Where Is My Child?* includes English intertitles or subtitles.

The film was produced by Abraham Leff and directed by Leff and Henry Lynn. Lynn wrote the screenplay, which he adapted from a story by Sam Steinberg and William Siegal. Lynn used a formula that had succeeded for him repeatedly in the past. He would cast a well-known stage personality with no prior film experience. He would then "sell" the movie based on the star's reputation, without concern about their ability to shine in this new medium. In this case, the famous personality was Celia Adler, who had made her name on stage, and who hailed from an illustrious theatrical family. Celia was past 40 when she played the part of this immigrant ingenue, but this dissonance did not dissuade Lynn.

Dismissed as an entrepreneur by film maven and prolific author J. Hoberman, Lynn possessed accurate intuitions about popular taste. Or perhaps he simply made astute observations about the box office (which likely made him a successful entrepreneur, at least for a while). This "potboiler" dominated Yiddish movie houses for five full months. In December 1937, *Where Is My Child?* opened in four separate movie houses simultaneously at the same time that it played in the former Yiddish Arts Theater. The film was favorably reviewed by the revered (and sometimes reviled) Abraham Cahan, editor of the Yiddish daily *Forverts* newspaper (which became better known as "The Forward" when translated into English). It also attracted the attention of the *Kansas City Jewish Chronicle* many years later, earning accolades from cultural critic and scholar Mashey Bernstein. In his writing for *The Jewish Chronicle* and in academic works, Bernstein often uses this film to discuss important sociological topics such as the rupture of the family, how the immigrant experience physically and psychologically separated families; Celia Adler's ability to elevate "low-brow" melodrama into a haunting exploration of loss; and reunion tropes with typical "happy coincidence" endings where the lost child is found, often in a position of high status (a doctor or a lawyer, perhaps), fulfilling the immigrant dream. "This film provides an insight into the concerns of Jews in the late thirties and their particular methods in playing out the reality of their situation," Bernstein writes, "for whatever the numerous advantages of life in the United States, inevitably there was a price to be paid in terms of health, family ties and religion."[4] When Hoberman calls this film "quintessential *shund*," he is not paying it a compliment but is distinguishing low-brow *shund* from the *literatishe* creations favored by "sophisticated" critics, whose opinions departed from the ticket-buying, movie-going public, whose patronage subsidized the Yiddish stage and screen.

Before delving into the specifics of *Where Is My Child?*, let me say a few words about Yiddish film in general, and more about this mysterious but easily recognizable *shund* slant. Yiddish cinema blossomed in America between the 1920s and 1940s, shortly after the heyday of mass Jewish immigration to the U.S. Such Yiddish films helped preserve Jewish cultural identity, as they relayed stories in the immigrants' native language. Yiddish cinema created a sense of belonging for these often-alienated new arrivals in the New World. At the same time, they dramatized doubts about their newly adopted homes and questioned the wisdom of abandoning familiar—yet perilous and pogrom-ridden—communities in Eastern Europe, as Mashey Bernstein summarized in his *Kansas City Jewish Chronicle* review.

Yiddish films that were made in America had other functions as well. They were often vehicles to highlight pressing social issues. (One can compare them to the "social realism" of painters and printmakers such as Ben Shahn [1898–1969].) As they added commentaries on contemporary Jewish life, they also broached controversial themes such as poverty, discrimination, intergenerational conflicts, and the pursuit of the American dream—even during the era of the Great Depression in America, a time when that so-called "dream" was closer to a nightmare. In addition, Yiddish cinema offered opportunities for Jewish actors, writers, and directors to showcase their talents and to tell authentic stories that "spoke" to communities that shared their language and culture. Importantly, Yiddish film and theater also provided jobs, which were all too scarce during the Great Depression and during the subsequent Roosevelt Depression.

Where Is My Child? was shot during the short-lived "Golden Age of Yiddish Film" (1936–1939). Those same years were anything but "golden" in Europe, for Hitler had already come to power. The Nuremberg Laws were in place in Germany and were becoming more and more restrictive as the years passed. Opportunities for Jewish participation in the arts, education, professions, and business ventures constricted under their yoke.

Kristallnacht, which marked the official start of the Holocaust (also known as the Shoah in Hebrew or the Churban in Yiddish) began in November 1938, when 91 Jews were murdered on that night alone, and when hundreds more were dragged away and sent to concentration camps, where they later met their deaths. On that day, Jewish businesses and synagogues were either debased or destroyed on the spot. American Jews who had faced discrimination and anti–Semitism and other unpleasantries, as the likes of Father Coughlin spewed hatred from his radio pulpit, were still safer than their European counterparts.

In *Where Is My Child?*, Celia Adler, doyenne of the Yiddish stage, stars as the film's hapless heroine, Esther Liebman. Esther had lost her husband while sailing to America and would soon lose her freedom after being institutionalized. She shares the same fate as the very American Elizabeth Packard, the minister's wife who was unfairly committed to an asylum and who later campaigned on behalf of other victimized women. But more importantly, Esther lost contact with her infant son because of a heinous plot perpetrated by two doctors, one who headed the mental hospital and the other who presided over the orphanage where she had entrusted her baby boy.

Celia Adler, with her stellar lineage and impressive stage career, was surely a name draw. She was the daughter of Jacob Adler, the "Great Eagle" ("Nesher Hagadol") of the Yiddish stage. The elder Adler began his theatrical career in Odessa (Russia) but left for London after Russia banned Yiddish theater in 1883. Jacob later relocated to New York. (Another daughter, Stella, opened an acting studio where she taught method acting in America to Marlon Brando and many others.)

While *Where Is My Child?* confronts contemporary social problems directly, its sentimentalism is typical of Yiddish film style, and of Yiddish *shund* films specifically. It might have been one of those "straight to video" movies, had it been made decades later. But it was socially relevant, having arrived at the peak of America's 1937–1938 "Roosevelt Recession" (to be distinguished from the "Great Depression"). Bread lines of impoverished people snaked through U.S. streets, while the Nazi regime passed suffocating "Nuremberg Laws" in Europe. That unanticipated timing turned out to be almost as important as the subject matter itself.

In the film, the heroine Esther (Adler) arrives in New York decades earlier, in 1911, at the height of mass Jewish immigration from Europe to America. Because the film's action is backdated by a quarter century, it implicitly reassures audiences (correctly or not) that the worst American experiences are over, and that they have survived and thrived in the New World despite other obstacles and so should expect similar success in the future.

When the newly widowed Esther arrives in New York, she is friendless and impoverished—and unfamiliar with the customs of this new country where residents speak an unfamiliar language. She is a loving mother but doubts her ability to meet the material needs of her newborn son. Desperate and depressed, she is about to throw herself and her baby off a bridge when a passerby intervenes. Conveniently, this passerby happens to be a physician (played by Morris Strassberg). Having saved her life, he suggests that she bring her child to an orphanage where the boy can be cared for. She accepts his seemingly helpful suggestions.

Minutes after signing the baby into the orphanage, Celia recants—but it is too late. A wealthy but childless couple is waiting in the wings, ready to adopt an available infant. Obsessed with the hope of reuniting with her son, Esther pines for him for the next six years. A letter carrier later alerts her to her son's whereabouts. The letter carrier performs the same function as a letter that reveals the plot, but he adds a human touch.

Relentless in her pursuit of her baby boy, Esther tracks down this address. Sadly, yet dramatically, Esther is spotted as she lurks near the affluent adoptive family's home. In today's world, she might be called a stalker, however justified her motivations may have been.

Fearing that he could lose custody of his adopted child, whom he has cared for so lovingly, the false father contacts the orphanage head, and the two men concoct a scheme to avoid discovery of the deception. The adoptive mother is never informed of this unethical strategy.

To offset anticipated interference by the biological mother, Esther, the orphanage head conspires with the head of a nearby mental hospital and arranges for Esther's involuntary admission. In an archetypal scene about psychiatric institutionalization, she is literally carted off by the "men in white coats" and shoved into an ambulance as she struggles.

In one of the film's more memorable scenes, Dr. Reisner of the adoption agency phones his psychiatrist colleague at the sanitarium, and the two strategize about ways to admit Esther into his asylum. When his skeptical assistant asks if the psychiatrist will comply with his request, Dr. Reisner says of the psychiatrist, "He'd sell his own mother for money." They then banter about the doctor not being a "real doctor," but rather a doctor who purchased his degree from a diploma mill. This dialogue leaves no doubt that the psychiatrist is as unscrupulous as the orphanage's medical director. It is equally likely that the allegation about his not being a real doctor is also true, for doctors did indeed purchase diplomas before Abraham Flexner's report spurred major reforms in medical education and closed down such "diploma mills."

After the men in white coats cart Celia away, the aides deliver her to the mental hospital, where she is declared to be delusional. This waiflike woman languishes in locked quarters for almost a quarter century, sitting in her room, cradling a bundled-up blanket in her arms, singing to it as if it were a baby.

Fast forward a few decades. Esther's son has grown to be a man and has become a doctor (played by Mischa Stutchkof). He somehow learns that he was adopted but learns nothing about his true parents, except, perhaps, that his biological father is deceased. In the interim, the young physician comments on the plight of poor immigrants, not knowing that their plight parallels the experiences of his birth parents. The finale occurs after he finishes his psychiatry training and starts his first full-fledged position as a staff psychiatrist.

When the young psychiatrist arrives at the hospital, he is introduced to a gray-haired woman who, he is told, harbors a long-held delusion about her stolen baby. But the doctor has already heard stories about his convoluted adoption through the letter carrier. He has previously voiced his suspicions that some asylum inmates might not belong in the institution at all. Soon enough, Esther and the newly minted doctor count the years, compare his age to hers, and piece together the facts. Not only do they realize that he is her long-lost son and that she is his mother, but the head of the institution confesses to the chicanery. Tears of joy (and sorrow) are shed.

Sentimentality and pathos aside, this film is cynical, to say the least. It is dismissive of psychiatric doctors (as well as orphanage directors). It matter-of-factly states that some doctors will sell out their own mothers. Importantly, it flat-out accuses doctors of buying degrees at diploma mills and thereby capitalizes on a fact that was well known to medical reformers of that era, when Dr. Abraham Flexner published his still-famous "Flexner Report" of 1910.[5] In the wake of the damning Flexner Report, a quarter of all existing medical schools were closed.

Apart from these curious but tangential details, this film focuses on the proverbial Jewish mother, whose love for her child—however long-lost—never ceases. In this case, the blameless victim cradles swaddling clothes for two decades, never abandoning hope of reuniting with her lost child. At least, that is how the National Center for Jewish

Film describes it.[6] As the website states, this film revolves around the "rupture and restoration of family ties," a subject that was especially important to immigrants to America, who literally left family members behind in the Old Country, as they established new roots in the New World.

This film is set in the past but does not romanticize it; rather, it reassures anxious audiences that earlier times were even worse, even though life in 1937 was not necessarily pleasant or easy. It reminds spectators that they surmounted hardships endured during early immigration and implicitly assures them that they can also triumph over the latest set of obstacles, which were mounting by the minute in 1937. Anti-Semitism peaked in America during the "Roosevelt Depression" (1937–8), as Father Coughlin preached his hateful diatribe on the radio. Some German Americans voiced support for Nazis, and German Bundists staged public rallies, such as the much publicized "Garden Party" at Madison Square Garden. Anti-Semitism inspired by the Lindbergh kidnapping case added to the furor.

Most importantly, Hitler was well established as Chancellor of Germany, where the Nazi Party was in power. Restrictions against Jewish physicians' practice of medicine progressively increased; at first they were permitted to treat Jewish patients only, and eventually they were stripped of their formal titles as doctors. However, psychoanalysts (who did not need to be medical doctors in Europe) were banned outright at the beginning—which ironically turned into a survival advantage in the long run because most fled Europe earlier than the physicians.

The official start of the Holocaust, which began with Kristallnacht, was still one year away, and the death camps would not start until 1941. Some prescient Jews from Central Europe trickled into America, having read the handwriting on the wall. Psychoanalysts who were not medical doctors were among the earliest European émigrés, having been banned from practicing their profession as early as 1933, when Hitler condemned psychoanalysis as "the Jewish science" and deemed it to be a philosophy rather than a medical treatment. He burned Freud's books early on, when the Nazis set the writings of anthropologist Franz Boas aflame.

As psychiatrists and psychoanalytic practitioners left Nazi-ridden Europe and sought refuge on American (or sometimes South American) shores, their presence increased Americans' awareness of psychiatry and psychoanalysis. A film that stridently disrespected psychiatric doctors, as this film did, raised concern about the risks of imparting too much power to that profession.

Just the same, for many viewers, *Where Is My Child?* is a film about the stereotyped Jewish adage of "my son, the doctor," which was rumored to be "every Jewish mother's dream." But even Borscht Belt comedians did not bother to joke about "My Son, the Psychiatrist," although a disproportionate number of American Jewish medical students chose to specialize in psychiatry in the second half of the 20th century. In this film, doctors (and adoption directors) are depicted as members of a privileged class that could—and would—exploit poor and unschooled immigrants, in ways that were loosely reminiscent of the banks that had confiscated homes and farms of errant borrowers only a few years before. Memories of the stock market crash of 1929 and record-high unemployment and long waits in bread lines were still fresh.

The payoffs to professionals in *Where Is My Child?* reflect generic populist concerns that permeated the Depression era (and that were rekindled during the Roosevelt Depression of 1937–1938). With its left-leaning message, this film spoke to an already radicalized Yiddish-speaking viewership that commonly embraced socialist ideology or at least supported trade unionism and social reform. It reminded 1930s-era Yiddish speakers that danger lurks on all sides, and that the vulnerable can be exploited by rich and powerful members of one's own group, and that anti–Semitism by outsiders should not be their sole fear. As per this film, profiteering professionals can be equally evil as outside agitators, and unscrupulous professionals can include Jewish doctors. Had this film appeared in 1957 rather than 1937, Senator Joe McCarthy might have seen a communist message hiding inside this populist plot.

The conspiracy concocted by the psychiatrist and the orphanage doctor in *Child* succeeds because other professionals pitch in and lend their skills or, at the very least, turn a blind eye. In this film, and in many others, the psychiatric institution operates as little other than a prison, just as philosopher Michel Foucault claimed in his seminal books on the subject. For those who are conversant with the history of psychiatry, it reflects the long-gone days before the storming of the Bastille during the French Revolution, when "insane" incarcerates were unchained and finally set free, more as a political statement of solidarity than as a deliberate clinical decision.

For those with more contemporary associations, it recollects events from 1975, when an administrator without clinical expertise was convicted of illegally incarcerating psychiatric patients without sound cause. In response to a suit brought by Kenneth Donaldson, who had been held for ten years, a Supreme Court decision in *O'Connor v. Donaldson* strengthened criteria for involuntary commitment to mental hospitals.[7] However, it should be noted that some claim that this controversial legal decision was not a total triumph and instead implicate it in the premature discharge of seriously ill patients from the safety net of psychiatric hospitals, leaving them to face even more social ills, such as homelessness and exposure to more dangerous street drugs.

The upshot of this landmark 1975 ruling is open to debate. But despite long-standing legal pressures to regulate involuntary commitment (which are currently being challenged by New York's governor's proposal to loosen such restrictions, as discussed in *The Guardian*'s April 2025 article), the fear of being locked inside an "insane asylum" persists in the public imagination and so is repeatedly exploited as a cinematic trope.

Yet some facts about Yiddish cinema are beyond argument. For instance, the fourth and best-known phase of Yiddish films coincided with the rejuvenation of the Polish film industry in 1935. The first Polish-Yiddish talkies catalyzed American Jewish filmmakers to dialogue with Warsaw, the literary capital of Jewish Poland. This interchange between American and Polish makers of Yiddish films continued until the eve of World War II and marked the so-called "Golden Age of Yiddish film." *Where is My Child?* stands smack in the center of that era, although it was overshadowed by even more famous Yiddish films such as the Polish production of *Der Dibuk* (*The Dybbuk*, 1937) and the American-made *Grine Felder (Green Fields*, 1937), which Hoberman discusses in his magnum opus on Yiddish cinema.

On that more upbeat note, I conclude this essay, and refer interested readers to full-length books on Yiddish films, including Goldman's revised edition of *Visions, Images and Dreams: Yiddish Film Past and Present*, revised edition,[8] and Hoberman's remarkably comprehensive catalogue, *Bridge of Light: Yiddish Film between Two Worlds*.[9] I also invite readers to respond to the evocative essay published by commentators from across the pond, after reflecting on this admittedly hyperbolic and maudlin film.

Notes

1. Timothy Hines based his 2015 film on this 1877 exposé, but the film did not earn the renown of the book that it was based on. The production earned an unimaginably paltry $12,165 at the box office, in spite of its $12 million production budget.

2. Jordyn Jensen, "The United States is witnessing the return of psychiatric imprisonment," *The Guardian*, April 27, 2025.

3. My very special thanks to the late Philip Miller, Ph.D., A.M.L.S., former director of the Klau Library at Hebrew Union College, who introduced me to *Where Is My Child?* when he hosted a seminar on Yiddish films.

4. "Where Is My Child? Vi Iz Mayn Kind?" The National Center for Jewish Film, https://jewishfilm.org/Catalogue/films/whereismychild.htm.

5. See Andrew H. Beck, "The Flexner Report and the Standardization of American Medical Education," *JAMA* 291, no. 17 (2004): 2139–2140. Also see Molly Cooke, David M. Irby, William Sullivan, and Kenneth M. Ludmerer, "American Medical Education 100 Years after the Flexner Report," *New England Journal of Medicine* 355 (September 2006): 1339–1344.

6. "Where Is My Child? Vu Iz Mayn Kind?" National Center for Jewish Film, https://jewishfilm.org/Catalogue/films/whereismychild.htm.

7. *O'Connor v. Donaldson*, 422 U.S. 563 (1975), https://supreme.justia.com/cases/federal/us/422/563, as discussed in David Behar's commentary in *Clinical Psychiatry News*, July 2023, 23.

8. Eric Goldman, *Visions, Images and Dreams: Yiddish Film Past and Present, revised edition* (Lynn-Reinner, 2011).

9. J. Hoberman, *Bridge of Light: Yiddish Film between Two Worlds*. (Brandeis University Press, 1991).

9

Frances

Memoir Movies (and Made-Up Madhouse Memories)

Eric J. Sterling

Frances (1982), directed by Graeme Clifford and starring Jessica Lange and Kim Stanley, concerns the quick ascent and rapid fall of the talented movie and stage actress Frances Farmer. In the film, which is based on William Arnold's liberally fictionalized 1978 biography *Shadowland*, Farmer (Lange) is portrayed as a self-confident, stubborn, and proud young woman prone to anger outbursts. William Arnold admitted that he embellished the plot to tell a better story. The film took even more liberties with the already distorted facts recorded in the "biography."[1] This admission by the author casts doubt on the film's veracity, turning both him and the filmmaker into unreliable narrators. Despite this caveat, we will discuss the film's details below, but when discussing psychiatric diagnoses and treatments, we will include more accurate and up-to-date data, as per psychiatric standards.[2] We will also address the standards that were reportedly in place when Frances sought treatment.

Frances's combative nature is diagnosed by her family and psychiatrists as mental illness, rather than being attributed to her substance misuse, which predated the onset of her behavior problems and which was subsequently exacerbated by supposedly helpful but apparently uninformed friends and coworkers who attempted to ameliorate her psychiatric symptoms by providing even more psychoactive substances, including alcohol. Substance use disorders are potentially treatable with targeted treatment techniques which are not necessarily interchangeable with standard treatments for "spontaneous" psychiatric disorders that surface in the absence of psychoactive substances. While substance use disorders are better understood at present, they were often overlooked in Frances's time, despite the attention accorded to alcohol use disorders in earlier films such as Billy Wilder's *The Lost Weekend* (1945),[3] or in somewhat later films about women with alcohol use disorders, such as *Smash-Up, the Story of a Woman* (1947)[4] or *I'll Cry Tomorrow* (1955),[5] each of which starred Susan Hayward.

Frances's mother Lillian (Stanley) also plays an important role in Frances's inadequate or inappropriate treatment. Lillian lives her life vicariously through Frances, refusing to relinquish her dream of being a movie star's mother—or a movie star herself—and punishing her daughter with involuntary institutionalization for leaving the film industry. *Frances* dramatizes how legal guardians can abuse their authority by involuntarily committing family members to mental institutions if their relative displeases them. This film shows how flaws in procedures used to incarcerate people in insane asylums can promote the mistreatment of the truly mentally ill and the presumptively mentally ill.[6]

The accuracy of Frances Farmer's mental disorder diagnosis, as presented in the film, is open to question, especially when we weigh in the probable contribution of alcohol overuse or stimulants, prescribed or nonprescribed. Continuous stimulant use can induce a clinical picture that is indistinguishable from paranoid schizophrenia, or at the very least can induce perceptions of paranoia, either fleeing or persistent. Alcohol withdrawal syndromes can also result in psychotic symptoms and hallucinations. Alcohol intoxication itself impacts behavior and disinhibits those who imbibe, leading them to behave recklessly and possibly destructively.

Clifford's film dramatizes coworkers' misguided efforts to relieve Frances's depressions. Their bad advice exacerbates her mental state and possibly bears some blame for her eventual institutionalization. For instance, her friends and movie colleagues, including her "studio-appointed guardian,"[7] Bob Barnes (Jack Riley), feel that the best way to elevate mood is make a depressed person feel happy and energized. So, when the actress shows signs of depression, Barnes and others provide her with alcohol and amphetamines like Benzedrine, which can induce psychosis, especially when used for protracted periods of time or in high doses. Even small doses of such stimulants can precipitate psychosis in someone with bipolar tendencies.

A well-known depressant, alcohol also increases the frequency and intensity of mood cycling in someone who is prone to bipolar disorder. Alcohol consumption worsens outcomes for individuals with bipolar disorder compared to those who abstain. Women of Frances's young age are extra vulnerable to the neurotoxic effects of alcohol when compared to men or older women.

The film, the book behind it, and Ussher's critique of the film suggest that psychiatrists like Dr. Doyle (Woodrow Parfrey) consider willful, obstinate, and independent women who violate cultural norms, which are constructed by the patriarchal society and allegedly designed to maintain male hegemony, to be mad. It is implied that women who possess a high level of self-worth and self-confidence—traits usually attributed to men—must have severe psychiatric problems.[8]

However, Farmer's behavior is undeniably aggressive, not only for women, but for men as well. For instance, when a motorcycle cop arrests Farmer for driving at night with her bright lights on in a dim-out zone in Santa Monica during a wartime blackout, she kicks him in the groin, knocks him to the ground,[9] and bites him.[10] She later punches a sailor.[11] It was rare for a woman to beat up a police officer and punch men aggressively—and such behavior shocked the media and her fans.

While Ussher's feminist interpretation of Frances's psychiatric treatment has cachet in many circles, it is noteworthy that studies show that comparable behavior in men is criminalized rather than pathologized. Men are likely to be arrested, whereas the same behavior in women more commonly catalyzes referrals for psychiatric treatment. Moreover, substance use disorders have historically been underdiagnosed in women, and alcohol use was believed to be uncommon among women, so its presence was often overlooked at the time and even in the present. Studies show that women are at least twice as likely to minimize reports of alcohol use as men, when queried about their medical and social histories by their treatment teams.

Although we can reliably relate much of Frances's aggressive behavior to alcohol

Anatole Litvak's award-winning and influential film *The Snake Pit* (1948) ultimately catalyzed state hospital reforms nationwide. Starring Olivia de Havilland (seen here), it was based on a memoir by Mary Jane Ward, who was hospitalized in New York's Rockland State Hospital (Juniper Hill), where she endured abhorrent conditions that mirrored the conditions chronicled by health journalist Albert Deutsch.

and amphetamine use, which probably compounded preexisting anger management problems, her evident self-destructiveness reinforces people's opinions of her alleged madness. As an example, when the actress bathes, policemen arrest her for a probation violation. They beat down the door to her hotel room and then the bathroom door. In the film—and historically—the police humiliate the actress by grabbing her while she is nude and then taking her to the police station, still disrobed. She is demonstrably rattled by the incessant violation of her privacy by relentless celebrity photographers who take pictures of her arrest, her booking at the police station, and even her time in a jail cell. The photographers' aggressiveness amplifies her violent and self-destructive behavior, adding to the impression that she is indeed psychotic. Humiliated by her arrest and the negative publicity from reporters, the angry Farmer worsens her situation by becoming even more rude and uncooperative.

When a police desk sergeant asks for her name, she retorts sarcastically, "You jerks drag me down in the middle of the night and you don't know who the hell I am."[12] A clever response, it shows her aggressive defiance of male authority, which was uncommon in a woman in that era. It also shows her disregard for social norms overall and her disrespect for the police, who can harm her by adding more criminal charges.

When the sergeant asks for her occupation, expecting her to say "actress" or "movie star," she shocks him by answering "cocksucker."[13] Subsequently, she mocks the judge, pretending that she is on a film set, not in court. Although she is presumably joking, the judge cannot discern if she is sane enough to distinguish between a movie studio and a courtroom. When the judge asks her if she has violated her probation by driving, Frances responds:

FRANCES: Who's writing this guy's [the judge's] lines?
JUDGE: Answer the question! Have you driven a car since you were placed on probation?
FRANCES: No, I couldn't get my hands on one.... Are you telling me you didn't have a little rum in your pineapple juice this morning? I can smell it from here, Your Honor.[14]

The film tones down her actual words as reported in her embellished "biography" upon which the film is based. Historically, when the judge asked if she was avoiding alcohol, she responded, "I put liquor in my milk. I put liquor in my coffee and in my orange juice. What do you want me to do, starve to death? I drink everything, including Benzedrine."[15] She then threw an inkpot at the judge, hitting him with it.[16]

Although presumably desperate to avoid jail time, Frances acts irrationally when she implies that she willingly violated her probation by driving while drinking. She then angers the judge by falsely accusing him of being drunk. Spectators ask themselves, "Would a sane person act rudely and belligerently to a judge who is sentencing her, bragging about her alcoholism, and hitting the judge with ink, as if this behavior is a virtue?" The average layperson believes that sane human beings demonstrate self-interest and self-preservation and do not try to hurt themselves and destroy their lives. Mental health professionals, on the other hand, are well acquainted with people who deliberately self-sabotage, even when not inebriated. The upshot is that Frances's purposeful self-destruction is perceived as madness.

The symbolism in the courtroom scene is a foreboding and interesting filmic device, for "the shadow of the Venetian blinds falls over Frances like prison stripes ... and also prefigures the use of Venetian blind shadows in the sanitarium."[17] Psychiatrists swiftly diagnose her with paranoid schizophrenia and institutionalize her. In their defense, it is worth recalling, once again, that prolonged stimulant use can produce a paranoid picture that is clinically indistinguishable from "real" paranoid schizophrenia, except for the fact that stimulant-induced paranoia can be far more protracted and treatment-resistant than spontaneously occurring symptoms of paranoia.

After Frances insults the judge, Lillian and her lawyer, Alma Styles (Sarah Cunningham), must decide between a jail or a mental institution for Frances. They choose the latter, sending her to Mountain View Convalescent Home. They assume—incorrectly—that a mental institution is more pleasant and safer than a jail. Although Frances is an adult, no judge or lawyer (or even her mother) asks her where she wants to go. Even as a grown woman, Frances has no agency or autonomy. She is present in her absence, because Lillian and Styles decide her fate by themselves, without consulting her, as if her opinions and desires are irrelevant.

Their implied conclusions are corroborated when the judge appoints her mother as her guardian. Styles callously informs Frances, "Your mother is now your legal guardian. In the eyes of the law, you no longer have any rights as an adult."[18] Frances's mother gains control over her life and fate and Frances herself has no power over her own life.

Lillian's refusal to consult Frances on these matters shows her push for authority over her daughter's life and her abuse of her role as guardian. When meeting with Lillian and Styles, mental health officials analyze only Frances's psychological health without considering her mother's mental health or motives. Had they done so, they might have seen Lillian as a jealous woman who commits her daughter to a mental hospital to avenge her daughter's refusal to make Hollywood movies and be a film star—which is Lillian's but not Frances's dream.

During a press interview about Frances's acting career, Lillian brags to a reporter, "I guess it's no secret that I'm proud. I like to think that she got some of it [Frances's acting talent] from me. I used to have theatrical aspirations myself, you know."[19] Although the spotlight is on Frances because of the premiere of her new movie, Lillian egoistically tries to make herself the center of attention. We see a significant contradiction when Lillian desperately wants Frances to regain her status as a Hollywood actress so that Lillian can once again be seen as a movie star's mother, and yet she repeatedly commits her daughter to mental institutions, thereby preventing Frances from returning to a successful career.

Other examples of Lillian's interference are shown in the film. For instance, when Lillian visits Frances at Dr. Symington's Mountain View mental asylum, she brings the actress's fan mail in hopes of inspiring Frances to return to Hollywood. Instead, Frances is unhappy that her mother has already opened, read, and answered the letters.

FRANCES: Why are these all open?
LILLIAN: Well, they needed immediate answers, Frances. It's good manners and good sense. You shouldn't be bothering yourself with these right now.
FRANCES: Then why did you bring them?
LILLIAN: It's your fan mail, little sister.
FRANCES: (looking off, under her breath) You kill me, Mama.[20]

"You kill me" is a colloquial phrase that signifies that the speaker has made the listener laugh; it is a common phrase of the era, often used by Holden Caulfield in the contemporary J.D. Salinger novel *The Catcher in the Rye* (1951). Although Frances remains calm and pleasant, she presumably feels frustrated that her mother has invaded her privacy, as if Lillian is not only nosy but trying to supplant her daughter as a movie star. Frances discerns, perhaps, that her mother is living her daughter's life vicariously, reading and answering fan mail as if Lillian, not Frances, is a movie star. We can surmise that Lillian fantasizes about being a young movie star like Frances, and so she always calls her daughter, who is the youngest of Lillian's five children, "little sister," when Lillian is obviously the actress's mother, not an older sibling.

The scene at the Mountain View asylum becomes even more disturbing when Frances requests permission from Dr. Symington (Lane Smith) to leave the sanitarium because she feels better. Symington declines Frances's request, claiming that after speaking with Lillian, he believes that Frances is too violent and paranoid to be released. Shockingly, Lillian has lied to the asylum director, claiming falsely that Frances said, '"Mama, you want to kill me.'"[21] Furthermore, although Lillian admits to Frances that she opened and read her daughter's mail, the mother tells Symington that Frances is paranoid and has falsely accused her of tampering with her mail. This report ensures that Frances remains incarcerated in the mental institution:

SYMINGTON: Your mother says you were sullen and uncommunicative. Whom do you think I should believe?
FRANCES: Doctor, ... my mother is a little batty.
SYMINGTON: Frances, you're still filled with anxiety. You feel guilty and hostile toward your family and friends. Consequently, I didn't recommend your release at the staff review.[22]

What happens when the mental patient is sane, but credulous psychiatrists like Symington receive dishonest and inaccurate information from a third party who is potentially mentally ill herself and a vengeful legal guardian who wants to punish her child? Symington's identification of Frances's guilt and hostility stem from Lillian's reports, not from his own interviews with the patient. To partly exonerate Dr. Symington in this instance, it is worth mentioning that it is standard practice in psychiatry to collect "corroborative information" from relatives or close associates and to factor such information into psychiatric assessments, since patients do not necessarily disclose all salient details about their lives and their thoughts.

Lillian knows that Frances wants her freedom, and she also knows that claiming that Frances expressed an unfounded fear of being killed and made paranoid accusations will prevent her immediate release. The psychiatrist ignores the unmistakable friction between mother and daughter and so Symington and other psychiatrists place their faith in the parent's report rather than in the identified patient without weighing in the possible secondary gain of the guardian.

Even more to the point, Symington himself possesses an ulterior motive for keeping Frances in his mental hospital: he seems obsessed with Farmer's fame. Hoping to bolster his self-esteem, and to gain the esteem of others, he plans to brag that he is treating a Hollywood star.

The mental hospital director confides in Frances:

> "I feel I've known you for a long time … you see, I've followed your career … you're a fascinating case.… I'm looking forward to resolving your predicament.… [T]he neuroses which fuel your [acting] talent can also generate certain character disabilities which … [can cripple your ability to function]."[23]

According to the film, Symington naively believes that he can accurately diagnose Frances because he has seen her movies and read stories about her in the tabloids and newspapers. He also stereotypes actors, assuming that all actors must be neurotic. Frances serves as his guinea pig, his "fascinating case." He treats her as a marketing tool, not as a human being, because she is a celebrity. It would be a significant boost to his career if he could boast that he treated and cured her. Otherwise, she will have to remain in his convalescent home until she acts in a way for which he can claim credit.

After Frances escapes from Symington's clinic, with the help of her dedicated friend Harry York (Sam Shepard), she makes the mistake of returning home to her mother. The truly insane behavior that Frances exhibits repeatedly in the film is her constant return to her home in Seattle, where the tension between Frances and her mother escalates, and her aggressive behavior resurfaces—even when she behaves normally and appears happy elsewhere.

Viewers might feel a sense of foreboding when they spot her mother looking out the window, searching obsessively for Frances, before she comes outside to meet her daughter and the fighting begins because Frances wants to quit acting while Lillian demands that she make a comeback and return to Hollywood.

In the film, Lillian is the aggressor, slapping Frances across the face after the actress states that she does not want to meet with an agent who plans to fly to Seattle and send scripts for a proposed comeback. The agent is scheduled to arrive early, along with reporters and photographers who can provide publicity for Frances. Biographer Peter Shelley notes that director "Clifford's staging of the confrontation … has Lillian on the staircase with Frances looking up at her. The camera is positioned behind Lillian to show that she has higher status, and that Frances is the weaker party—as if she needs her mother's approval to reject Hollywood."[24]

Toward the beginning of this scene, Lillian tells Frances that she is cured and must return to Hollywood, but only minutes later, when Frances says that she doesn't want to be a movie star, the mother decides to commit her daughter again to a mental hospital, presumably out of revenge.[25] As uniformed asylum workers come to take Frances back to Western State psychiatric hospital, she tells her mother, "You can send me away, Lillian, you can pretend I'm crazy and pretend I'm still your little girl who can't take care of herself, but one thing you can't pretend anymore. You can't pretend I love you because I don't. I can't. Not after what you've done to me."[26] Lillian seems shocked, as if she can't think of anything she did wrong. Yet as her legal guardian, Lillian is the person who tenders information to Frances's psychiatrists upon which they base their decisions and diagnoses.

To show the arbitrariness of Frances's most recent incarceration, it should be noted that the actress was prohibited from leaving Western State Hospital in Lakewood, Washington—44 miles from Seattle—because she was deemed insane, yet when Lillian suffered a debilitating stroke and needed a caretaker, Frances was suddenly diagnosed as sane enough to be released to care for her mother. Furthermore, Clifford's film suggests that Judge Hillier (James Karen) committed Frances to a mental institution not because of inherent mental illness but rather as revenge for harboring communist sympathies that he despised and for publicly insulting Judge Hillier's wife in front of reporters at the Seattle premiere of Frances's movie, *Come and Get It* (1936).

Even if Farmer were not mentally ill, being confined in mental institutions and convalescent homes could have compromised her self-esteem and self-confidence. Some self-doubt could stem from forcible insulin treatments as well as medications prescribed for a presumptive diagnosis of schizophrenia. Still, she somehow recovers from her symptoms, perhaps because those treatments were as effective as expected, or perhaps because she never needed them in the first place. As an aside, insulin coma therapy was initially devised by Manfred Sakel, M.D., in the 1930s to treat morphine addiction and was later repurposed for schizophrenia treatments.

Ralph Edwards (Donald Craig) asks her on national television (*This is Your Life*, 1958) if she is mentally unstable:

> EDWARDS: Finally your mother finds it necessary to commit you to a state mental institution. Were you mentally ill, Frances?
>
> FRANCES: No, Ralph. I don't believe I ever was sick. But when you're treated like a patient long enough, you're apt to act like one.[27]

Because this is such a powerful moment, Lange reenacts this excerpt from the television show in the film. Frances questions her sanity because she is incarcerated in an insane asylum. Because she is surrounded by mentally ill people, she herself starts to act crazy, or so she suspects. The film implies that her recent episodes of psychotic behavior—which immediately preceded her hospitalization—could reflect mistreatment, poor medication choices, or other mismanagement while in the mental institutions.

Mountain View Convalescent Home seems sedate on the surface, but a nurse lies to Frances, telling the actress she is using a hypodermic needle to give her a shot of vitamins when it is actually an insulin treatment that makes her nauseated and forces her body into insulin shock.[28] Insulin treatments were designed to drop the blood sugar and to send the recipient into "shock" or coma to restore, or reset, the brain back to normalcy. Although these treatments at Mountain View are terrible, the film shows that life at the Western State Mental Hospital is dramatically worse. In these scenes, the color in the film disappears, as if this section of the movie is filmed in black-and-white. The movie's vibrant colors are replaced with white walls, dark shadows, mold and fungus, and holes in the ceilings. The audience sees the inmates dressed in white smocks. The walls have no paintings or color, just white and a drab light green.

The windows have bars, mirroring the venetian blinds in the earlier courtroom scene and likening the building, which used to be a fort, to a prison. Patients in straitjackets scream. The beds are simple cots, close together, with many patients tied to them by cloths. They cry incessantly and look malnourished, unbathed, and haggard. More than a dozen women are confined to one room, leaving them with nowhere to go for privacy. Being imprisoned in the same dull and chaotic room with very distressed and mentally disturbed people, coupled with such drab and bleak surroundings, could possibly push even a sane person to the breaking point. Frances appears to be affected negatively by what she witnesses while locked in an asylum.

Patrick Agan says that "Frances was a readmission case; she was treated as incurably insane and was subjected to outrageous treatment by staff and inmates alike.... She was assigned to the violent ward, where she was forced to work long, inhumane hours in the clothing dispensary, watched over every moment of the day by sadistic matrons who tormented her with verbal and physical abuse. At first, she ... [was] screaming nights away until they put her into solitary confinement, a mean cell which didn't even contain a toilet.... Surrounded by the hopelessly insane, women who had torn themselves apart emotionally and were now doing it physically, fighting at the fence at the end of the ward for a few scraps of almost inedible food, Frances fought, too, for the food and against the injustice."[29]

How could anyone be expected to escape damage from these experiences? Furthermore, the actress claims that she was raped often and had to fight the other inmates in the asylum because food was scarce. Farmer says that the asylum orderlies acted as pimps, receiving money from soldiers at a nearby military base for allowing them into the women's ward to rape the actress and other female patients. Unfortunately, these accused perpetrators were not arrested and tried in a court of law, where other patients with similar experiences would be called to testify and to confirm (or contradict) the events relayed by Frances. Because Clifford admitted to embellishing his accounts, and to sensationalizing the narrative for the sake of a "good story," viewers are left wondering about the accuracy of the horrifying events described below. This omission is especially concerning, given that paranoid women frequently believe that they are prostitutes. And we know that protracted use of stimulants—like those used by Frances—can induce paranoia. With all respect to today's "Me Too" movement, and the need to respect victims' reports, we need more definitive data before confirming Frances's allegations. But one thing is beyond dispute: these sensational sex scenes in *Frances* attract audiences and portend bigger box office receipts.

Farmer insists that she "was raped by orderlies, gnawed on by rats, and poisoned by tainted food." "I was chained in padded cells, strapped into straitjackets and half-drowned in ice baths."[30] The sexual abuse is dramatized in *Frances*, with orderlies taking cash payments for allowing the soldiers to rape female inmates. In the film, the directions read:

> Soldiers laugh as Frances lies naked and spread-eagled on the floor. Four hospital ATTENDANTS pin her arms and legs. A SOLDIER, his pants down around his ankles, is squirming violently on top of her. Frances' eyes are open but glazed, her face turned away from her attacker.... Two of the SOLDIERS, waiting their turn, are smoking cigarettes, and chatting idly.
>
> SOLDIER #1: Best deal I ever made. Twenty bucks to fuck a fuckin' movie star.
> SOLDIER #2: Yeah, it's worth it, I guess.
> SOLDIER #1: What's she saying, anyway?
> SOLDIER #2: Who knows. She's crazy, ain't she?

Frances keeps reciting [Sonya's prayer monologue from Anton Chekhov's play *Uncle Vanya*] as one rapist gets off [of Frances's body]. The Soldiers cheer as another quickly takes his place.[31]

Farmer is the main target of the asylum's orderlies and the soldiers because of her beauty and fame. Men want to brag to their friends that they had sexual intercourse with such a star—never saying, of course, that the sex was nonconsensual. Given that even a single rape negatively impacts mental health, one can infer that repeat rapes could do even more damage. The action portrayed in the film suggests that her stay in the mental institution harmed, not helped her.

The scene is disturbing not only for the violence toward the women, and particularly toward Frances, but also the dehumanizing mistreatment of the women, with the implication that they are devoid of feelings. To retreat psychologically from the pain of the rape and to dissociate from the horrors of the mental institution, Frances recites a monologue, returning (in her mind) to a happier time when she was a young actress without troubles. The callous behavior of the orderlies and soldiers is extra horrific because attendants are expected to protect patients.

When the psychiatrists see that their female patients such as Frances are not improving (while being raped and starved), the next recourse presented in the film is lobotomy. (The film follows William Arnold's fictionalized biography by dramatizing Frances's lobotomy, which never occurred in real life, and which was directly disputed by Frances's father, as noted below.)

In the film, Symington, superintendent of Western State Hospital, casually tells his fellow doctors that "one merely inserts the leucotome beneath the eyelid and presses up into the prefrontal lobe, manipulating it to sever the nervous connections between the thalamofrontal radiation and the body of the brain."[32] Although operating on the brain itself is typically complicated and requires the skills of a trained neurosurgeon, transorbital lobotomies are not difficult and could be performed in an office setting with minimal advanced training. Symington is nonchalant, using the word "merely" as if he is simply pulling a tooth or treating a hangnail. To the spectator, his casual attitude toward lobotomy represents his indifference and lack of care for his patients. The film does not provide useful information about the straightforward procedure itself to help spectators better understand the specifics. Instead, it sensationalizes the procedure and adds to the drama.

Symington brags that he can perform ten lobotomies in less than half an hour, without sedating his patients. It is implied that he regards this as a medical breakthrough or a positive psychiatric measure. The spectator who does not know that there are no pain receptors in the brain and that neurosurgery is ordinarily performed without anesthesia might conclude that the doctor does not care about his patients' feelings when he operates on their brains without sedating them. That assumption is unjustified. Medical specifics aside, it appears that Symington, like the soldiers, uses Frances to satisfy his own ego and for his own pleasure, with his pleasure being financial profit and acclaim as a supposedly great psychiatrist and surgeon.

On screen, Frances stares emotionlessly as the leucotome, resembling an ice-pick, is placed into her eye. Symington claims that the lobotomy "works best on patients with extreme overreactions to emotional stimuli.... [M]y technique severs the nerves which give emotional energy to ideas. Along with the cure comes a loss of affect ... a kind of emotional flattening."[33] The lobotomy breaks her spirit, but Frances's free-spirited nature and creativity make her unique and talented as an actress. Her creativity, emotions, reactions to stimuli, and her affect have made her successful and happy and added to her acting abilities—and made her Frances Farmer.

Symington sums up his lecture at Western State Hospital at Lakewood with a catchy phrase: "Lobotomy gets 'em home."[34] But at what cost? As the film concludes, color is restored to the screen because Frances has been released from Western State. But in a heartbreaking final scene, the actress encounters her lover, Harry. Although she recognizes him, her passion for him and her emotional energy are gone; the lobotomy (which never took place in real life) has destroyed her personality, leaving her a dull and flat semblance of her former self. She has left the asylum, but the lobotomy robbed her of her passion for life.

Arnold and Clifford include the lobotomy in their book and film, respectively, although they realize that records indicate that Farmer never underwent the procedure. Clifford admits that the lobotomy never happened, but he decided to include it anyway: "We didn't want to nickel-and-dime people to death with facts."[35] Frances's sister Edith Elliot recalls that "the doctors there [at Western State] were seriously proposing to perform a lobotomy on Frances."[36]

In a letter to Edith, Farmer's father Ernest wrote that he "was over to see Frances a week ago [at Western State] and we had a wonderful visit. She is just about as crazy as I am but try and make those damned doctors believe that.... I got there just in time to head them off from some danged experimental brain operation on her. I notified them one and all if they tried any of their guinea pig operations on her they would have a danged big lawsuit on their hands. [Ernest's brother] doesn't think much of the doctor in charge of the ward Frances is in and says he ought to be in the ward himself. We will get her out of there or know the reason why."[37]

Frances's father kept trying to get his daughter discharged from the mental institution while his wife continually committed her. Because her parents were divorced and not on good terms, Frances was caught in the middle of their contentious relationship. Ernest's letter proves that Frances never had a lobotomy, despite what her biography and *Frances* (the film) claim. Both the biography and film choose to portray the fictionalized lobotomy because it is poignant and sensational, adding sympathy for and interest in Farmer. It is good for sales and for profits. The horror of the procedure makes their work more marketable.

In summary, despite having the good fortune to escape the lobotomy depicted in the biography and film, Frances Farmer was misunderstood by her mother, reporters, judges, and psychiatrists. She deserved better than the cruelty inflicted upon her.

Notes

1. Peter Shelley, *Frances Farmer: The Life and Films of a Troubled Star* (McFarland, 2011), 212.
2. As noted in the introduction, criteria for involuntary—and even voluntary—admission to psychiatric wards have changed significantly since the time when Farmer was hospitalized. However, concerns about safeguards against guardianship abuse persist.
3. *Lost Weekend* (1945), Billy Wilder.
4. *Smash-Up, the Story of a Woman* (1947), Stuart Heisler.
5. *I'll Cry Tomorrow* (1955), Daniel Mann.
6. Jane M. Ussher, "Diagnosing Difficult Women and Pathologizing Femininity: Gender Bias in Psychiatric Nosology," *Feminism & Psychology* 23, no. 1 (2013): 64.
7. Eric Bergren, Christopher De Vore, and Nicholas Kazan, *Frances*, screenplay, http://www.sellingyourscreenplay.com/wp-content/uploads/screenplay/scripts/Frances.pdf, 70–71.
8. Ussher, "Diagnosing," 66.
9. Bergren, *Frances*, 76–77.
10. Bergren, *Frances*, 81.
11. Bergren, *Frances*, 81.
12. Bergren, *Frances*, 86.
13. Bergren, *Frances*, 87.
14. Bergren, *Frances*, 88–89.
15. Bergren, *Frances*, 88–89.
16. Bergren, *Frances*, 88–89.
17. Shelley, *Frances Farmer*, 213.
18. Bergren, *Frances*, 114.
19. *Frances*, directed by Graeme Clifford (Lionsgate, 1982). Lillian's line is in the film but not in the screenplay. Kim Stanley might have ad-libbed the line.
20. Bergren, *Frances*, 101.
21. Bergren, *Frances*, 101.
22. Bergren, *Frances*, 103.
23. Bergren, *Frances*, 96.
24. Shelley, *Frances Farmer*, 214.
25. Bergren, *Frances*, 121, 123.
26. Bergren, *Frances*, 144.
27. Bergren, *Frances*, 150–51.
28. Bergren, *Frances*, 100.
29. Patrick Agan, *The Decline and Fall of the Love Goddesses* (Pinnacle Books, 1979), 27.
30. Maxine Harris and Christine L. Landis, *Sexual Abuse in the Lives of Women Diagnosed with Serious Mental Illness* (Harwood Academic, 1997), 146.
31. Bergren, *Frances*, 44.
32. Bergren, *Frances*, 47.
33. Bergren, *Frances*, 148.
34. Bergren, *Frances*, 148.
35. Graeme Clifford, "Commentary," *Frances*, DVD, directed by Graeme Clifford, 1982 (Anchor Bay Entertainment, 2001).
36. Edith Farmer Elliot, *Look Back in Love: The True Story of Fame and Misfortunes of a Brilliant, Talented, Beautiful Actress and Her Family* (Gemaia Press, 1978), 153.
37. Elliot, *Look Back*, 153.

10

Romanticized Renditions vs. Realistic Depictions

The World of "Weepies"

Sharon Packer

Whenever I speak at conferences and mention "madhouse movies," the audience often grimaces and squirms in their seats, and I can sense unspoken assumptions that I am speaking of horror films only, or of sadistic melodramas that revolve around the mistreatment of the mentally ill. Of course, everyone is entitled to their own associations with those words, but there is much more to be said on the subject.

Specifically, we can find madhouse movies about benevolent and beneficial institutions. Venom-spewing cinemas such as *Bedlam* (1946) or *The Snake Pit* (1948) or *One Flew Over the Cuckoo's Nest* (1975) get the lion's share of attention, both in film studies classes and in lectures for psychiatrists in training, yet positive portrayals of sanitarium life or rest home cures are among our most memorable movies. These positive portrayals do not represent the majority of madhouse movies, but they definitely do exist. Some such films swayed public sentiment not only in their own time, but in decades to come, as with Philippe de Broca's comedic *King of Hearts* (1966), which continues to attract attention 60 years later.

King of Hearts is fiction, even if it weaves in real-life events of the past. Like other movies of its ilk, it emerges from the imagination. Other positive portrayals are based on nonfiction memoirs, or semiautobiographical accounts of firsthand experiences.

Some films (or the memoirs that inspire them) romanticize sanitariums and establish unreachable expectations that do not exist in real life. Rather than offering encouragement, as it might seem on the surface, such themes set ailing patients up for disappointment and demoralization when their real-life experiences do not match their cinema-inspired idealization. Firstly, patients may blame themselves for not progressing faster. Trust in their treatment team can be shaken even before treatment begins. Using sophisticated statistics-based analyses, we can prove that rifts in doctor-patient rapport can compromise clinical care and decrease the likelihood of successful outcomes. Moreover, when expectations are high, dopamine rises, but when those expectations are not met, that surge of dopamine drops like a lead balloon, promoting depression that follows such disappointments.[1]

For instance, in the sanitarium scenes in *Now, Voyager* (1942), Claude Rains plays the kindly psychiatrist who transforms Bette Davis's dowdy and downtrodden Aunt

In *Now, Voyager* (1942), Bette Davis (standing) stars as the dowdy and downtrodden Aunt Charlotte, who is intimidated by her demeaning and domineering mother (Gladys Cooper, seated), until she undergoes a dramatic transformation, thanks to her stay in a sanitarium headed by a caring psychiatrist played by Claude Rains.

Charlotte into a self-assured woman of the world who can finally escape the psychological shackles imposed by her mother. Rains's heroic role as Capt. Louis Renault in Michael Curtiz's 1942 wartime classic *Casablanca* earned him an Academy Award nomination for Best Supporting Actor and paralleled his sensitive portrayal of the savior psychiatrist in *Now, Voyager.* Rains's rendition of Dr. Jack Griffen, in his 1933 breakout performance in James Whale's *The Invisible Man* (an interpretation of H.G. Wells's 1897 novel), adds to his credibility as an iconoclastic and daring (albeit damned) physician.

Now, Voyager's Dr. Jaquith enjoys greater professional success on the screen than the disappearing Dr. Griffen, who became psychotic in response to his self-experiments. The pillorying of Dr. Jaquith's character occurred much later in time, when his paternal approach to his patients came under attack by feminist critics and women's studies courses.

In the film, Dr. Jaquith is not a miracle worker whose patients reap instant benefit. The rest cure he recommends requires two tries, instead of just one, and when Charlotte leaves the hospital and embarks on a lengthy cruise, a heartrending romance ensues.

On that cruise, Charlotte meets an unhappily married man who has no plans of abandoning his wife, despite his affection for Charlotte. Besides offering an evening's entertainment, the film functions as an advertisement for Freudian-style family interventions that were fashionable in that era, which were put to rest (more or less) by a landmark lawsuit—*Osheroff v. Chestnut Lodge*—in the mid–1980s. We will elaborate on that lawsuit soon enough, but for now, let us simply say that *Now, Voyager* shows a positive snapshot of sanitarium life, and it was also lauded—at the time of its release—for its sympathetic treatment of mental illness.

Now, Voyager is believed to be Bette Davis's best film and one of her most beloved, but is also one of the most rebuked, having caused controversy over the years. In 2007, this film was selected for preservation by the National Film Registry of the Library of Congress because it is "culturally, historically, or aesthetically significant."

Deemed one of the 20th century's top love stories by American Film Institute, *Now, Voyager* is representative of the delightful 1940s "weepies" that were replaced by daytime TV melodramas in the mid–1950s, when televisions appeared in most American homes. Those "soaps" earned their nickname because they sold soap during commercial breaks. They captivated housewives who had recently "earned" the luxury of remaining at home, contemplating the nuances of housekeeping, rather than working in factories and laboring for the war effort, Rosie-the-Riveter style. This and other World War II–era "women's films" were geared toward female audiences who frequented movie theaters while their men were away at war.

Now, Voyager may be one of the best-known "women's films," but it is also one of the more maligned—unjustly, in my opinion. It has been subject to divergent interpretations. It became the bane of feminist critics, who bristle at the patriarchal role played by Bette's psychiatrist who took charge of her care and challenged the dominion of her mother. It is easy to understand the (pre-feminist) appeal of *Now, Voyager*. The film offered solace to solitary women during the wartime era. It spoke to shuttered women of later eras, who strove to free themselves from the shackles of overbearing and undermining matriarchs, who might not be as wealthy or as pompous as Charlotte's mother but were pernicious in their own ways. Many spectators could identify with the plight of the oppressed female lead.

Despite the opprobrium that *Now, Voyager* elicited from feminist critics, after the fact, it is safe to say that this film offered hope and assured those (mostly female) moviegoers that even unlikely settings, such as rest homes or psychiatric sanitariums, could redirect their lives, free them from Charlotte-style self-doubt, and enable them to pursue loftier goals than their own mothers foresaw. And to add yet another interpretation, let me suggest that the sanitarium in *Now, Voyager* functions as the iconic telephone booth that transforms the meek and mild Clark Kent into the muscular superhero who flies through the skies, after being jostled by bullies and insulted by the likes of Lois Lane. This analogy may be more apt than it seems on the surface, since Jerry Siegel and Joe Shuster's Superman had surfaced in comics only a few years before *Now, Voyager* appeared on the big screen. Such superhero stories promised (mostly male) soldiers that they, too, could cast off their stuffy suits and spectacles to become as spectacularly successful as the spandex-clad voyager from Krypton.

Now, Voyager epitomizes the romanticized rendition of a sanitarium, where patients luxuriate in lovely surroundings, busying themselves with looms, symbolically weaving new tapestries of life. Such a film reflects our highest hopes about private (not public) hospital stays. Even people who never saw *Now, Voyager* firsthand often harbor fantasies about an equally unhurried, uncrowded respite that is far removed from the realities of our current day.

The year 1962 brought an equally romanticized rendition of a psychiatric facility, this time based on a novel written by a psychiatrist with a dramatic flair, Theodore Isaac Rubin, M.D. In *David and Lisa*, a young man fears being touched and believes that a touch will kill. In the psychiatric facility, he meets an equally ill young women who has very different symptoms. Her ability to communicate is severely compromised, and she speaks exclusively in rhymes. Yet the two "meet cute" and cure one another, defying all psychiatric expectations and violating all rules of probability. Because this film was released in the early 1960s, before the sexual revolution came to full fruition a few years later but shortly after oral contraceptives came on the market, it was still plausible that a touchless romance could bloom between these two troubled youths—but uncertainty about lay ahead for David and Lisa in the years to come added tension to the plot.

In 1963, the film earned director Frank Perry a nomination for the Academy Award for Best Director. His writer-wife, Eleanor Perry, was nominated for Best Screenplay. Despite its cinematic success, this film evoked the ire of later generations of psychiatrists who were not swayed by R.D. Laing's anti-psychiatry sentiment, which would gain traction by the mid-sixties. The movie set itself and the protagonists' interactions evoke images of Laing's innovative (yet ultimately ineffective) treatment at Kingsley Hall, where patients were encouraged to act out their psychosis and where they lived, side-by-side, with their psychiatrists.

Laing's Kingsley Hall would open in London in 1965, three years after this film premiered. However, this experimental treatment setting, housed in a community center that once welcomed Gandhi, would soon be shuttered, and Laing himself would admit defeat. Even before Kingsley Hall rose and fell, more scientifically minded psychiatrists (whose numbers multiplied over the decades) bristled at the suggestion that schizophrenia could be cured by love alone.[2]

Still, the film itself was engaging. It assured audiences that quick fixes are available for the asking at a psychiatric sanitarium, even for the most serious and seemingly untreatable conditions. All that is needed are compassionate fellow patients and sagacious psychiatrists who are willing to step aside and postpone their professional intervention. This ethos was in tune with the reigning (but since dismissed) theories about the causality of psychosis as well as its cure.

In *David and Lisa*, the delusional young man who believes that a touch will kill avoids all skin contact. He is also obsessed with clocks and plagued by recurring nightmares of blade-like clock hands that decapitate heads projecting from the clockface's surface. It takes little imagination and a sprinkle of art history and cinema savvy to connect this clock imagery to Salvador Dali's surrealistic paintings about melting clockfaces, or to Hitchcock's disturbing dream scenes in *Spellbound* (1947), with their more diabolical Dalí-esque clock imagery.

Lisa, who speaks in rhymes, resides in the same sanitarium. Lisa suffers from the proverbial "split personality," a diagnosis that does not appear in standard psychiatric terminology, but which was made fashionable via popular films such as *Three Faces of Eve* (1957). *Eve* is based on another psychiatrist-written novel that takes extensive liberties with the true story of Chris Costner Sizemore. Sizemore subsequently refuted details from the film and emphasized that her psychological troubles did not fully disappear, although the "happily ever after" ending of the film suggests otherwise.

Hoping to cure the comely Lisa of her affliction, David parrots her symptoms and communicates with her in rhymes. Eventually, he succeeds, and Lisa responds in prose. Conveniently (but not credibly), this interchange cures David in the process. He now permits her touch. Rather than riding off into the sunset together—to borrow a meme from TV westerns that were popular on small screens of that era—the two sanitarium patients meet on the steps of the Philadelphia Museum of Art and are forever freed from the constraints of severe mental illness.

The irresistible role of hope in this plot—and in assuring its success on the screen—is obvious even to the most uninformed. It is a feel-good film, for sure—for everyone except those who themselves suffer from chronic schizophrenia or delusional disorders. Those people might be left wondering why they have been left out in the cold, uncured, unlike David. The potential impact of such unmet expectations on afflicted patients is equally obvious, albeit in retrospect. But this film was released in an era when even enlightened professionals spoke of "schizophrenogenic mothers" (a term coined by Dr. Fromm-Reichmann, a European-born and educated psychiatrist from Chestnut Lodge, who will be discussed below). A decade earlier, so-called "refrigerator mothers" were (falsely) accused of causing their progeny's autism, based on since-debunked theories espoused by Bruno Bettelheim from University of Chicago. However, scientific studies today find unrelated genetic changes in up to 80 percent of such patients with ASD.

Other chronological correspondences added to the film's superficial credibility. For one thing, *David and Lisa* appeared as the civil rights movement was sweeping across America. Advocates argued that biology was *not* destiny and cited studies that human behavior and learning abilities are acquired, not inborn, and that social changes, along with appropriate education, could alter the destiny of almost any individual. Only a year earlier, Stanley Kramer's acclaimed *Judgment at Nuremberg* (1961) dramatized the genocidal role of Nazi doctors who believed that biologically based, intergenerational "degeneration" was the cause of inheritable and thereby incurable mental illness. As the televised Nuremberg trials implied, the Nazi doctors thereby justified the annihilation of mentally ill patients in Aktion (Operation) T4, via gas chambers that were specifically built for this purpose. Because clergy protested these policies, the gassing of mental patients and otherwise disabled people would grind to a halt, and those gas chambers would subsequently be reappropriated for the "ultimate solution" and the attempted annihilation of the entire Jewish "race" (as well as the Romani people). That heinous legacy further predisposed the public to disbelieve in the biological basis of mental illness and to embrace the romanticized rendition dramatized in a fictional film such as *David and Lisa*.

Some years later, *David and Lisa* was remade as a made-for-television film, but without the fanfare of the 1962 original. Oprah Winfrey produced the TV film. The legendary Sidney Poitier stars as Dr. Swinford. The setting shifts from Philadelphia to Los Angeles, and the Museum of Natural History substitutes for the Philadelphia Museum of Art. But important shifts that took place in the landscape of psychiatry by 1998 mitigated the appeal of the plot. Psychiatric theory and practice were forever disrupted by *Osheroff v. Chestnut Lodge*, which challenged psychoanalytic theories espoused by Chestnut Lodge and impugned the underlying premise of *David and Lisa*. Even a lovely, sunny LA-style setting, with a revered cast and an esteemed producer, could not compete with the seismic shift that had occurred in psychiatry between 1962 and 1998. The plot of *David and Lisa* was no longer plausible, if indeed it ever was, and spectators from 1998 could not suspend disbelief long enough to enter "movie mode." More about the history-making and profession-shaping *Osheroff* legal decision a little later.

Not long after the premiere of the original *David and Lisa*, an entirely unrelated film, *King of Hearts*, arrived in 1966. The story of a World War I soldier who decides that the inmates of the Belgian sanitarium are "saner" than the war-plagued world that exists outside of the institution, *King of Hearts* remains a prime example of romanticized renditions of sanitarium life. *King of Hearts* also reflects the rebellious spirit of the American anti-war era and the belief that the reigning authorities are invariably wrong and that the counterculturists, iconoclasts, and insane asylum inmates are correct. The American anti-war generation that marched against government policies pertaining to Vietnam embraced the message of the movie. *King of Hearts* became a cult classic that still speaks to many who saw it. Baby boomers reminisce about this influential film, as noted by the award-winning social psychiatrist, H. Steven Moffic, M.D.

Yet the 1960s youth culture and the baby boomer generation were not the first to challenge the logic or the ethics of war. The carnage of World War I made many people question the sanity of the authorities' decisions to wage a senseless war that sent so many young soldiers to certain death, using them as cannon fodder, apparently not expecting them to return home in anything other than a body bag, if that.

Art forms such as Surrealism and Dadaism emerged in those years, partly in response to the insanity of war in general and to World War I specifically.[3] The charlatan psychiatrist of *The Cabinet of Dr. Caligari* (1919), that German Expressionist masterpiece, also directly relates to World War I. According to scholars, *Caligari* implicitly comments on the policies of the heartless Austrian military psychiatrists who forced fearful soldiers to return to the front, by administering sadistic "Kaufmannization" shock treatments to goad them back to battle.[4] Such shock treatments would not be interchangeable with today's ECT (electroconvulsive therapy), which would be invented in 1938, and which relies on brain wave data from EEGs (electroencephalograms) that were discovered well after World War I ended. "Kaufmannization" shocks (named for their inventor) were simply electric shocks, intended to induce pain and produce avoidant behavior, not to cure mental disorders directly.

As for *King of Hearts* itself, Alan Bates plays a solider who has been dispatched to deactivate a bomb in war-ravaged Belgium. In the process, he falls in love with a beautiful and jovial asylum inmate. "Saner" city residents have fled for safety, while the sanitarium's patients have remained in town, playing gleefully inside and outside of the institution and dancing in the streets, as if nothing were amiss. Even the nuns who run the asylum have disappeared.

As the film ends, Bates's soldier disrobes and stands naked at the asylum's entryway. He holds a birdcage in one hand, hoping to be admitted to an institution that is "saner" on the inside than the psychotic wartime goings-on on the outside. Rather than condemning asylum life, à la *Cuckoo's Nest*, this film applauds the paradoxical freedom afforded by a locked building that blockades the noxious influences of the "real world" outside the asylum walls.

The psychiatric asylum portrayed in *King of Hearts* is a true psychological sanctuary, an asylum, as the term was intended. Several copycat films with similar themes surfaced over the years, but none could compete with the cachet or cult status of *King of Hearts*.

King of Hearts appeared in 1966, two years after the 1964 publication of an equally beloved memoir by Joanne Greenberg under the name Hannah Green: *I Never Promised You a Rose Garden*. Years later, Greenberg divulged her given name and publicly commented on the 1977 film adaptation of her book.

Greenberg's story is straightforward if we discount the diagnostic disputes that surfaced after its publication, when the memoir invited debates among armchair psychiatrists who "evaluated" Greenberg's symptoms as described in the book (but not the medical records). For years, Greenberg had been a patient of Dr. Frieda Fromm-Reichmann at Maryland's once esteemed but now defunct—yet historically significant—Chestnut Lodge. She based her book on her slightly embellished firsthand experiences. The book became a bestseller and was required reading for many high school classes. It was a favorite of teenaged readers, long before the film debuted.

The film adaptation that followed in 1977 could not compete with *King of Hearts*' appeal, despite its nominations for Oscars and Golden Globe awards. One of the executive producers of the film of *I Never Promised You a Rose Garden* was Roger Corman. Corman was extraordinarily productive, with hundreds of films to his credit (or sometimes discredit). He directed *The Trip* in 1967, starring Peter Fonda and Jack Nicholson (who would star in *One Flew Over the Cuckoo's Nest* in the next decade, and in many more films). *The Trip* was a psychotronic film if there ever was one, and a worthy prelude to the Land of Yr described in *Rose Garden*. More than anything else, Corman's ability to improvise economically is the stuff of film legend. (For instance, to simulate a frightening fire-breathing dragon whose nostrils exhaled smoke, Corman filmed a tea kettle that released steam as the water boiled.)

Always aware of the popular pulse, the incredibly clever Corman reportedly got the film version of *Rose Garden* funded because of the success of *One Flew Over the Cuckoo's Nest*. Apparently, it was irrelevant that Corman's proposed film would be reverential, while *Cuckoo's Nest* reviled psychiatry. *Rose Garden* premiered in 1977, two years after *Cuckoo's Nest*. *Rose Garden* was nominated for an Academy Award for Best Adapted Screenplay. Two Golden Globe nominations for Best Picture and Best Actress for Kathleen Quinlan followed. At the time, the critics' responses were mixed, but the film's significance to the history of psychiatry persists, if only because of its link to the landmark *Osheroff v. Chestnut Lodge* case, as we shall discuss below.

To Greenberg's chagrin, the 1977 film is not totally true to her memoir. The movie omits references to Judaism and to the anti–Semitism experienced by the protagonist, who is renamed "Deborah Blake." Joanne Greenberg objected to these omissions and transpositions and other obvious liberties taken by the filmmakers. The story changes Dr. Fromm-Reichmann's name to a thinly disguised "Dr. Fried." Apart from that switch in nomenclature, plus the casting choice of a decidedly Nordic-looking actor, Bibi Andersson, as the German-Jewish Dr. Fromm-Reichmann, the psychiatrist's portrayal was more or less accurate—in contrast to the very unreal Kingdom of Yr that propels the plot.

A refugee from Nazi Germany who relocated to the U.S.—as did over two hundred European analysts who escaped the Reich—Dr. Fromm-Reichmann had been reared in an Orthodox Jewish family that encouraged her secular education. She was known to practice "Torah therapy" or "Torah-peutics," as her approach was mockingly called. Then she fell under the sway of her husband, Erich Fromm.

Fromm had been Reichmann's supervisee prior to their marriage (in a boundary-breaking union that would not be tolerated by today's standards and that might even promote the loss of one's professional license). Fromm was the son of an orthodox rabbi, but he later became an equally devout socialist. Fromm was also a full-fledged psychoanalyst, having trained in Europe, where medical degrees or even psychology degrees were not prerequisites for entering analytic training. He was not a physician. Over time, he evolved into more of a social scientist/cultural commentator than a clinician. In response to Fromm's influence, Reichmann's earlier emphasis on religiously inspired righteousness veered toward the socialist ideology espoused by Fromm.

In the interim, Dr. Fromm-Reichmann coined the once popular but since contested concept of the "schizophrenogenic mother." That term fell by the wayside over the years, and its use became a badge of the discredited old guard. Despite later denunciation of such analytic constructions, Dr. Fromm-Reichmann's memory is still cherished by the remaining—but greatly diminished—Chestnut Lodge community. The doctor was once called "the Queen of Chestnut Lodge." A house on the grounds bears her name.

Reichmann's much-quoted phrase, "I never promised you a rose garden," was spoken to the film's Deborah Blake (and to Hannah Green, in the memoir), who demanded an explanation for the abusive behavior displayed by one the facility's guards. Dr. Fried then cajoled her reluctant patient to rejoin the real world and renounce her idyllic yet illusory land of Yr.

In contrast to her elaborate delusions—which attracted the attention of director Roger Corman, someone who was known for his fantasy films—it was a straightforward suicide attempt that prompted Joanne Greenberg's admission to Chestnut Lodge. Once in the lodge, she continued to self-harm when the opportunity arose, as seen in the film's bathroom scene, where an unkempt and unconcerned attendant leaves her unsupervised for a few minutes.

In the film, the facility itself is simple, but certainly not squalid. This is not the decrepit British-based adult home that houses Ralph Fiennes in *Spider* (2002), where he is haunted by hallucinations and by the accusatory voice of an uncaring custodian who supervises the facility. Nor is it the luxury-laden sanitarium of *Now, Voyager*, discussed earlier. Likewise, it is not the elegant mansion from Hitchcock's *Spellbound* (1945) where the disgruntled, soon to be retired senior psychiatrist points a gun at a perceptive young female psychoanalyst who realizes that it was he who had murdered the doctor intended to replace him in the sanitarium.

The nondescript board games played by other simply dressed residents in the day room of Chestnut Lodge recollect day rooms that were standard in psychiatric wards of the 1970s, before the advent of video games. Despite the descriptions of a guard's bad behavior, this place is worlds away from Bridgewater State Hospital in Massachusetts, where ragged, unkempt and sometimes naked patients were force-fed and confined to barren, overcrowded cells, as featured in the controversial black-and-white documentary, *Titicut Follies* (1967).

In *Rose Garden*, the protagonist's internal delusional world is far from simple. The teenaged character (Blake/Green/Greenberg) believes that she and a pantheon of deities inhabit the Kingdom of Yr. Mesmerizing recordings of a Balinese Kecak dance performance, the ceremonial chant of the sacred monkey story from the Hindu Ramayana, play during the Yr scenes. This musical accompaniment adds a mysterious, otherworldly dimension to her delusions. One might assume that the Kecak ritual dates to ancient ancestral Hindu traditions, presumably preserved by this tiny, largely Hindu island situated in the world's most populous Muslim-majority country (Indonesia), but that is not so. The Kecak ritual was constructed in the 1930s by Dutch artist Walter Spies, who lived in Bali and turned the island into an anthropological destination.

Sitting across from Miss Coral (Sylvia Sidney) as she demonstrates the iconic hospital pastime of basket weaving is the patient-protagonist Deborah Blake (Kathleen Quinlan) of *I Never Promised You a Rose Garden* (1977), a movie based on Joanne Greenberg's memoir about her stay at once fabled but now defunct Chestnut Lodge.

The choice of this specific performance was probably not coincidental, for the Kecak dance serves to exorcise evil spirits. One might say that it is an exotic version of the Jewish *Dybbuk* legend, which was penned as a play by S. An-sky and performed on stage in 1921, a year after An-sky's death. The story in *The Dybbuk: Between Two Worlds* revolves around malevolent spirits (*dybbuks*) that simulate psychotic states. According to Jewish lore, those clinging spirits or *dybbuks* can be expelled from the possessed via appropriate rabbinical rituals. The parallels between the two geographically separate and divergent traditions are obvious.

Critics later attacked Greenberg's symptoms, claiming that she fabricated her Yr story to impress her psychiatrist, Dr. Fromm-Reichmann. Dr. Fromm-Reichmann's temporary substitute was not as taken with her history as Freida was, and so the new psychiatrist challenged the patient's claims to have invented her own language de novo. Regardless, the youthful Greenberg was diagnosed with schizophrenia while in residence at the Lodge. That diagnosis was commonly applied as a catch-all before later iterations of the DSM delineated diagnostic criteria more precisely. Her diagnosis was subsequently redacted, and in hindsight, her symptoms were reinterpreted as borderline personality disorder or as major depression with psychotic features.[5]

Chestnut Lodge itself came under attack in the mid–1980s, when Dr. Raphael Osheroff filed suit against the much-storied bastion of psychoanalysis that had treated Joanne Greenberg as an adolescent. Already well-known among mental health professionals and Greenberg's many readers, the Lodge garnered even more attention through that landmark lawsuit and the controversies it generated among medical professionals.

Legal scholars, plus the public at large, also took note. It was discussed in psychiatric training programs, psychiatric journals, and the mainstream media, such as the *New York Times*[6] and elsewhere.

Ironically, the memoir *I Never Promised You a Rose Garden* had already played a pivotal role in Dr. Osheroff's life well before he filed suit against Chestnut Lodge. Dr. Osheroff had experienced intermittent depressive episodes in the past. At the insistence of his wife, he was searching for a psychiatric hospital that could relieve his persistent depressive symptoms that did not remit with outpatient appointments only. Over the course of two years, he had been treated by Nathan Kline, M.D., a prominent psychopharmacologist, who prescribed tricyclic antidepressants that were reportedly not taken as prescribed.

Dr. Kline recommended hospitalization, as did Dr. Osheroff's wife. Osheroff specifically chose Chestnut Lodge because Green/Greenberg's memoir about her stay at that institution impressed him. As shown in Greenberg's pseudonymously written book and in the film that followed, Chestnut Lodge offered psychoanalytic approaches only and eschewed prescription medications (until it shifted its seemingly sacrosanct strategies after settling the Osheroff lawsuit some years later).

Unfortunately, the outcome of Dr. Osheroff's treatment at the Lodge was not as salubrious as Hannah's (in the memoir), Deborah's (in the film), or Joanne Greenberg's in real life. His mental and medical conditions deteriorated during his seven-month hospitalization at Chestnut Lodge. Dr. Osheroff reportedly paced relentlessly, slept little, and lost 40 pounds. His analyst nevertheless pressured him to regress, in a futile attempt to peel away his maladaptive personality traits that presumably propelled his outward symptoms. Rather than recovering, the man who had been a successful nephrologist and owner of 11 dialysis centers lost control of his business and eventually lost his entire medical practice.

Most significantly, according to reports provided to this author by Dr. Osheroff's attorney, Philip Hirschkop, who was one of the country's most prominent civil rights attorneys, he also lost his relationships with his sons. Those all-important relationships were never repaired.

After the Lodge refused Dr. Osheroff's mother's last-ditch recommendation to add psychotropic medications, his mother arranged his transfer to Silver Hill Hospital, which had a different approach to treatment. There, his symptoms remitted with a mere three weeks of medications. After a course of tricyclic antidepressants combined with a phenothiazine, he was discharged in three months. Now divorced by his wife (the same wife who pressured him into admitting himself to a hospital), Dr. Osheroff attempted to recapture his prior professional success, and to proceed with his life without that wife. He was never rehospitalized and did not attempt suicide, but his story did not have as happy an ending as one might wish. Writing for *The Guardian* in October 2022, Rachel Aviv elaborates on the convoluted events that followed.

A sea change in psychiatry followed Dr. Osheroff's lawsuit and the debates that it catalyzed. The Maryland Health Care Arbitration Panel had ruled in Osheroff's favor, but that was not the end. Legal proceedings lingered for years before his suit was finally settled in his favor without being adjudicated by a court of law. Psychiatrist Peter Kramer, the author of the bestselling book *Listening to Prozac* (1993), deemed to be one of the century's most important psychiatry-related books, later compared the case's significance to *Roe v. Wade*.

Shifts in psychiatric practice were spurred in large part by the much-quoted testimony provided to the panel by psychiatric luminaries, such as Gerald L. Klerman, M.D., who subsequently published an influential journal article about "The Psychiatric Patient's Right to Effective Treatment: Implications of *Osheroff v. Chestnut Lodge*." Dr. Klerman opined that the central issue of the case was not psychotherapy versus psychopharmacology, but rather "opinion versus evidence." His article implies that issues related to ethics and doctors' obligations to patients are as important as clinical decisions that dictate treatment.

Dr. Osheroff's legal case attracted national attention largely through the all-star cast, which included not only Klerman (Harvard professor; director of research at Mass General) but also William Potter (chief of psychopharmacology, National Institute of Mental Health [NIMH]), Frank Ayd, M.D. (professor of psychiatry who pioneered the use of chlorpromazine), Donald Klein, M.D. (professor of psychiatry, Columbia; director of NY State Psychiatric Institute), and more. These titans implicitly indicted traditional psychoanalytically based psychiatry when they testified on behalf of the physician-turned-patient-turned-plaintiff. Several well-known psychiatrists testified in support of the institution's treatment plan and some posited other explanations for Osheroff's clinical improvement.[7]

Osheroff's case proved that psychiatry was a house divided. Civil war raged as Dr. Alan Stone, a former president of the American Psychiatric Association, attributed Dr. Osheroff's recovery to a better therapeutic alliance with his new psychiatrist, rather than medications. Dr. Stone later told reporter Rachel Aviv that "no psychiatric malpractice lawsuit has attracted more prominent expert witnesses than Ray's.... The case became 'the organising nidus' around which leading biological psychiatrists 'pushed their agenda.'" Another psychiatrist opined that Osheroff improved after his dalliance with a female patient at Silver Hill increased his self-confidence.

Dr. Klerman's succinct statement became a rallying cry in psychiatry: "the issue is not psychotherapy versus biological therapy but, rather, opinion versus evidence."[8] The ramifications of that statement cannot be emphasized enough. In essence, Klerman recapitulated the philosophical concept of epistemology, without using that opaque term. With that single pronouncement, the hallowed walls of psychoanalysis came tumbling down.

"Evidence-based medicine" became the buzzword in psychiatry. The catechism voiced by devotees of "St. Sigmund" frayed at the edges. In time, Dr. Fromm-Reichmann's term about "schizophrenogenic mothers" who spurred schizophrenic breaks in their progeny likewise vanished from psychiatry's vocabulary and moved to history of psychiatry seminars.

In hindsight, this paradigm shift in psychiatry was not as sudden as it seemed. Psychiatry was already changing course and veering into turbulent waters when Osheroff entered Chestnut Lodge in 1977. Also in 1977, APA's then-president Mel Sabshin, M.D. urged psychiatrists to "return to their medical roots." DSM-III appeared in 1980.[9] Intending to encourage a more scientific psychiatry, DSM-III delineated diagnoses carefully, omitting the metaphorical language of psychoanalysis. Dr. Osheroff filed suit two years after DSM-III's publication,[10] and his attorneys accepted an out-of-court settlement on his behalf in 1987. The 1990s were subsequently dubbed the "Decade of the Brain."

The Lodge stayed afloat for another decade before it officially closed in 2001, but it had already been sold to CPC Health in 1997. The latter-day Lodge was in part a victim of managed care's shortened stays that made its practice model financially unsustainable. Although it eventually prescribed medications to almost all patients, in the aftermath of Osheroff's victory, its overall adherence to outdated treatment techniques that did not withstand the test of time and that lacked the endorsement of evidence-based medicine sealed the fate of this historic institution.[11] About a year after Dr. Osheroff's death, almost to the day, *Psychiatric Times* published editor James L. Knoll IV, M.D.'s, article on "The Humanities and Psychiatry: The Rebirth of Mind."[12] He links the late 20th-century gyrations in psychiatric approaches to *Osheroff v. Chestnut Lodge.*

Other sentimental celluloid hospitals remain in our collective consciousness, and the names of certain characters have entered our everyday vocabularies, having become signifiers for specific personality traits.[13] The plot of *Rain Man* (1988) revolves around a troubled family, a long-term residential facility, and a "kidnapping"-cum-road trip. Charlie Babbitt (Tom Cruise) hopes to reclaim a relationship with his mysterious older sibling, autistic savant Raymond (Dustin Hoffman), who has been sequestered inside an asylum for as long as he can remember and whose imago was reduced to his childlike mispronunciation—"Rain Man"—of Raymond's name.

After their father dies, Charlie carts his brother away from the institution that has housed "Rain Man" for much of his life. Charlie drives them in the car that he inherited from his acrimonious father, who left him this car and little else. The father bequeathed the bulk of his sizable estate to the institution. En route to Las Vegas, Charlie hears Raymond mutter one unforgettable quote after another, as they stop at roadside diners along the way. Raymond's mathematical skills serve him well in Las Vegas, but not well enough.

"Tuesdays are pancakes," Raymond/"Rain Man" announces, before Charlie realizes that his seriously impaired brother needs his hospital setting more than he needs his freedom—and far more than he needs his estranged brother's affection. What a switch from Miloš Forman's *One Flew Over the Cuckoo's Nest* (1975), which changed both public and professional attitudes toward psychiatric wards, and instigated California's anti–ECT laws.

We come away from *Rain Man* with positive feelings toward a benevolent institution that is there when needed and is run by an understanding and patient psychiatrist. Most viewers also find the depiction of Rain Man—which was based on a real person who was born without a corpus callosum that connects the two sides of his brain—endearing, and far from stigmatizing.

Even the inspiration for the Rain Man character, Kim Peek, a real-life savant, approved of his portrayal in the film. Hoffman spent time with Peek to learn more about Peek's life and character. When Hoffman won an Oscar for his performance, he specifically thanked Mr. Peek in his acceptance speech. Barry Marrow, the screenwriter who won an Oscar for the screenplay, gave his trophy to Peek to acknowledge the inspiration that Peek had provided him. Thrilled with his Oscar statuette, Mr. Peek carried it with him to all public appearances over the next 21 years before he died of a heart attack at age 58. By then, Peek was a well-regarded celebrity himself.[14]

In hindsight, it was believed that Kim Peek himself was not exactly autistic, but that his exceptional memory abilities and other skills resulted from a rare anatomical anomaly of the brain. He himself stated that his life was changed because of *Rain Man*, and he is still fondly remembered by so many people who learned of his life, thanks to his positive portrayal and thanks to the attention showered on him by some of America's most renowned actors.

Another award-winning film that privileges life in a mental hospital over home life with a dysfunctional family is *Ordinary People* (1980). Directed by Robert Redford, who had previously earned a lasting reputation as an actor (and an activist), this film won four Oscars, including one for Best Picture, along with several other Academy Award nominations and five Golden Globe awards. This film focuses on the release of a young patient, Conrad, from a protracted stay in a mental hospital. Conrad (played by Timothy Hutton) reminisces about his hospital stay, which included electroshock. Speaking to his psychiatrist, Conrad confesses that he misses the place "because nobody hid anything there"—in contrast to his undermining mother (played by Mary Tyler Moore). Some psychiatrists dissed this film, calling it "saccharine sweet," but the impressive box office returns showed otherwise.

Regardless of how readers view this film, it is safe to say that it is nearly impossible to compete with the graciousness of the screenwriter who handed his hard-earned Oscar to Kim Peek, or with the real-life charm of Kim Peek, who carried this Oscar with him for the rest of his life, demonstrating his appreciation of the film, and its actors and screenwriters, virtually every day that he lived thereafter.

Notes

1. It is unclear if such dopamine drops have the same beneficial effects on schizophrenic symptoms, which can be quelled by medications that block dopamine, although it appears that dopamine drops correlate with depression.

2. Without denying the biological basis of schizophrenia, it is worth noting that data confirms that family support for people who had schizophreniform psychotic breaks is as important as medication in determining prognosis. But family support is not the same as the romance depicted in *David and Lisa*.

3. Michael White, *Generation Dada: The Berlin Avant-Garde and the First World War* (Yale University Press, 2013); Book review by Sharon Packer, *Metapsychology Online*, 2013.

4. Sharon Packer, *Cinema's Sinister Psychiatrists* (McFarland, 2012).

5. Dava Sobel, "Schizophrenia in Popular Books: A Study Finds Too Much Hope," *New York Times*, February 17, 1981.

6. Miriam Shuchman and Michael S. Wilkes, "Dramatic Progress Against Depression," *New York Times*, October 7, 1990.

7. Rachel Aviv, "Psychiatry wars: the lawsuit that put psychoanalysis on trial," *The Guardian*, October 11, 2022, https://www.theguardian.com/society/2022/oct/11/psychiatry-wars-psychoanalysis-antidepressants-rachel-aviv.

8. John M. Oldham, "Editorial: Psychodynamic Psychotherapy for Personality Disorders," *American Journal of Psychiatry* 164 (2007): 1465–1467; G.L. Klerman, "The psychiatric patient's right to effective treatment: implications of *Osheroff v. Chestnut Lodge*," *American Journal of Psychiatry* 147, no. 4 (1990): 409–418.

9. "DSM: History of the Manual," http://www.psychiatry.org/practice/dsm/dsm-history-of-themanual.

10. Personal electronic communication, Jonathan Mook, Esq., June 14, 2013.

11. Joanna Greenberg, *I Never Promised You a Rose Garden* (New American Library, 1964).

12. James L. Knoll IV, "The Humanities and Psychiatry: The Rebirth of Mind," *Psychiatric Times*, March 15, 2013.

13. In the television series *White Collar*, Neal (Matt Bomer) refers to his pal Mozzie as "Rain Man," with the expectation that audiences will immediately recognize that Neal is comparing Mozzie to the autistic-like savant portrayed in *Rain Man*.

14. Bruce Weber, "Kim Peek, Inspiration for *Rain Man*, Dies at 58," *New York Times*, December 26, 2009.

SECTION V

Politics and Polemics

11

Mad Studies Perspectives on Madhouse Movies

Ashley Barry

In the December 1975 issue of *Madness Network News*, page 17 displays two columns of "NAPA Notes," or updates from the Network Against Psychiatric Assault.[1] This section includes information on the NAPA Legal Action Committee's work to ban involuntary psychosurgery, meeting dates for former psychiatric inmates, promotion for a documentary filmed at a California State psychiatric institution, a statement of support for Patty Hearst, and a paragraph on the bottom corner titled "One Flew Over the Cuckoo's Nest."[2] The paragraph reads:

> The new movie based on Ken Kesey's book will open December 17 with a benefit for the San Francisco Mental Health Association. NAPA expects to be present—at least with literature (a NAPA Shock Packet has already been printed: for a free copy, send us a self-addressed envelope), and hopefully with guerrilla theatre. Regardless, we will need help in maintaining a regular presence at the theatre. Good literature should help the audiences better understand what Kesey wrote about so well—and the need to fight for fundamental change.[3]

The release of *One Flew Over the Cuckoo's Nest* came right in the middle of deinstitutionalization, 12 years after the passing of the JFK's Community Mental Health Act of 1963 and thirteen years before the advent of Prozac (fluoxetine).[4] Stretching from the 1950s to the late 1980s, the goals of deinstitutionalization were trifold: "the release of these [mentally ill] individuals from hospitals into the community, their diversion from hospital admission, and the development of alternative community services."[5] *Cuckoo's Nest*, both the film and the novel, was one iteration of art that raised public consciousness of the abuses faced by psychiatric patients, accompanied by documentaries and published exposés.[6] These representations and investigations were crafted by "experts" who were not themselves actual psychiatric patients, but experienced the institution as an outsider looking on, or occasionally as an undercover reporter. What was much less likely to reach the public was the work of former psychiatric patients who constituted the Consumer/Survivor/Ex-patient, or C/S/X, movement. The 1970s saw a plethora of activism organized by groups of former patients; their work was not exclusive to asylum abolition but covered a range of abuses faced by folks with psychiatric or developmental disabilities.[7]

The legacy of deinstitutionalization was based on good intentions and failed executions. While there was a significant decline in the number of patients living in public institutions, the promised alternative of community health centers did not live up to its promises, due partly to inadequate funding and partly to an overly optimistic estimate of families' abilities to help.[8]

I argue that in 21st-century rhetoric and popular film about mental illness, the political dimension has been erased. The psychiatric survivor movement, which occasionally gained national attention in the late 20th century, exists now in small community circles and online networks, but these efforts rarely culminate in large protests or guerrilla theater. Their efforts should not be confused with the goals of Scientologists, who religiously stage protests at psychiatric conferences; the impetus behind their objections is religious, rather than political. Essentially, Scientologists promote their own religion as an alternative to psychiatric treatment.

Critiques of the psychiatric system have become both commonplace and fringe; while many new psychologists and patients vocalize discontent with diagnostic frameworks like the DSM, the push for psychiatric abolition that was voiced half a century ago would now be dismissed as extreme. So, how do these tensions manifest in narrative film?

We can differentiate representations of asylums in fictional films as pre-deinstitutionalization, during deinstitutionalization, and post-deinstitutionalization. The pre-era mostly consists of thrillers and character-driven dramas, starting with the 1920 German film *The Cabinet of Dr. Caligari* and the 1926 Japanese film *A Page of Madness*, which both embrace surreal and expressionistic aesthetics to depict the strange, warped environment of the asylum. Both feature the theme of wrongful imprisonment, while *Caligari* directly questions power dynamics and the fraught relationship between sanity and insanity. The *Mabuse* franchise, begun by Fritz Lang in 1922, shortly after *Caligari* premiered, and historically more popular in Europe than in the United States, specifically identifies the bad doctor who aspires to world dominion and who manipulates the stock market as a psychoanalyst. In his role as a psychoanalyst, Dr. Mabuse seduces and exploits his patients and induces one to commit suicide but is eventually institutionalized himself.

Films in the following two decades depicted psychoanalysis, the need for the asylum reform, and an evolving understanding of post-traumatic stress,[9] which was known as shell shock or battle fatigue in the World War I era and which became even better known during and after World War II, when half of all veterans who were deemed "disabled" suffered from psychiatric rather than physical disabilities.

These divergent tropes are mostly unrelated to one another, other than by chronological coincidence. Examples of the first category include Hitchcock's *Spellbound* (1945) and *Possessed* (1947), starring Joan Crawford and told in flashbacks, to be distinguished from a much earlier Crawford film from 1931. *Bedlam* (1946) is a horror film about asylum reform set in 1761 London (although the film's iconic horror star Boris Karloff characterized this film as "historical" rather than "horror"). *The Snake Pit* (1948), set north of NYC in Rockland County, is another classic film that called (successfully) for asylum reform and that catalyzed changes in state hospitals.

As for films about PTSD, excellent examples include the dark British drama, *Mine Own Executioner* (1947). *Random Harvest* (1942) is a tearjerker that revolves around a shell-shocked and amnesiac World War I veteran who is admitted to an asylum—but staff suddenly abandon the asylum to celebrate the war's end, leaving the unsupervised protagonist to wander off. *Random Harvest* was based on a novel by James Hilton, who also wrote the bestselling *Lost Horizon*. *Identity Unknown* (1945) is another film about

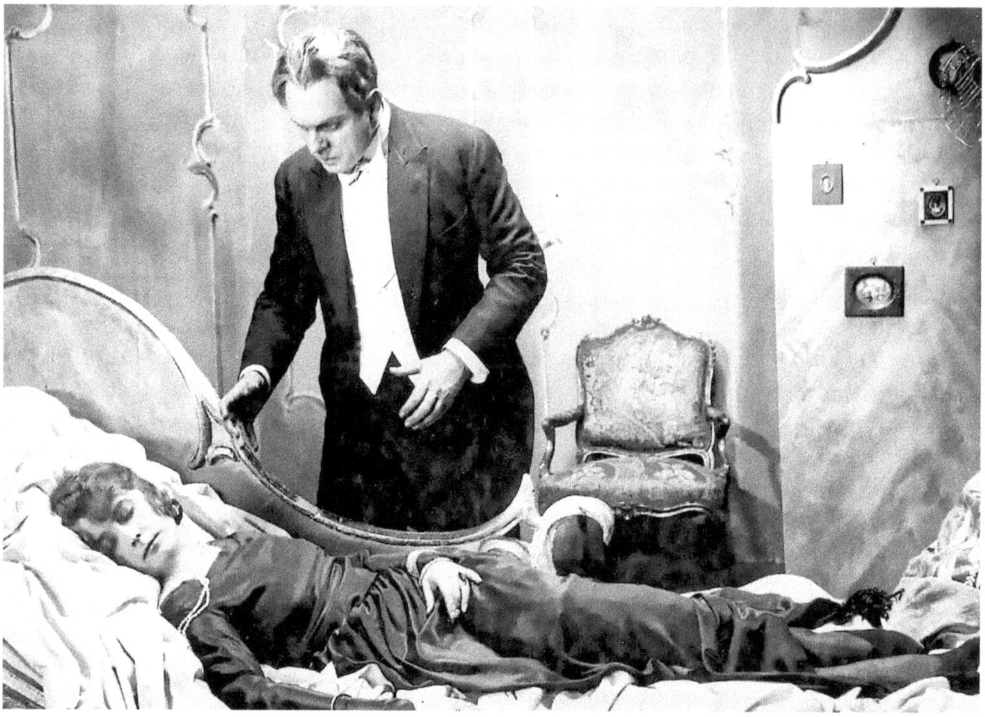

Dr. Mabuse, the Gambler (1922) is one of many Fritz Lang films that feature an unscrupulous psychoanalyst (Rudolf Klein-Rogge), who stands above his reclining patient, Countess Dusy Told (Gertrude Welcker), and otherwise seduces patients, goads some to suicide, and manipulates the stock market in his quest for world dominion before he is incarcerated in an asylum himself and experiences even stranger events once inside.

PTSD-related amnesia, as is *Somewhere in the Night* (1946), with its twist ending that explains the civilian identity of yet another unnamed amnesiac veteran.

During deinstitutionalization, the trope of asylum-as-spectacle continued, cementing itself into the bona fide genre of asylum horror that continues to this day.[10] Examples include *Asylum* (1972) and *Tales That Witness Madness* (1973). By showing the asylum as a place of intrigue or horror, films during deinstitutionalization assumed their audiences shared a general idea that psychiatric wards are bad places to be. In some narratives, the fear or chaos comes from the unpredictable, violent patients; in others, blame is placed on the structures of the asylum, typically either a particularly abusive nurse or inhumane treatments such as coerced ECT, straitjackets, isolation, or forced medication.

Some films prey on spectators' fears that deinstitutionalized people—or recently released patients—could pose threats to society. The spectacularly successful slasher film, *Halloween* (1978), which generated several sequels and spin-offs, revolves around an escaped asylum inmate. The remake of *House on Haunted Hill* (1999), adapted from the 1959 original, fits into this timeline and mirrors this theme, although the setting of the asylum, with its horrific unethical experiments, is backdated to 1931.

Toward the end of deinstitutionalization, some notable American movies featuring asylums or other psychiatric institutions veered toward science fiction, while most films about mental illness shifted to the outpatient setting, which is how most care was delivered. Science fiction films include *Terminator 2: Judgment Day* (1991) and *12 Monkeys* (1995). In contrast, romance and comedy films that focus on the clinic setting (as opposed to an institutional setting) include *The Couch Trip* (1988); *What About Bob?* (1991); *Mr. Jones* (1993); *As Good as It Gets* (1997); *Analyze This* (1999); *Me, Myself, & Irene* (2000); and *Analyze That* (2002).

The beginning of the 21st century saw the successful debut of the young adult bildungsroman asylum film with 1999's *Girl, Interrupted*, as well as the prestige biopic of schizophrenic mathematician John Nash in 2001's *A Beautiful Mind*.

In the subsequent two decades, the genre of the psychological thriller has crystallized around characters with dissociative identity disorder or unreliable protagonists who are revealed to be psychotic. DID-focused thrillers include *Identity* (2003), *Secret Window* (2004), and *Split* (2016). Psychotic, unreliable protagonists appear in *Black Swan* (2010) and *Shutter Island* (2010).

One of the three works I analyze here, *Unsane* (2018), fits into this latter category, whereas *It's Kind of a Funny Story* (2010) follows the tradition of *Girl, Interrupted*—an adaptation of a book that is a semiautobiographical account of a teenager in a psych ward—and *Horse Girl* (2020) exists in a hybrid genre of psychological drama and science fiction.

Narrative films rarely address the political dimension of mental health treatment. By following a young, privileged man with anxiety and depression, *It's Kind of a Funny Story* prioritizes destigmatizing teen mental illness, but it does gesture toward Mad politics (which prioritizes the direct experiences and narratives of people deemed "mad" over the diagnoses imposed on them by professionals and other outsiders). By offering a subtle critique of the disease model and challenging dangerous taxonomies of mental patients,[11] this film nods to the "Mad politics" mentioned early in this essay. This film is based a popular book by Ned Vizzini, which NPR recognized as one of the "100 Best-Ever Teen Novels." Sadly, Vizzini died by suicide at age 32.

Unsane centers a woman who is a victim of both sexual harassment and profit-driven insurance exploitation, but the film muddles these two important themes for more surface-level thrills, valuing the audience's shock over its empathy.[12] *Horse Girl*, a mumblecore drama, provides something that the other two do not: context. In this last film, the protagonist experiences mental illness symptoms while contextualizing these phenomena in her family history and in the history of national health care policy.[13]

The goal of this essay is to ask of three recent narrative films that at least partially take place in asylums:

- What types of relationships are possible for the protagonist? Is Mad History invoked? And how so, if we trace "Mad History" to the countercultural "Mad persons'" movement of the late 1960s/early 1970s, when Mad Liberation coalesced and WBAI's *Madness Network News* aired on the radio and the Consumer/Survivor/Ex-patient, or C/S/X, movement gained steam—but before "Mad Studies" became a bona fide subject of study in universities and before college departments of "Mad Studies" surfaced and before disability studies spawned a distinct discipline of "Mad Studies"?
- Does the asylum function as prison or voluntary treatment?
- What taxonomies of "mental patient" are established?
- Do these representations say anything about the histories of psychiatry?

- What can we say about the political and discursive implications of different representations of asylums and psych wards?
- How do filmmakers and audiences imagine the psychiatric ward functioning in the 21st century, when Nurse Ratched is more of a bogeyman than a symbol of institutional violence?

"I Really Don't Think I Belong Here"

In the opening scene of *It's Kind of a Funny Story*, a white teenage boy with a neat haircut and a fresh button-down shirt follows a nurse down a hospital hallway and avoids eye contact with two older men who are now his fellow patients.[14] The first is an elderly white man wearing sunglasses, a Backstreet Boys T-shirt, a worn flannel button-down shirt, and a beard down to his chest. He makes a zapping noise at the nurse, and the nurse zaps back. The second is an older Black man with an awkward posture and a shaking hand, focusing on someone who is not there; he enthusiastically says, "It'll come to you." After the nurse tells our protagonist, Craig, that this latter man is schizophrenic, Craig asks, "Is there a place here for people more like me?"

A few scenes later, Craig meets his roommate Muqtada.[15] Muqtada lies in bed, wrapped in a thin blanket, facing away from Craig, but turns around briefly to acknowledge his entrance into the room. As Craig settles in and attempts to make small talk, he receives mumbled responses. The camera occupies Craig's position, so only a few inches of Muqtada's hair is visible poking out from the blanket. The frame cuts back to Craig, who looks increasingly uncomfortable, and then back to Muqtada's side of the room, specifically a woven hat on his nightstand with a fly buzzing around it. Simultaneously, the music track begins, unharmonious strings that emphasize the fly's buzzing. This track gets louder over the next few shots. We next see a close-up of Muqtada's worn, dirty slippers on the tile floor, and a brief cut to Craig's eyes shifting, landing on the reverse-shot of Muqtada's feet. Only a few toes peek out under the blanket, and the skin looks dry or unwashed, disturbing enough to prompt Craig to immediately leave the room to find the head psychiatrist and demand to leave.

The meme of "I really don't think I belong here" is a well-worn trope, both in real life and in reel life.

Released in 2010, *It's Kind of a Funny Story* is an adaptation of Ned Vizzini's 2006 book of the same name, which was inspired by Vizzini's own experience as a patient in a psychiatric ward. The film is a distant descendant of *One Flew Over the Cuckoo's Nest*, occupying a genre that is closer to a coming-of-age romantic comedy than a psychological thriller. There is never a real sense of danger or coercion in the hospital ward where Craig stays, even as he takes a while to adjust to being around people who are, in his words, "seriously messed up."[16] The staff are friendly, and Craig's main point of contact is a nurse named Smitty who is dressed in everyday clothes: worn corduroy pants, a flannel, a hoodie, and a porkpie hat. Smitty resembles more of a peer counselor and wields authority only by giving and taking back "points" from the patients, a system that rewards good behavior with prizes like time in the rec room and gift shop visits.

It's Kind of a Funny Story is a mixed bag when contextualized in Mad History. While *It's Kind of a Funny Story* does not critique specifically institutionalization, it emphasizes the social model over the disease model of mental illness, shows the importance of patient solidarity, and deconstructs sanist taxonomies of mental patients, which privileges explanations offered by so-called "sane" people over the lived experiences of people deemed to be "non-sane."

First, Craig admits himself to the hospital voluntarily, and actually pushes the ER nurse to admit him.[17] Craig enters the hospital with a particularly medical understanding of mental illness, as he first asks the nurse, "Can't you just give me something?" implying that there is a medication that will immediately help his suicidality.[18] When he is referred to outpatient care, he insists that he may not be safe if he leaves the hospital. However, Craig's understanding of hospitalization is inaccurate, as he thinks he will be able to leave later that evening; a few scenes later, he is directly told that he will need to stay for a minimum of five days.

Craig had assumed that psychiatric care could function acutely, that the hospital could be a fast-acting corrective to his mental suffering: "I thought you guys could do something quick, like give me some medication to feel better ... or.... Look, I didn't think that I'd be committed. I really don't think I belong here."[19] The head psychiatrist with whom Craig works during his stay, Dr. Minerva, is shown to be kind and firmly entrenched in a traditional diagnostic framework. When Craig expresses fear of his friends finding out where he is, she responds, "There's nothing to be ashamed of, Craig. Depression is a medical illness. If you were diabetic, would you be embarrassed by that?"[20]

When Craig first visits Dr. Minerva's office, the first shot is a close-up of a bookshelf featuring files of "Reports," "Violent Incident Reports," and "Progress Reports" alongside copies of the DSM-III and DSM-IV.[21] The next shot begins on the base of a phrenology bust, tilting up to reveal the labeled subsections of the human skull. However, Dr. Minerva functions more like a non-medical psychotherapist than a psychiatrist throughout the film, and there is minimal focus on medical interventions during Craig's time in the ward. It is implied that Craig goes back on Zoloft (sertraline) as the film shows him waiting in line for meds, but the bulk of his treatment consists of group therapy sessions and individual meetings with Dr. Minerva.

Additionally, Craig himself finds support and hope by reframing his life through conversations he has both with the psychiatrist and his fellow patients. While he does ask to be admitted to 3 North, he is initially desperate to leave after seeing the type of people who are patients. Even on his second day there, Craig says in the voice-over, "I shouldn't be lining up for meds behind schizophrenics and sociopaths."[22] However, he develops a personal connection with several of the patients throughout the film, specifically Bobby and Noelle.

Bobby is a middle-aged, homeless man with schizophrenia who befriends Craig and helps him acclimate. Bobby shows Craig how to play the system, how to sneak out, and how to interact with other, more "unusual" patients. In return, Craig comes to realize how much his class privilege has affected him when Bobby panics over his interview for acceptance into a residential home to live in after his discharge from 3 North. Craig loans Bobby one of his father's clean button-up shirts for the interview, for which Bobby is immensely grateful. At the film's close, Bobby and Craig have a mutual understanding that their friendship exists solely in the ward and will not continue back in the "real world," but both seem to have benefited from their bond.

Noelle is one of Craig's love interests in the film, as well as a fellow patient. Before admitting himself, Craig was nursing a crush on his best friend's girlfriend, Nia.

However, when he enters 3 North and meets the only other teen patient, a blonde girl, he bonds with her as well. It seems easy to compare the two young women, as one represents Craig's outside world, which is a large source of stress, and the other represents his new understanding of mental health and happiness, but the film complicates these characterizations, as both Nia and Noelle are mentally ill themselves. Craig only finds out that Nia suffers from depression when he calls her from the hospital. She confesses that she sees a therapist, even though "it's pretty embarrassing."[23] Craig confesses in turn that he takes Zoloft (sertraline), to which Nia enthusiastically responds, "Shut up. Oh my god, we're like so screwed up!"[24] Nia is also excited about visiting Craig, and her tone implies that she is more interested in the spectacle of the psych ward than in seeing Craig himself. When she does visit later in the film, she fetishizes the environment, placing her hand on Craig's thigh while explaining she is attracted to him because he's "really, really screwed up."[25] The two begin to make out in Craig's room until they are interrupted by Craig's roommate, prompting Craig to vomit from anxiety. Where Craig's mental illness was previously a turn-on, Nia now shouts, "What's wrong with you?" and leaves.[26] Although she is a patient herself, albeit in a clinic setting, Nia is depicted as othering Craig once she understands the reality of psychiatric illness.

Noelle, on the other hand, is visibly mentally ill. She has self-harm scars across her left cheek as well as on her arms. For better or worse, Noelle is obviously a "mental patient." The third act of the film follows Craig as he apologizes to Noelle for kissing Nia, and as discussed prior, part of his future is based on his continued relationship with Noelle. It is with her that Craig concludes that the source of his anxiety and depression, an ultra-competitive high school career, is not worth it.[27] In this sense, we can see Nia and Noelle as two different kinds of patients; Nia "passes" as non-mentally ill and fetishizes Craig's experience at the hospital, while Noelle embodies a life of understanding and working through mental illness.

The film also works through Craig's evolving perception of mentally ill adults. While 3 North is depicted in a sanitized manner, the demographic of patients is realistic. Most folks are older and implied to be living in poverty. While Jimmy, the Black man with schizophrenia, is mostly played as comic relief, his existence in the world of the film reflects the real problem of discriminatory diagnostic practices.[28] Black patients are more likely to be diagnosed with schizophrenia whereas white patients more commonly receive affective diagnoses, such as bipolar disorder. Similarly, Jimmy has a humorous (to Craig and his mother) encounter with an unnamed Black trans woman, who would, in real life, be more vulnerable to institutionalization.

Lastly, we return to Muqtada. Craig initially sees Muqtada as a symbol of the disgust and stigma he associates with the psychiatric ward, especially when Muqtada violently interrupts Nia and Craig's hook-up. By the end of the film, Craig has learned that Muqtada is Egyptian and likes Egyptian music, so he acquires an Egyptian record to play at his going-away party, which Muqtada greatly appreciates.[29] These gestures in the film show a form of patient solidarity and Craig's unlearning of stereotypes, and an argument could be made that the film values human connection over medical treatment for psychiatric disorders. That said, institutionalization and mental illness are presented as apolitical phenomena in *It's Kind of a Funny Story*, which prioritizes a destigmatizing narrative of a suicidal teen over any particular portrayal of a psychiatric ward.

"Is She or Isn't She?"

Steven Soderbergh's 2018 film *Unsane* starts with a young white woman, curled up in the fetal position on a metal hospital bed, her grippy-sock-clad feet barely touching a young Black man who sits up next to her.[30] The rest of the frame is composed of beige, white, and brown rectangles. A dingy white wall is interrupted by a brown bathroom door, then a dingy white column, a white wall in the background with a clock and an illegible sign, the ceiling a series of cooler white tiles. The man, Nate, comforts the woman, Sawyer, as she awakens from a sedative-fueled nap. The camera is still, the frame static apart from the two patients' small gestures. When Sawyer finds out she broke the ward's television, she fears she "must be insane."[31] Nate responds, "Oh, no, no. You're not insane. I know the difference between people who are supposed to be here and the people who end up here, and you're definitely in column two."[32]

The two discuss their pasts, and the static shot cuts into a sequence of short scenes, a flashback as Sawyer narrates what has brought her to the psychiatric ward.[33] As a college student, Sawyer volunteered at a hospice where she met David Strine, the son of one of her patients, who began stalking her after his father died. The montage depicts Sawyer meeting David, his father's funeral, multiple acts of stalking and harassment, and lastly, a detective giving Sawyer a laundry list of tasks she must do to protect herself. Back in the psych ward, the camera places Sawyer sitting up in the background with Nate in the foreground, comforting her again. He affirms, "Column two. For life."[34]

Unsane is a classic psychological thriller about the terrifying possibilities of madness. It was shot entirely on an iPhone 7 Plus, and the action appears to be more or less contemporaneous with the making of the film. Its tagline, vague yet succinct, reads: "Is she or isn't she?" The film intertwines themes of stalking, gaslighting, and psychosis to make the audience question if the protagonist, Sawyer, is a reliable narrator, as the surrounding characters position her as either a victim of a psychiatric conspiracy or a typical patient suffering from hallucinations and paranoia. Indeed, these two categories are made explicit by Nate, her fellow patient at Highland Creek Behavioral Facility.

Unsane follows a young woman who is revealed to be a victim of stalking, which prompts her to move across the country for a new job. She experiences PTSD symptoms and seeks help from a counselor, who offers guidance and empathy. However, when Sawyer finishes this first appointment, she is given additional paperwork to fill out, described to her as "boilerplate."[35] From here, she is brought to an examination room, where her personal belongings are confiscated and exchanged for a hospital gown. Sawyer is then taken to a psychiatric ward, insisting all the way that she is not supposed to be admitted and was simply in the building for therapy. It is revealed that her "routine" paperwork covered involuntary admission, causing her pleas to leave to be interpreted as a symptom of mental illness, and further convincing the staff that she needs to be committed.

Early in her stay, Sawyer sees David Strine, her stalker, posing as a nurse. While the rest of the staff is convinced this is simply paranoia, and it is initially unclear to the audience whether Sawyer is right. It is eventually revealed that it is indeed David who took this job to gain access to Sawyer. He kills Nate and abducts Sawyer, and their violent encounter ends in David's death.

The other plot in the film follows Nate's investigation into Highland Creek, which is tricking patients into voluntarily committing themselves so the hospital can make a profit from insurance payments. Nate is an undercover journalist, and despite his death, the story comes out, leading to the head hospital administrator's arrest.

These parallel stories speak to significant issues in psychology and psychiatry. First, Sawyer represents a long history of abused and harassed women who are further gaslit by legal and medical institutions. We can trace this theme all the way from ancient diagnoses of hysteria to contemporary instances of victim-blaming and discrediting of victims in the post–#MeToo era. For the last century, feminists have fought for sexual harassment and abuse to be taken seriously and to combat stereotypes of weak, neurotic, or overly emotional women. *Unsane* succeeds in portraying this narrative, as we see Sawyer's insistence that David works at the hospital as just another symptom of mental illness. However, the genre of the psychological thriller, exemplified by the question in the tagline—"is she or isn't she?"—is prioritized over any type of feminist agenda. In the very last scene of the film, a year after Sawyer has killed David, she lunches with a coworker and believes she sees David on the other side of the restaurant. She approaches, ready to attack, before realizing he is a stranger.[36] While this could be a statement on the lasting effects of trauma, the spectacle of violence and the constant ambiguity of Sawyer's sanity fuel diagnostic voyeurism over compassion.

The insurance conspiracy in *Unsane* has a similarly fraught relationship to real life and probably reflects popular perceptions—and misperceptions—about insurance carriers, without introducing more up-to-date data about insurance coverage or legislative changes that challenge such pervasive knee-jerk reactions. On the one hand, there have been major problems in how insurance companies cover—or do not cover—mental health services (or medical services, for that matter). Previously, many health insurance policies capped reimbursement for inpatient psychiatric stays at 30 days, but in the "post-parity" world, insurers are required to provide mental health benefits that are equal to medical benefits.

In the post-managed-care world that began late in the 20th century, it became increasingly common for health insurance policies to establish large monetary "deductibles" for both mental and medical care, causing many patients to postpone necessary treatment or to forgo treatment entirely. On the other hand, we may wonder if insurance payments are enough to incentivize hospitals to keep patients longer than necessary, or to hospitalize people who do not need inpatient care, but as we shall see below, such deceptive tactics are not entirely unheard of.

In the majority of articles on this matter, authors focus on parity between mental health and physical health coverage, which had been a genuine concern before legislation such as the MHPA (Mental Health Parity Act) of 1996 and MHPAEA (Mental Health Parity and Addiction Equity Act) of 2008 outlawed such practices. Details about these complicated laws are available on Medicare's website at https://www.cms.gov.

Other articles emphasize pre-authorizations that can act as barriers to inpatient care, which privilege outpatient treatment in what is known as the "least restrictive setting," and which specify the stringent circumstances that qualify for "medically necessary" voluntary hospitalization that is covered by insurance benefits, when available. One of those criteria of hospitalization includes "failed" (non-beneficial) attempts at outpatient treatment. Others stress the dearth of available beds and staff in psychiatric inpatient settings.[37]

One strange parallel that was nearly identical to the events depicted in *Unsane* was originally pointed out by Jordan Hoffman. A team at BuzzFeed News investigated a scandal from 2014 to 2016,[38] a few years before the theatrical release of *Unsane* but recent enough to have conceivably colored the plot of *Unsane*. The lead journalist, Rosalind Adams, conducted 175 interviews with former and current employees of Universal Health Services, the largest chain of psychiatric hospitals in the United States, researching claims that employees were instructed to "trick" patients into voluntarily admitting themselves.[39] Many of Adams's participants claimed that the facilities "tried to keep beds filled even at the expense of the safety of their staff or the rights of the patients they were locking up" in order to acquire additional payments from insurance companies.[40] In other words, the patient's stay would be exactly as long as their insurance would pay for; no more, no less. Since BuzzFeed News published their findings, Universal Health Services has conducted a major public relations campaign to dispute the allegations and repair their public image.[41] Although there is no direct evidence that *Unsane* drew inspiration from this controversy, the film is correct in pointing out the complex, problematic relationship between insurance coverage and mental health care.

Lastly, the taxonomy of mental patients presented in *Unsane* perpetuates dangerous and inaccurate rhetoric around mental illness. The mere differentiation of "Column 1" and "Column 2" implies that the insurance conspiracy is only dangerous to "sane" people who don't "deserve" to be confined against their will. Sawyer herself claims that she should not be "locked up with psycho rapists." Another patient, Violet, serves as a minor antagonist as she mocks and harasses Sawyer, which includes throwing a used tampon at her. In the third act, once David has abducted Sawyer, Sawyer manipulates him into raping Violet instead; it is revealed that Sawyer only wants to get Violet there to obtain her shank to attack David. While this is a positive turn, it does not indicate that Sawyer has a new perspective on her fellow patients. She is "column 2, for life."

"Reagan Closed Down All the Hospitals"

The 2020 film *Horse Girl* tells two different stories, depending on your interpretation. If you follow the protagonist's version, or if you believe what is presented on the screen as the literal version of events, *Horse Girl* is science-fiction noir. Like a plot from *The X-Files*, the protagonist discovers she is a clone of her grandmother created by aliens. In her journey for truth, she finds a fellow alien abductee, and by the end of the film, she willingly allows herself to be taken once again, her body floating up a shaft of light into the unknown.[42]

If you do not take the protagonist's experiences at face value, *Horse Girl* is a tale of transgenerational trauma and mental illness. Sarah is a young woman of the age when predisposed people typically start experiencing symptoms of schizophrenia. She knows that she has a strong genetic predisposition, given that her grandmother was diagnosed with paranoid schizophrenia and later died homeless, and her mother had chronic depression. A year before the events in the film take place, Sarah witnessed her mother's suicide and has had trouble adjusting since. As her symptoms worsen, Sarah becomes delusional and spends some time in a psychiatric ward. The distinction between her hallucinations and the film's reality blurs until the film concludes in the strange UFO scene.

In the scope of this essay, *Horse Girl* is both the most abstract and the most direct compared to *It's Kind of a Funny Story* and *Unsane*. While very few scenes take place in a psychiatric ward, Sarah's encounters in this setting are quite relevant. First, Sarah directly acknowledges the role that deinstitutionalization has played in her family's history and in their downward trajectory. In this scene, she sits across from the desk of Ethan, her social worker.

While discussing her grandmother, Sarah says, "She got put in a place like this, and then, you know, Reagan closed down all the hospitals, and she got put out on the street, and she died as, like, a homeless woman, in the streets."[43] (It is not necessarily relevant that Sarah appears to be unaware that deinstitutionalization began with a benevolent initiative by John F. Kennedy, whose political posture differed dramatically from Reagan's conservative stance.) This political dimension of mental health treatment is rarely addressed in narrative film, as we can see in the two other films discussed. *It's Kind of a Funny Story* focuses on destigmatizing teen mental illness, and *Unsane* is myopic in its sensationalization of an insulated controversy.

Horse Girl provides something that the other two do not: context. The sociopolitical context of mental illness is often obfuscated, so we rarely think about the historical factors behind psychological and psychiatric discourse. Specific mental illnesses are conceptualized as groups of symptoms that can be isolated and categorized, while the history behind different diagnoses, and even the disease model itself, is considered insignificant. In one sentence, in an offhand comment to a counselor, Sarah connects the personal to the political. Her specific symptoms are connected to a history that is much larger than her own; her grandmother's life was shaped not just by biological or genetic or even epigenetic factors, but by governmental policies of institutionalization and deinstitutionalization, which presumably secondarily affected Sarah's mother, who went on to commit suicide. Curiously, this implicit condemnation of deinstitutionalization counters the stance of many Mad activists, who historically decried institutionalization and especially opposed involuntary hospital admissions that override the potential patient's personal choice.

Horse Girl is also the most abstract in its narrative and presentation. Much of the second act appears to be a type of dream sequence. The audience experiences time loss along with Sarah, and it is impossible to delineate between what she is hallucinating and what is occurring in the world of the movie. This is further complicated when Sarah meets her roommate in the psychiatric ward, a woman she recognizes from the dreams she has every night.[44] This woman does not know who Sarah is but is shocked when Sarah describes these dreams, because she has had the same ones. The two conclude that they are both experiencing supernatural phenomena and take relief in confirming each other's sanity. It is difficult to call this solidarity between patients, as their brief connection in the hospital does not affect the plot. This scene serves to further confuse the viewer, since somebody else is verifying the protagonist's perception, which could otherwise be easily dismissed as hallucination.

The film's opacity may serve both its genre and the purpose of the production. As an independent drama, *Horse Girl* did not have such prescribed expectations as might a coming-of-age film or psychological thriller. Additionally, *Horse Girl* was cowritten by its director, Jeff Baena, and its leading actor, Alison Brie. Brie herself has a family history with mental illness, which served as inspiration for the screenplay.[45] This autobiographical component also appears in *It's Kind of a Funny Story*, as the film is based on a novel by Ned Vizzini which itself was inspired by his own time in a psychiatric hospital. However, the goals of these two texts are very different. Vizzini's, and by extension the filmmakers', rhetorical purposes are trifold: to inform, to entertain, to persuade. First, Craig's experiences at 3 North may enlighten viewers as to what happens when someone goes to the hospital feeling suicidal, or at least what happened when Vizzini did. Second, the film is a comedy, even going as far as to include a musical sequence. Third, the anti-stigma message is strong, as Craig learns to humanize his fellow patients and accept his own struggles. Compared to these easily identifiable motivations, *Horse Girl* is harder to pin down. It seems more like a reflection or an exploration of what it might feel like to inherit mental illness, whether that inheritance consists of genes or family memories. The asylum setting plays a much smaller role, but the protagonist's own articulation of her family history vis-à-vis mental institutions conveys an understanding of psychology and psychiatry's history that is missing from other narratives.

Conclusion

It is difficult to imagine ex-patients gathering outside a screening of any of the three films discussed to hand out "good literature" to moviegoers, as described in the NAPA notes mentioned at the start of this essay.[46] *It's Kind of a Funny Story* could be accompanied by anti-stigma material, which would serve one rhetorical purpose but not challenge any institutional factors faced by mentally ill people. *Unsane* could pair with information on insurance company scandals but might prefer promotional materials that reinforce the fear of mental illness, rather than the fear of how mental illness is exploited. Lastly, while the writers of *Horse Girl* could articulate the connections between neoliberalism and deinstitutionalization, such analysis is reserved for academic settings, not popular entertainment. Each film makes gestures toward a critique of different psychiatric norms and practices but prioritizes genre conventions over attempts at Mad or Disabled justice. As we move farther from deinstitutionalization but deeper into the 21st century, psychiatric discourse and the public's relationship to mental illness and its institutions will be both reflected in and shaped by popular narrative film.

Notes

1. "NAPA Notes," *Madness Network News* 3, no. 4 (December 1975), https://madnessnetworknews.com/archives/archives-vol-3/.
2. "NAPA Notes," 17.
3. "NAPA Notes," 17.
4. The 1963 Community Mental Health Act sought to phase out admissions and long-term stays at psychiatric hospitals or other institutions and transition to smaller community centers that would function more like typical outpatient offices.
5. H. Richard Lamb and Leona L. Bachrach, "Some Perspectives on Deinstitutionalization," *Psychiatric Services* 52, no. 8 (August 2001): 1039, https://doi.org/10.1176/appi.ps.52.8.1039.
6. For a non-exhaustive list, see Bibliography: Bly, Deutsch, Goffman, Rivera, and Wiseman.
7. Mel Starkman, "The Movement," in *Mad Matters: A Critical Reader in Canadian Mad Studies*, ed. Brenda A. LeFrançois, Robert Menzies, and Geoffrey Reaume (Canadian Scholars' Press, 2013), 27–37.
8. Lamb and Bachrach, "Some Perspectives," 1039.
9. Examples include *Spellbound* (1945), *Bedlam* (1946), *Possessed* (1947), *Mine Own Executioner* (1947), and *The Snake Pit* (1948).
10. Early examples of asylum horror include *Asylum* (1972) and *Tales That Witness Madness* (1973), and the most popular contemporary representation is the television show *American Horror Story: Asylum*, which aired from 2012 to 2013.
11. *It's Kind of a Funny Story*, directed by Anna Boden and Ryan Fleck (Focus Features, 2010).
12. *Unsane*, directed by Steven Soderbergh (Bleecker Street, 2018).

13. *Horse Girl*, directed by Jeff Baena (Netflix, 2020).
14. *Funny Story*, 10:12 to 10:50.
15. *Funny Story*, 13:38 to 15:17.
16. *Funny Story*, 16:39.
17. *Funny Story*, 7:43 to 8:29.
18. *Funny Story*, 7:54.
19. *Funny Story*, 15:07.
20. *Funny Story* 15:40.
21. *Funny Story*, 20:24.
22. *Funny Story*, 23:45.
23. *Funny Story*, 30:58.
24. *Funny Story*, 31:57.
25. *Funny Story*, 1:12:40.
26. *Funny Story*, 1:14:28.
27. *Funny Story*, 1:26:29 to 1:26:55.
28. See Jonathan Metzl, *The Protest Psychosis: How Schizophrenia Became a Black Disease* (Beacon Press, 2010).
29. *Funny Story*, 1:32:56.
30. *Unsane*, 51:51.
31. *Unsane*, 51:56.
32. *Unsane*, 52:00.
33. *Unsane*, 52:33 to 58:15.
34. *Unsane*, 58:31.
35. *Unsane*, 13:07.
36. *Unsane*, 1:36:22.
37. See Amy Funkenstein, et al., "Prior Authorization for Child and Adolescent Psychiatric Patients Deemed to Be in Need of Inpatient Admission," *The American Journal of Emergency Medicine* 34, no. 5 (2016): 915–16, https://doi.org/10.1016/j.ajem.2016.02.027; Sherry Glied and Richard G. Frank, "Shuffling toward Parity — Bringing Mental Health Care under the Umbrella," *The New England Journal of Medicine* 359, no. 2 (2008): 113–15, https://doi.org/10.1056/NEJMp0804447; Jay Greene, "Groups Study Fixes for 'ER Boarding' of Psych Patients," *Crain's Detroit Business* 35, no. 1 (2019): 11+; Jessica A. Scarbrough, "The Growing Importance of Mental Health Parity," *American Journal of Law & Medicine* 44, no. 2–3 (2018): 453–74, https://doi.org/10.1177/0098858818789432; and Claude Solnik, "Timothy's Law Failing to Protect Mentally Ill in N.Y.," *Long Island Business News*, 2011.
38. Jordan Hoffman, "'Unsane' Gives a Real-World Medical Conspiracy a Big Final Twist," *Thrillist*, March 23, 2018, https://www.thrillist.com/entertainment/nation/unsane-review-endingsteven-soderbergh.
39. Rosalind Adams, "Intake: 'What the Fuck Just Happened?'" *BuzzFeed News*, December 7, 2016, https://www.buzzfeednews.com/article/rosalindadams/intake.
40. Adams, "Intake."
41. Rosalind Adams, "Nothing to See Here! How a Giant Psychiatric Hospital Company Tried To Spin Us—And Silence Its Staff," *BuzzFeed News*, December 27, 2017, https://www.buzzfeednews.com/article/rosalindadams/how-a-giant-psychiatric-hospitalcompany-tried-to-spin-us.
42. *Horse Girl*, 1:37:58.
43. *Horse Girl*, 1:14:15.
44. *Horse Girl*, 1:30:36.
45. Rachel Handler, "Alison Brie Based *Horse Girl* on Her Own Mental Health History," *Vulture*, February 7, 2020, https://www.vulture.com/2020/02/alison-brie-based-horse-girl-onher-mental-health-history.html.
46. "NAPA Notes," 17.

12

Countercultural Commentaries

King of Hearts *and* Cuckoo's Nest

LAURA E. COLMENERO-CHILBERG

More often than not, popular culture views mental institutions as horrendous places that actively suppress an individual's self, withdrawing all sense of autonomy and agency, and that result in damaging and traumatic effects on top of already existing mental disorders. They have traditionally been portrayed as warehouses for individuals who are seen by society as awkward, difficult to deal with, weird, and unable to exist in the outside world. Sometimes they have been depicted as places where unwanted spouses, children, and a variety of opponents can be locked away and forgotten.

King of Hearts (1966), a French film directed by Philippe de Broca from a script written by Daniel Boulanger,[1] takes this often-accepted perspective and turns it upside down. Set in Europe at the end of World War I, the movie was released four years after Ken Kesey's highly regarded and popular novel *One Flew Over the Cuckoo's Nest* (1962),[2] and it takes a position diametrically opposed to the more traditionally accepted one presented by Kesey in his novel and in the later movie of the same name. While Kesey exposes mental institutions as being harmful, even deadly, for their inhabitants, *King of Hearts* shows the institution as a place of protection, of social support and lively interaction. The real insanity is found outside of the mental institution.

A History of Madness

Madness is a powerful and frightening word that can interest, entertain, and terrify us. It brings a torrent of images to mind spanning millennia, many of them found in our popular culture. Norse berserkers who in battle displayed violent frenzies where they would yowl, foam at the mouth, and gnaw their shields. The ancient Greek Dionysian mysteries, whose secrets are still debated today, and the drunken frenzy and violence of its adherents, the Maenads. King Lear's senile dementia and the suicidal madness of Ophelia. How about the life of writer Virginia Woolf, who suffered from such severe mental illness that one day she filled her pockets with stones to weigh herself down as she walked into a pond to drown herself, leaving behind a suicide note saying, "I feel certain that I am going mad again. I feel we can't go through another of those terrible times. And I shan't recover this time. I begin to hear voices, and I can't concentrate"? Another writer, poet Sylvia Plath, solved her deepening depression and suicidality by blowing out the pilot light in her oven, carefully sealing off the kitchen from the rooms where her children slept, and putting her head in the oven. Maybe your memory is the straitjacketing of a schizophrenic patient abandoned to *The Snake Pit* in the movie of the same name, the attempted suicide and institutionalization of a troubled teen in *Girl, Interrupted*, or the psychotic break and suicide of a prima ballerina in *Black Swan*. There are many other representations of mental illness and the institutions in which we place them in our popular culture.

What Do We Do with Them?

Historically, madness has been a topic of great interest, with three questions guiding the discussion: What is it? Why do people suffer from it? What do we do about it? These challenges have been debated for millennia, literally. Fiction or nonfiction, the issue often debated in the present day is "How should we handle people who are mentally ill?"

Traditionally, of course, the idea was to lock people away—sometimes due to their potential to harm others, but often because of the embarrassment they provided for their families or the inconvenience they presented to their community. "Locking them away" could mean in your own home if you were wealthy enough to have the space to keep them isolated from the world. Those who did not have the resources did the best they could, but many who were mentally ill wandered the streets, stigmatized powerfully by members of their community, often defined as possessed. If they became inconvenient enough, they were thrown in prison.

The idea of an institution solely for the mentally ill was a long time coming. Prior to Great Britain's scrutiny of asylum conditions and subsequent reforms in the early 19th century, the most usual "lock-up" was the local penal institution. Prisons were crude, filthy, and lacking in basic sanitation. They were dangerous, putting men, women, and children guilty of a wide range of crimes, from simple theft to rape and murder, in a single "warehouse" where they were likely to be chained or handcuffed. There was no such thing as rehabilitative treatment for either the convicted criminals or the mentally ill.

Great Britain's Lunacy Act of 1845 made a critical semantic change in identifying the mentally ill, classifying them as patients in need of care rather than as inmates. Other countries followed suit, but while some aspects did improve, these institutions continued to be warehouses to hide people considered an embarrassment, a danger, political opposition, intellectually disabled, as well as for women seen as unruly and unwomanly and therefore an embarrassment to their family or community.

Perhaps intended in the best interests of the mentally ill, new forms of treatment were developed such as lobotomies and electroshock therapy, but these techniques could do more harm than good, to the point that lobotomies are rarely if ever used today, although some types of psychosurgery are still available for very extreme situations. In contrast, ECT, when used appropriately and according to standard guidelines, can be lifesaving for acutely suicidal people or for those whose medical conditions prohibit use of medications.

In addition, eugenics, a popular theory of the time, was often applied to female inmates/patients. Eugenicists promoted the idea that to improve the quality of the human population, individuals who were potentially a danger to the gene pool (the poor, feebleminded, persistently criminal, physically and mentally disabled) should not be allowed to procreate. This was meant to stem the spread of these "weak genes" that would harm society. Forced or secret sterilization was commonly used to prevent members of these groups from procreating.

20th-Century Mental Health Treatments

The number of mental institutions increased substantially until the mid–20th century, when the cost of maintaining these asylums began to be seen as prohibitive, prioritizing economics over the welfare of the mentally ill and intellectually disabled. What took its place was the deinstitutionalization movement, which rapidly emptied out the asylums, putting patients into a community care system that was unprepared for them and that they did not understand and often were unable to navigate on their own. The development of the medical model of psychiatry that promoted the use of psychiatric medications, like chlorpromazine, became the new solution to the mental health problem: drug them up so they would not act "abnormal" and make trouble.

In addition, a new generation of scholars began to investigate the idea that it was not necessarily the mentally ill who were the problem, but instead a society that was uncomfortable interacting publicly with people who behaved normatively different from the "average" citizen. In their social discomfort, communities selected one of two choices: (1) drug them so they would not be behaviorally awkward, or (2) warehouse them in the few remaining locked institutions. These places were overseen by medical and psychiatric personnel who created rigid rules, withdrawing all sense of personal and civil rights from patients upon their entrance to the asylum, often for the convenience of the staff and the smooth running of the asylum.

Psychiatrist Thomas Szasz in his two books, *The Myth of Mental Illness* (1961)[3] *and The Manufacture of Madness* (1970),[4] believed that the problem was not those labeled mentally ill. Instead, he pointed a finger at society, identifying those with mental disorders not as flawed but as humans who had behavioral difficulties living in normative society. Szasz believed society constructed definitions of madness which were then applied to people with these problems. This labeling of mental illness then supported their stigmatization and removal from the general population. It was not that Szasz felt that mental illness did not exist, but that only those with the most serious and dangerous forms should be subjected to involuntary incarceration.

Like many who came before him, such as the French psychiatrist Philippe Pinel who unchained the insane to show sympathy with the French Revolution, Szasz's psychiatric theories were also politically motivated, since he was swayed by the intolerable fascism that he witnessed in his native Hungary. Because he refused to rotate through hospitals with locked psychiatric wards, he did not have direct contact with the most seriously ill patients during his psychiatric residency and based many of his best-known ideas on theoretical inference rather than on direct clinical experience. According to Szasz, those with other less serious and more treatable forms of mental illness should not be placed into asylums because society found them unusual, awkward, differently abled, etc. They could find their place as productive members of their communities while at the same time receiving the help they needed in those communities.[5]

Sociologist Erving Goffman, in his 1961 study of mental institutions, *Asylums: Essays on the Social Situation of Mental Patients and Other Inmates Studied*,[6] looked at both the harms created by placement in a total institution and how its patients redefined their own roles from "normal" to "crazy" as they tried to salvage some sense of self torn away from the moment of their institutionalization. "Upon entrance, he is immediately stripped of the support provided by [certain stable social arrangements] ... he begins a series of abasements, degradations, humiliations, and profanations of self. ... Territories of self are violated."

Psychologist David Rosenhan's pseudo-patient experiment, described in his 1973 article "On Being Sane in Insane Places,"[7] published at the height of the counterculture, was highly influential in its day, even if it is discredited today for reasons that will be explained below. Rosenhan concluded that what really mattered was the initial labeling of mental instability that resulted in institutionalization. In his study, he supposedly followed individuals who had been prepped to pretend to have symptoms of schizophrenia and as a result were placed in a mental asylum. After institutionalization, these subjects dropped all performances of schizophrenic symptoms and acted as normal "sane" people. As per Rosenhan's publication (which did not reference a person who reported benefit from hospitalization and which did not disclose that he himself was one of his experimental "subjects"), the sane behaviors evidenced later were discounted and ignored by the authorities in charge of the institution; the label "insane" was already immovably in place). Significant problems for the pseudo-patients arose when the asylum authorities refused to redefine the subjects' fake presentations for several weeks before finally accepting that these were ruses and allowing them to leave the wards.

Recent findings have questioned Rosenhan's findings, showing that he cherry-picked data to support his thesis that psychiatry and mental institutions were worthless. Whether or not Szasz has been totally misunderstood, and whether Rosenhan's findings need to be completely revamped and potentially disregarded, the perception of psychiatric mismanagement of the mentally ill gained a significant foothold in popular culture.[8]

Out of these overwhelmingly negative images of the mentally ill, and the institutions in which they were placed or the streets on which they were abandoned, came a strong anti-mental asylum reaction, probably most strongly articulated in popular culture in Ken Kesey's novel *One Flew Over the Cuckoo's Nest* (1962) and the 1975 movie of the same name. Kesey's representation of these institutions was harsh, identifying them as warehouses for embarrassments to families (Billy), a place to hide for homosexuals not accepted by their families (Harding), a hiding place for lazy criminals seeking to bypass the hard labor of a criminal sentence (McMurphy), and lockup for patients who suffered from such severe anxiety that it could lead to suicide (Cheswick). Many of the individuals chose to hide within the walls of this dysfunctional institution, where they were bullied and berated by the nurse responsible for their care and rehabilitation (Nurse Ratched), where they were medicated, electroshocked, and in some cases lobotomized on the say-so of the nurse who used these treatments as methods of social control or punishment, not as legitimate treatment. The reason most continued to stay? Because even with the horrendous and destructive techniques of control used against them, some said that even these otherwise untenable events were superior to the horrible stigmatization they faced in the outside "normal" society.

Just before the "I want my cigarettes" scene in *One Flew Over the Cuckoo's Nest* (1975) erupts into mayhem, patients played by actors William Redfield, Sydney Lassick, Jack Nicholson, Christopher Lloyd, Vincent Schiavelli and William Duell (left to right) lounge around the psych ward in the film that profoundly changed public attitudes toward psychiatric hospitals and that even led to a time-limited ban on ECT in California.

King of Hearts

Into this highly controversial arena comes a French film, *King of Hearts* (1966), script by Daniel Boulanger and directed by Philippe de Broca. Meant to be an anti-war film, this movie, initially unpopular with French audiences, soon became an American cult favorite with the focus not primarily on the war theme but instead on that of housing the mentally ill.

Set at the end of World War I, German forces occupy the small French town of Marville, the location of a mental asylum run by nuns. At a distance but closing in is a company of Scottish soldiers who plan to take back the town and free it from the occupation of the Germans. Unfortunately, the Germans, led by the eccentric and unstable Colonel Von Krack and supported by his underlings Lieutenant Hamburger and Captain Adolf Hitler (yes, that Hitler!), decide that if they cannot have the town, then neither can the enemy. In one last violent response, they plan to destroy the village and bridge with a bomb hidden in a disguised blockhouse. It is set to go off that evening when the knight on the town clock strikes midnight.

The barber, a member of the Resistance, warns the townspeople, including the nuns in charge of the asylum. He also contacts the approaching Scots by shortwave radio and in a bizarre and garbled message, warns them, "The mackerel likes frying. The mackerel likes frying. Germans blowing up munitions dump … tonight before midnight. The knight strikes at midnight! The knight strikes at midnight! For God's sake, don't enter the town!" But before he can explain more, he is caught and shot as the Germans retreat from the town, with Von Krack giggling in delight about the surprise he has left behind for the Allied forces. Then the townspeople evacuate, leaving behind only the patients in the asylum. They do, however, in a slight gesture of humanity, unlock its gates, allowing the patients the opportunity to venture out.

Meanwhile, the Scots, led by Colonel Mac Bibenbrook with Sergeant Mac Fish as his second in command, focus on the single item they can understand: "The Germans are planning to blow up the town!" Rather than mobilizing and sending his troops, the strategically prudent move, he instead decides to endanger only a single soldier, the one who speaks French, Private Charles Plumpick, who is a lover of poetry and the carrier pigeons for which he is responsible. Mac Bibenbrook directs his sergeant to force Plumpick to "volunteer" for the mission to disarm the bomb. Clearly working off a script of his own, the colonel is so out of touch with reality that he is perpetually unable to remember that the private's name is NOT Pumpernickel. He also ignores all of Plumpick's gentle suggestions.

> "I wonder if perhaps one of the chaps from ordinance ... may not do the job just a wee bit better, sir."
> "You're asking me to risk the life of two of my troops? ... Did you or did you not volunteer?"
> "Well, as a matter of fact, sir—" ... "But I wonder, sir, if you do have the right Plumpick, sir. You see, about the explosives—"

As is obvious from the beginning of their conversation, the colonel's script of reality wins out, and Plumpick, in his regulation kilt uniform, with his gun and his cage of carrier pigeons, heads off toward Marville. Finding that the Germans have not all left, he temporarily hides in the asylum, so as to appear as one of the "crazies." He names himself the King of Hearts, receiving an overwhelming positive response from the inmates. Once safe, he leaves the asylum.

However, almost magically, Marville has begun to transform into something new and unique. The inhabitants of the asylum have gradually wandered into the town, slowly discarding the things that mark them as inmates and replacing them with markers of the new roles they have taken on—clothing, hairstyles, makeup, styles of speech. The mental institution has not disappeared; it has just expanded to fit the available space of the town. The asylum is not a physical structure but is instead defined and constructed by the behavior of the people who inhabit it and how they are perceived by the outer world.

Plumpick initially fails to recognize that the town members he was encountering were the very patients he had first met when he entered the town and was forced to hide. There is Monseigneur Marguerite, the religious leader; Monsieur Marcel, the barber; the Duke de Trèfle and his wife the Duchesse; Madame Eglantine, the brothel owner; Poppy and other women, who are the prostitutes; General Géranium, in charge of the military, and a variety of other characters. They put on the clothing, the makeup, the personality, and take ownership of the town space that is appropriate for their new position. And then they live ... joyfully. They create a coronation for the new King of Hearts and provide him with a Queen, Poppy, the young prostitute and tightrope walker who always wears a yellow tutu.

Plumpick shifts back and forth between these two worlds, wildly trying to get these people to take their endangered situation seriously and at the same time drawn into their contagious happiness and obvious love of life. "God's pleasure is joy. We have decided to be happy, and nothing can stop us," the Monseigneur tells Plumpick.

Plumpick points out, "Yesterday, you were in the asylum!"

"Are you jealous?" asks the Duke. "Yesterday you were out there with them."

King of Hearts demonstrates that it is those in the outer world who are insane, not those inside the asylum. Instead, the asylum is a location of joy and sanity. As the Monseigneur says, "I already knew that to love the world, you must leave it."

Desperate to save these gentle and innocent people, Plumpick argues, cajoles, and begs them to help him find the bomb, but they are uninterested, focused only on the present. Failing that, he attempts to get them to leave town, and they follow him, but just to the edge of Marville. They recognize the crazed violence of the war outside their community.

Philippe de Broca's cult classic, *King of Hearts* (1966), as illustrated by a playing card poster, stars Alan Bates as a World War I–era soldier who concludes that life inside the insane asylum is preferable to the psychotic goings-on witnessed in the wartime society outside.

"Sir, come back. There are wild beasts! Can't you hear them? They're blood thirsty. ... There's a wall between us and the world out there. It's too dangerous. ... You have no idea how wicked they are out there. ... Sire, what's the point of traveling when everything you want is at home?"

Plumpick returns, choosing to spend his final hours with those who have become "his people." As Poppy happily responds when Plumpick points out that the bomb will explode at three minutes to midnight. "Three minutes is great," she says. She then mentions that he should watch for the knight who will come out and ring at midnight. It falls into place when Plumpick prevents the knight's hammer from ringing and, in doing so, stops the ignition of the bomb. Marville is saved!

In a fit of anger, the German Colonel Von Krack, who has been excitedly waiting for the bomb to go off, orders Lieutenant Hamburger executed as punishment when it fails to explode. The Scots, also waiting for the explosion, happily enter the town, congratulate Plumpick, and spend the evening celebrating with those who they think are the citizens of the town. At dawn, the Germans come to investigate, meet the Scots, and both sides engage in a truly insane form of military strategy—the line battle—killing everyone except Plumpick, who has been gagged and tied up by his subjects, begging the question, who really is insane?

Slowly the inmates of the asylum make their way back to the gates of the institution, unhurriedly shedding their costumes, makeup, props, and behaviors, replacing them with those uniforms they have been issued. They lock the gates behind them. The legitimate citizens of the community trickle back into town and pick up the lives they had left behind.

The French liberators enter Marville and honor both Plumpick and his remaining pigeon with medals, ordering him to the front. Plumpick lines up with the soldiers, but silently slips out of the group, slowly shedding his own clothing and military paraphernalia and arriving at the gates of the asylum, naked, and carrying the bird cage with his pigeon.

In the last scene, Plumpick has accepted the transition to his new role, King of Hearts, and asks General Géranium, "What now?"

Géranium replies, "It's your turn, Your Majesty."

Still confused, Plumpick says, "I still don't understand the rules."

"There aren't any," answers Géranium. "Well, you're here now. And you won't be running off anymore."

"I'm staying here, General. I'm not going anywhere."

In the final line of the movie, the Duke de Trèfle summarizes the true value of the institution: "The most beautiful journeys … are taken through the window."

Kesey, Szasz, Goffman, and Rosenhan all identify mental institutions as cruel, dehumanizing prisons. Boulanger and de Broca's message is clearly in direct opposition to that. The real insanity of the world is not found inside an asylum, but instead outside in what we have chosen to define as the "normal" world. For the King of Hearts and the other patients of this asylum in Marville, France, their institution, whether it is behind the gates of a single building or within the walls of a whole town, is a place of protection, of social support, of lively and creative interaction, and joy. It is a true asylum.

Notes

1. *King of Hearts* (1966), directed by Philippe de Broca, written by Daniel Boulanger, https://www.scripts.com/script/king_of_hearts_11837.
2. Ken Kesey, *One Flew Over the Cuckoo's Nest* (Viking Press, 1962).
3. Thomas Szasz, *The Myth of Mental Illness* (Harper and Row, 1961).
4. Thomas Szasz, *The Manufacture of Madness* (Syracuse University Press, 1970).
5. Sharon Packer, "How Anti-Semitism and the Shoah Helped Shape Twentieth Century Psychiatry," in *Anti-Semitism and Psychiatry: Recognition, Prevention, and Interventions*, ed. H.S. Moffic et al. (Springer Nature Switzerland, 2020), https://doi.org/10.1007/978-3-030-37745-8_7.
6. Erving Goffman, *Asylums: Essays on the Social Situation of Mental Patients and Other Inmates Studied* (Anchor Books, 1961).
7. David Rosenhan, "On Being Sane in Insane Places," *Science* 179 (January 1973): 250–258.
8. Susannah Cahalan, "The Flawed Experiment That Destroyed the World's Faith in Psychiatry," *New Scientist*, February 5, 2020, https://www.newscientist.com/article/mg24532680-700-the-flawed-experimentthatdestroyed-the-worlds-faith-in-psychiatry/.

13

Titicut Follies

What Was and What Could Have Been

Ashley Barry

If ever there were a poster child film for the anti-psychiatry and anti-asylum movement that began in earnest in the early 1960s, it would be Frederick Wiseman's 1967 documentary *Titicut Follies*. The film was banned for 20 years not only because its negative depiction of state hospital wards offended political sensibilities, but also because of its flagrant violation of emergent patient privacy policies. With its raw black-and-white footage of institutionalized people who suffer seemingly endless indignities in state hospitals, *Follies* catalyzed discourse both on psychiatric treatment and the injustice of censorship in documentary film. But this catalysis was delayed because of unexpected legal complications.

Follies was one of Wiseman's first films and the start of a long and storied filmmaking career that focused mostly on social issues. Its subject matter and its sentiment were very much in keeping with the anti-psychiatry zeitgeist of the era. We will first review details about this film and its filmmaker, along with the reasons why it caused such controversy at the time and why banning the film delayed social reforms that might have followed from greater exposure. From there, we will trace the somewhat winding road between 1960s- and 1970s-era anti-psychiatry, with its multifaceted origin point, through its later incarnations as the mostly British-based critical psychiatry movement that attracted mental health professionals rather than mental health consumers, with more recent manifestations in academic MAD STUDIES departments that came into full force in Canada and emerged intermittently in American universities, along with a lively internet discussion board, spearheaded by a related book (*Mad in America: Bad Science, Bad Medicine, and the Enduring Mistreatment of the Mentally Ill*) written by an American journalist, Robert Whitaker.

Frederick Wiseman began his career teaching law at the Boston University Institute of Law and Medicine. He frequently brought his students to Bridgewater State Hospital for the Criminally Insane, and in 1965, he spoke to the hospital's superintendent about featuring the institution on a documentary.[1] After gaining permission from the institution and the Massachusetts government, Wiseman spent a month observing and filming the living conditions of the inmates, always accompanied by corrections staff who would determine whether individual subjects could consent to being filmed.[2] *Titicut Follies* was screened at the 1967 New York Film Festival and received its first set of negative reviews from critics who found "that the film violated decency and had no reason to exist beyond legislative and non-artistic consequences."[3]

As the film gained negative publicity, the Massachusetts government brought Wiseman to trial, alleging both that *Follies* invaded its subjects' privacy and that the state was supposed to have authority on the final cut.[4] When the judge ruled that the negative should be destroyed, Wiseman appealed to the Massachusetts Supreme Court, which ruled that "the film had value, but could only be seen by special audiences, consisting of doctors, lawyers, judges, legislators, people interested in custodial care, and students in these and related fields."[5] For the next ten years, *Follies* was only shown in limited environments, mostly restricted to college campuses and medical school classes. It was not until 1977 that the film had its first public screening in the state where it was filmed, and not until 1992 that it was aired for a general audience on PBS.[6]

Nearly 60 years after its initial release, *Titicut Follies* remains a staple in the history of documentary film not only for its subject matter, but also for its approach to filming and representing that subject. Wiseman calls his filmmaking style "reality fiction," which means a policy of nonintervention in the behavior observed at Bridgewater alongside a neutral depiction in the film, i.e., a lack of commentary to contextualize or condemn the abuses presented. These abuses consist of the guards' verbal humiliation of the patients, the deprivation of clothing and beds, and force-feeding.

While Wiseman does not force a clear narrative structure onto the footage, it is hard to avoid the temptation to compare the documentary to the fictional *One Flew Over the Cuckoo's Nest*. On a narrative level, *Cuckoo's Nest* protagonist Randle McMurphy pretends to be mentally ill so he can be placed in an institution like Bridgewater instead of incarcerated on a work farm. Additionally, McMurphy discovers that his original sentence limitation does not apply once he is in the mental hospital. In a parallel vein, a major controversy that emerged about Bridgewater was holding inmates long after their imposed penal terms had expired (as is typical of forensic psychiatric facilities, which use different standards for release into the community).[7]

As discussed in the opening of my earlier essay in this essay collection, *Cuckoo's Nest* became a cultural touchstone for the American public's reconsideration of psychiatric practices. However, since *Titicut Follies* was banned from public viewing for years after its production, it was unable to make a similar—if not potentially bigger—impact on the American moral conscience, given that it included footage from an actual institution and was not a fictionalized narrative, à la *Cuckoo's Nest*. Psychologist Salvatore B. Durante argues, "Given the momentum of the anti-psychiatry movement and the issues with the inhumane treatment of individuals with mental health concerns in hospital and forensic settings, it is possible that a wide distribution of *Titicut Follies* in 1967 could have led to public outrage and reform of psychiatric treatment and institutions." From 1986 to 1987, at least eight Bridgewater patients died; three of the deaths were ruled suicides.[8] Durante hypothesizes that these deaths could have been prevented if not for the censorship of *Titicut Follies*; if the American public was given the opportunity to be outraged by the abuses depicted in the film, there could have been a critical eye on Bridgewater much earlier, possibly leading to reforms.

Wiseman himself drew the connection between censorship and social change in an interview with Ted Koppel in 1987, the same year the alarmingly high number of "unexplained deaths" at Bridgewater were reported. He says, "The censoring of *Titicut Follies* or any other film prevents people in a democracy from access to information which they might like to have in order to make up their minds about what kind of society they'd like to live in—it's as simple as that."[9] While the concern for patient privacy is valid, this particular story played out in such a way that prioritized political reputation over the welfare of actual patients. One must especially consider the dearth of information about what happened in institutions mid-century and the power that exposure could hold in this era. While institutionalized people remain on the fringes of society in the 21st century, social media and the internet have made it much easier for people to share their stories and advocate for change.

In *Titicut Follies*, the audience meets Vladimir, a patient/inmate "who avers that he is better and blames the institutional environment as the cause of his mental health distress."[10] While he does experience symptoms of schizophrenia, he believes that Bridgewater is exacerbating his mental health symptoms, not mitigating them. His complaint is met with an increased dosage of his psychiatric medication.[11] Vladimir and Wiseman are part of an important but often ignored social movement advocating for the rights of mental patients. As noted elsewhere, films have played a critical role in swaying public opinion, but *Titicut Follies* was pulled from distribution before that could happen. The rest of this essay explores the contemporary academic subfield of Mad Studies, which evolved out of disability studies. We will trace a timeline of Mad History that is often marginalized in conversations of other liberation movements.

Overview

One history might start with Elizabeth Packard and Charlotte Perkins Gilman, the former an unfairly incarcerated wife of a minister who petitioned her way out of Illinois's first psychiatric hospital and went on to found the Anti-Insane Asylum Society in 1867, the latter a staple of English classrooms, whose own experiences with hysteria and the "rest cure" informed her 1892 short story "The Yellow Wallpaper."

Others look to the academic work of Michel Foucault and Erving Goffman, whose discursive and sociological analyses challenged the typical positionality of scholarly considerations of the mad; similar shifts were seen in practicing psychiatrists like R.D. Laing and Thomas Szasz, who sought experimental and nondogmatic approaches to mental illness. The reclamation of the previously pejorative term "Mad" originates with activist groups of psychiatric survivors who began working in the 1970s to organize for collective rights, fulfillment of basic needs, and protections against psychiatric abuse.

Expanded Timeline of Mad History

Mad Studies does not fit into a neat chronology or taxonomy. Mad histories are not codified or canonized, and the use of today's Mad language will always be anachronistic. Additionally, the histories are inherently multiple: to understand madness, you need both a history of psychology and a history of the critique of each stage of psychology. Discourses are layered, and the easiest way to pull them out seems to be a focus on voices. Which voices were given legitimacy or epistemic authority? Which were not, but were somehow still preserved? And which are forgotten or erased completely, left only to our speculative imaginations? To cite the originator of the term "Mad Studies," I offer Richard Ingram's reflection on in/disciplinarity of the field: "There are two sides to this equation: on the one side, showing that there is method in our madness; and on the other side, preserving madness in our method."[12]

I map out seven stages that we can call survivor research, proto–Mad Studies, or general work that takes a critical position when analyzing the mechanics of psychology and psychiatry. These stages include (1) early anti-asylum work; (2) mid-century academic critique; (3) radical psych; (4) mid-century patient activism; (5) the late-century lull; (6) new millennium mad studies and pride; and (7) Mad Studies. I would like to clarify that this mapping is not definitive or exhaustive and is simply one manifestation of what a Mad Studies history could look like.

Early Anti-Asylum Work

With a contemporary scholarly lens, one could see this early period as a feminist, anti-carceral approach. Nérée St-Amand and Eugene LeBlanc offer a profile of three women who were unfairly institutionalized in their *Mad Matters* essay, "Women in 19th-Century Asylums: Three Exemplary Women; a New Brunswick Hero." Elizabeth Packard is a key figure here, committed to Illinois's first psychiatric hospital from 1860 to 1863 after disagreeing with her husband's conservative views on child rearing, family finances, and slavery. Because her husband had legal authority over her, Packard was not granted a public hearing but was eventually able to "prove her sanity," at which point she was discharged and able to regain custody of her children.[13] After her time institutionalized, Packard "published several books and was responsible for 34 bills protecting women from undue hospitalization and treatment." She also founded the Anti-Insane Asylum Society, an organization that advocated for the rights of mental patients.[14] St-Amand and LeBlanc refer to Packard as a "mad-positive" individual, who did not herself suffer from mental illness, but remained aligned with patient rights after her reentry into sane society. While it is difficult to find information about the Anti-Insane Asylum Society, one source reports that the alleged pledge members had to agree to includes not consenting to "enter an asylum as a patient," not giving consent to institutionalize relatives or friends, to take care of insane family members in their communities, and that the society itself would provide financial support for caretakers.[15] These principles are core to today's psychiatric survivor movement, and one can imagine these oaths being replicated in a contemporary mutual aid organization.

Additionally, I consider Charlotte Perkins Gilman's 1892 "The Yellow Wallpaper" to be a proto-mad-feminist text. The short story follows a woman who has been sentenced to the "rest cure" due to her postpartum depression. The protagonist's sanity slowly declines until she believes there is a woman living in the walls, and she herself becomes that woman. Gilman herself had a similar experience, and she considered this story a form of protest and awareness-raising for the public. In this facet, she succeeded, because the doctor most known for the rest cure, Silas Weir Mitchell, ceased prescribing it. Gilman's narrator is more mad-identified than mad-positive. Gilman offers a critique of the psychological practices she had experienced at the time, locating a patriarchal alliance between psychological "experts" and oppressive gender norms, both of which served only to exacerbate her suffering. Gilman's experiences of home confinement parallel similar rest cures offered at some sanitariums.

Mid-Century Academic Critique and Radical Psych

The academic works most frequently cited in contemporary publications on Mad Studies, anti-psych, and post-psychiatry are written by Michel Foucault, Erving Goffman, R.D. Laing, Thomas Szasz, and Frantz Fanon. Fanon particularly straddles a couple of categories, and I include Phyllis Chesler's *Women and Madness*, although she appears in bibliographies much less than the aforementioned group. Additionally, Laing and Szasz are typically cited alongside Foucault and Goffman in the Mad Studies canon but can be more accurately located as early thinkers in critical psychiatry, as will be elaborated below. The academic critique comes from multiple disciplinary locations: Goffman was a sociologist, Foucault a philosopher, Fanon both a psychiatrist and political philosopher, Laing and Szasz both working psychiatrists, and Chesler a psychologist.

It is impossible to generalize about these thinkers, as they did not align their work with one another. While I group Laing and Szasz together in my syllabi, it is on record that Szasz loathed Laing's ideas and actively confronted him at speaking events.[16] Additionally, the terms used now to describe these theories were directly disavowed by the writers. For example, all are listed under "Golden Age of Antipsychiatry," even though Laing and Szasz refused to apply the term "antipsychiatry" to their own work. Theoretically, Laing, Szasz, Fanon, and Chesler might have fit into today's Critical Psychiatry Network as practitioners with critiques of the system, but it is once again inappropriate to make that assumption.

The first publication in this grouping is R.D. Laing's *The Divided Self*, published in 1960. This text argues against an overmedicalization of experience, instead articulating a form of existential phenomenology that would prioritize patient narratives and seek to work through their problems with them, instead of placing the sole value on cure.[17] Laing also saw sanity as socially constructed, schizophrenia as a result of family dysfunction, and psychosis as an opportunity for growth and breakthrough. Laing's thick descriptions of mental illness are relevant, although he is frequently made the poster boy of a dangerous, LSD-obsessed school of anti-psych. (Ironically, psychedelics have resurfaced in mainstream psychiatry and are undergoing reevaluation as well as garnering hype.) Laing's envisioning of what a radical psychotherapy (as seen in Kingsley Hall) could look like remains fruitful when we consider what lies beyond institutional psychiatry, but we cannot overlook the fact that Laing himself closed Kingsley Hall when he saw that his theories did not work out in practice. Additionally, the work of Mary Barnes, a one-time resident of Kingsley Hall, is useful for understanding the "crazier" sides of crazy, compared to the now ubiquitous cultural experience of anxiety and depression.

The next year, 1961, saw the publication of Thomas Szasz's *The Myth of Mental Illness*, Erving Goffman's *Asylums*, and Michel Foucault's *Madness and Civilization*. While working as a psychiatrist, Szasz argues that mental illness simply does not exist, and its emergence as a medical entity is a categorical mistake due to the broadening of the idea of disease to include "functional disease" and the subsequent medicalization of mental distress, hence the invention of the term "mental illness."[18] Szasz believes the role of psychologists and psychiatrists should not be medical, but rather a way of helping patients with moral problems.[19] Additionally, Szasz argues that "psychiatric diagnoses are stigmatizing labels," that there is no concrete entity that can be identified as psychopathology, that psych and law must remain completely separate, and that all forms of involuntary psychiatric treatment are "crimes against humanity."[20] When we dive deeper into Szasz's politics, it becomes difficult to label him a mad thinker. He identified primarily with libertarianism, believed in carceral solutions to social problems, and became deeply aversive to authoritarian approaches after witnessing the fascist takeover of his native Hungary.[21] It is especially valuable to consider Szasz's unusual psychiatric residency training as well, given that he refused to rotate on inpatient wards where patients were mandated to treatment, and so he bypassed customary exposure to hospitalized people with serious mental illness. However, psychiatric survivors of the time found great value in his ideas, and Leonard Roy Frank, the founder of the Network Against Psychiatric Assault, called Szasz "an oasis in the desert of modern psychiatry" after having seen Szasz talk in 1972, as published in *Madness Network News*.[22] Additionally, Szasz's name continues to appear in modern bibliographies, if only for an early articulation of a critique against the medical model of mental illness.

On the other hand, Goffman remains as citable today as he was when his work was originally published. In one way, *Asylums* fits into a legacy of 19th- and 20th-century social activism that includes Dorothea Dix, Elizabeth Packard, Nellie Bly's 1887 *Ten Days in a Mad-House*, and Albert Deutsch's 1948 *The Shame of the States* due to the shared goal of exposing poor conditions in mental asylums and other institutions where the "mad" might end up. Goffman used his time working at St. Elizabeth's Hospital in Washington, D.C., "to try to learn about the social world of the hospital inmate, as this world is subjectively experienced by him," explicitly aligning himself with patients instead of doctors or nurses.[23] One can compare St. Elizabeth's Hospital to Bridgewater State Hospital, as depicted in *Titicut Follies*, but the comparison is inexact, since Bridgewater operates under the aegis of the Department of Correction and has a custodial focus, whereas St. Elizabeth's is more closely aligned with the public mental health system, with an emphasis on rehabilitation and research.

Goffman's critique of modern psychology and psychiatry lies in the system's inability to "treat" the mind as one might a different organ or physiological disorder in the human body. The presence of custodialism, forced treatment, and stigma make the practice of psychiatry more likely to socially other its "clients" rather than provide a curative function. By focusing on power dynamics in the asylum setting, Goffman is able to tie his observations to the larger disciplinary structures present in society's approach to madness, eventually declaring, "Mental patients can find themselves crushed by the weight of a service ideal that eases life for the rest of us."[24] It is clear why Goffman continues to be cited, and there is much more to be said about his conceptualization of total institutions and his work in *Stigma* that continues to be reworked today.

Foucault's *Madness and Civilization* is an early version of discourse analysis that historicizes the developments of psychology, putting these trajectories into conversation with the religious and legal norms to which they developed in parallel. When I taught "Introduction to Mad Studies," we used this text to develop a pre-psych timeline, following Foucault's narrativization of leper colonies, religious explanations of madness during the Renaissance, the era of the General Hospital and Great Confinement, the birth of the asylum, and the formation of modern psychoanalysis. I continue to find value in the idea of undifferentiated confinement to consider both the mechanics of modern biopower and the coalitions formed to resist them. To consider that these three texts (*The Myth of Mental Illness*, *Asylums*, and *Madness and Civilization*) were published in the same year is to understand a broad, interdisciplinary, and cognitively dissonant set of intellectual critiques of mid-century psych practices and philosophies.

We can conclude this section with Frantz Fanon and Phyllis Chesler. While their frameworks and positioning are very different, they share similar beliefs that psychology is not inherently wrong or evil but rather requires a deeper understanding of gender and race politics both when treating individual patients and when developing theories of psychopathology. In 1961's *The Wretched of the Earth*, Fanon argues that mental illness is indeed real and is, at least in colonial Algeria, generated by the psychic and physical warfare perpetrated by colonial forces. Fanon believed that institutional psychotherapy could be useful by incorporating both medical treatments and social/political contexts, and by actively encouraging patient participation in institution management. In Femi Eromosele's article "Frantz Fanon in the Time of Mad Studies," he concludes that Fanon's critiques of psych, developed as he worked within the system, are useful for proving the brutality of colonialism and involuntary psychiatric treatment. Eromosele writes, "To articulate normative mental conditions as a construct—as the anti-psychiatrists would later do—would undermine his position that racism, colonialism and the wars they foster are direct sources of harm to both the colonized and the colonizer."[25] Fanon is under-cited in Mad Studies, but Eromosele is correct in explaining why Fanon has been much more visible in anticolonial and decolonial scholarship.

Lastly, Chesler's 1972 *Women and Madness* offers less of an anti-psych critique than a feminist critique of psychology, which works alongside Fanon's colonial critique. She considers the legacies of hysteria and the use of psychology as a patriarchal tool to delegitimize, punish, and restrain women. Chesler writes of Elizabeth Packard, mythology, and witch hunts, moving to a Foucauldian analysis of asylums and gendered differences in diagnostic practices. She also considers the makeup of professional psychology and psychiatry, considering how the overwhelmingly male majority [at the time when she wrote] has cemented sexist ideas in their practices. Since the publication of *Women and Madness*, the gender breakdown of these fields has dramatically changed: as of 2016, 65 percent of psychologists are female,[26] and more recent data show that about 80 percent of psychologists are female; master's degree practitioners such as psychiatric social worker and mental health counselors include even more women.

Chesler does critique Laing's theory of the schizophrenogenic mother while espousing Szasz's theory of psychiatric imperialism and sexocide. Chesler's critique is liberal (and essentialist) in desiring a particular female conceptualization of the psyche alongside a politics of equality in the profession of psychology.

Mid-Century Patient Activism

Much of the specific history of the psychiatric survivors' movement comes from several sources: Mel Starkman's 1981 essay, "The Movement"; an interview between Lanny Beckman and Megan J. Davies in "Democracy is a Very Radical Idea"; and the documentary *The Inmates are Running the Asylum*, as well as archival research of the newsletter *Madness Network News*.

This movement has been referred to as the psychiatric survivors' movement, mad pride, the C/S/X (Consumers/Survivors/Ex-Patients) movement, and the mental patients' liberation movement. It began in the early 1970s and included several different organizations working through similar issues and questions. Common themes include fighting for accessible housing and employment, fighting against involuntary hospitalization and treatment, and dismantling sanist stigma. The Mental Patients Association (MPA) followed a radical politic by organizing with a nonhierarchical structure, buying property for supportive housing, and running a 24/7 drop-in center that functioned independently of medical or legal authority. Other groups included the Mental Patients Liberation Front, which was cofounded in 1971 by Judi Chamberlin, whose 1978 *On Our Own: Patient-Controlled Alternatives to the Mental Health System* offered a patient-centered analysis of the mental health system, its role in "creating" patients, and how both individuals and organizations can create sustainable alternatives. Psychiatric survivors Leonard Roy Frank and Wade Hudson founded the Network Against Psychiatric Assault (NAPA) in 1974 and succeeded in banning involuntary ECT in Berkeley, California, for a few months in 1982.

Madness Network News was a newsletter that ran from 1972 to 1985, founded by Tulia Tesauro and Jennifer Gleissner, two inmates from California's Agnews State Mental Hospital. It was explicitly anti-psychiatry, operating in the same building as NAPA. The journal featured art and writing by dozens of psychiatric survivors.[27] Special issues covered topics like workers' rights and conditions, ECT, antipsychotic drugs, women's experiences as patients, colonialism, racism in psychology, and lesbian parenting. Available in an open-access digital archive, the ideas in MNN are as relevant today as they were 50 years ago, which speaks to how little the experiences of psychiatric survivors have changed.

Mel Starkman's 1981 essay "The Movement" was an early attempt to document the many strands of activism going on at the time. He identifies three primary priorities: psychiatric survivors are trying to identify themselves to each other, define their struggle, and "decide whether the system is reformable or whether they need to create an alternative community."[28] Starkman specifically cites a number of sources that served as inspiration for those organizing, including feminist consciousness-raising, work against hysteria, R.D. Laing, Erving Goffman, Thomas Szasz, and the gay liberation movement.

The Late-Century Lull

The late 1980s and 1990s see much less public writing and action in Mad Studies and organizing. This period was shaped mostly by the introduction of Prozac (fluoxetine) in 1987 and the psych focus on recovery and community support, which could have provided a new version of psych post-deinstitutionalization but has been deemed a failure by several Mad scholars. This time was also designated the "Decade of the Brain," and thus became the era of biopsychiatry, leading to the 1994 publication of the DSM-IV.

New Millennium Mad Studies and Mad Pride

The new millennium saw a resurgence of interest in Mad pride as well as some of the roots of a Mad Studies discipline. *Mad Pride: A Celebration of Mad Culture* was published in 2001 and includes a series of personal essays, a guide to interacting with psych professionals, and a particularly useful essay by Ben Watson, "Towards a Critical Madness," which puts madness into conversation with other ideologies of liberation. This was also the point where Mad Studies became an institutional history of Toronto's Ryerson University, where Geoffrey Reaume taught a "Mad People's History" course from 2002 to 2003, which was adapted into "A History of Madness," taught by David Reville at the same institution. Notably, Mel Starkman was invited to audit these courses; he accepted and enjoyed.

The year 2003 saw two notable developments: the formation of the Icarus Project and the 2003 Hunger Strike against the American Psychiatric Association (APA), as documented by Bradley Lewis. The Icarus Project was created by individuals with bipolar looking to create a community of like-minded folks. What started as an online group led to the 2007 publication of *Navigating the Space Between Brilliance and Madness*, which features member essays on madness and practical guides for handling crisis without coercion from police or hospitals. The Hunger Strike was organized by David Oaks and the Support Coalition International, and served as a form of protesting the international domination of biological approaches to psychiatry and increasing use of prescription drugs; their goal was to get the APA, the National Alliance of the Mentally Ill (NAMI), and the U.S. Surgeon General to provide evidence of a biological evidence of mental illness, or what we now understood as neurotransmitter theory. The APA eventually responded that modern neurology is not yet capable of providing physical evidence of psychopathology, but there has only been an increase in the prevalence of biopsychiatric frameworks.

Additionally, it was around this time that terms began to formally crystallize. The Critical Psychiatry Network was formed by a group of British psychiatrists in January 1999. The term "critical psychiatry" describes professionals who work in psych while maintaining serious critiques of the system. While critical psychiatry itself is limited to care providers, they tend to work closely with service user groups. We also see the publication of Patrick Bracken and Philip Thomas's 2001 article "Postpsychiatry: A New Direction for Mental Health," which served as the major inspiration for Bradley Lewis's 2006 *Moving Beyond Prozac, DSM, and the New Psychiatry* (note: Bracken, Thomas, and Lewis are all members of the Critical Psychiatry Network). Bracken and Thomas see post-psychiatry as emphasizing social and cultural contexts, prioritizing ethical concerns over technological, and minimizing patient coercion. However, they do position themselves as specifically *not* anti-psych and emphasize opening room for new voices within psych, primarily the voices of service users and survivors. Lewis builds on post-psychiatry by offering a "theorized postpsychiatry," which has roots in poststructuralism, postmodernism, and postdisciplinarism. He advocates for a cultural study of psychiatry, and himself conducts a discursive and rhetorical analysis of the DSM-III, which "legitimized and scaffolded the new psychiatry's embrace of the disease model."[29] Thinkers like Lewis see great value in challenging oppressive structures within psych and empowering survivor narratives as valid sources of knowledge. The concerns of critical psychiatrists have spread to the wider population of professionals and practitioners. For example, the 2022 annual meeting of the American Psychiatric Association centered on the social determinants of mental health, expanding beyond a medical model of mental illness to incorporate the role of factors including politics and environmental concerns.

It is worth mentioning the work of Robert Whitaker, a journalist who has not only published his own award-winning analyses of contemporary psychiatry but also sought to raise other voices in the C/S/X community. His 2002 *Mad in America: Bad Science, Bad Medicine, and the Enduring Treatment of the Mentally Ill* provided a history of treatment for mental illness with a particular focus on the questionable efficacy of antipsychotics, white his 2010 *Anatomy of an Epidemic: Magic Bullets, Psychiatric Drugs, and the Astonishing Rise of Mental Illness in America* questions the continual increase in the population of Americans with mental illness despite increasingly accessible treatment. Since 2012, the webzine www.madinamerica.com has hosted a variety of "news of psychiatric research, original journalism articles, and a forum for an international group of writers—people with lived experience, peer specialists, family members, psychiatrists, psychologists, social workers, program managers, journalists, attorneys, and more—to explore issues related to this goal of 'remaking psychiatry.'"[30]

Mad Studies

According to Mad Studies lore, the term was first used by Richard Ingram at a conference on disability studies in 2008, although he does not take complete credit, viewing the term as a culmination of years of work by other scholars. Ingram himself had worked with David Reville at Ryerson University and was speaking from his position as a recently institutionalized and unemployed academic. He reflects on this moment in his 2006 article, "Doing Mad Studies: Making (Non)sense Together," drawing on work from Margaret Price and Liat Ben-Moshe, who are not self-identified Mad scholars but whose contributions on disability have expanded the conversation in vital ways.

Mad Matters: A Critical Reader in Canadian Mad Studies was published in 2013. In the introduction, editors Robert Menzies, Brenda A. LeFrançois, and Geoffrey Reaume offer the following: "Mad Studies can be defined in general terms as a project of inquiry, knowledge production, and political action devoted to the critique and transcendence of psy-centered ways of thinking, behaving, relating, and being."[31] They consider the field to be grounded in the contemporary Mad movement of the 1960s and 1970s and the work of thinkers like Goffman, Laing, and Szasz. They identify a set of common themes, which include the following:

1. criticism of psy-centered ways of thinking
2. an approach that is interdisciplinary and multivocal
3. work done by the people affected
4. an understanding of the relations of sameness and difference
5. critical pedagogy and knowledge
6. historical memory work to liberate, connecting the past to now
7. an effort to engage relations of power
8. frameworks that are dialectical, intersectional
9. a desire for transformation and radical restructuring
10. work that stays grounded in the "immediate practicalities of everyday human struggle"[32]

Other Mad Studies edited collections have been published in the years since, including the 2014 *Psychiatry Disrupted: Theorizing Resistance and Crafting the (R)evolution*, the 2015 *Madness, Distress and the Politics of Disablement*, and the 2016 *Searching for a*

Rose Garden: Challenging Psychiatry, Fostering Mad Studies. The specific stances differ within these collections, so it is common to find anti-psych thinkers alongside critical psych and post-psych, all under the functional umbrella of Mad Studies. I believe anti-psychiatry is the last term for me to offer a definition of, and I draw from Bonnie Burstow's chapter "The Withering Away of Psychiatry: An Attrition Model for Antipsychiatry" in the 2014 anthology.[33] Burstow explains how those within the anti-psychiatry camp hold "that psychiatry is unqualifiedly untenable, untenable as it stands today, untenable even if it improved itself substantially."[34]

Anti-psychiatry advocates for the abolition of the psychiatric system, and Burstow offers an attrition model that considers progress to be any work that moves us closer to abolition or narrows the scope of psychiatry. When we work with Burstow's definition, it makes sense to consider Szasz anti-psych, although he called the movement quackery. Fanon and Chesler would not be anti-psych, because they both see psych as playing an important role in treating suffering caused by racism and sexism, although they do have major critiques of its functioning.

The complex history of the C/S/X movement means that not all psychiatric survivors would identify as anti-psych. Today's population of people diagnosed with mental illness includes every demographic, and each individual has their own unique relation to the systems of psychology and psychiatry. What Mad Studies and Mad activism seek to remedy are the systemic forces that deny voice and autonomy to consumers, survivors, and ex-patients. Indeed, the legacy of *Titicut Follies* holds 60 years later not only because it exposed the conditions of the institution but because it provided a platform for the voices of the institutionalized to be heard.

Notes

1. Carolyn Anderson, "The Conundrum of Competing Rights in *Titicut Follies*," *Journal of the University Film Association* 33, no. 1 (Winter 1981): 16.
2. Anderson, "Conundrum of Competing Rights," 17.
3. Salvatore B. Durante, "The Historical Significance of *Titicut Follies* in Psychiatric Treatment: An Anti-Censorship Perspective," *Psychological Reports*, 2023.
4. Marc Mohan, "Frederick Wiseman Talks 'Titicut Follies,'" Oregon Artswatch, April 18, 2016, https://archive.orartswatch.org/frederick-wiseman-talks-titicut-follies/.
5. Mohan, "Frederick Wiseman Talks."
6. Anderson, "Conundrum of Competing Rights"; Durante, "Historical Significance of Titicut Follies."
7. Jennifer Honig, "The History of Bridgewater State Hospital," Massachusetts Association for Mental Health, October 2, 2023, https://www.mamh.org/library/the-history-of-bridgewater-state-hospital.
8. Durante, "Historical Significance of *Titicut Follies*"; "Deaths at a Prison Hospital Lead to Inquiries," *The New York Times*, 1987, 32.
9. Barry Keith Grant, *Ethnography in the First Person: Frederick Wiseman's* Titicut Follies (Wayne State University Press, 2014), 265.
10. Durante, "Historical Significance of *Titicut Follies*."
11. Durante, "Historical Significance of *Titicut Follies*."
12. Richard A. Ingram, "Doing Mad Studies: Making (Non)Sense Together," *Intersectionalities: A Global Journal of Social Work Analysis, Research, Polity, and Practice*, 2016, 13, emphasis added.
13. Nérée St-Amand and Eugene LeBlanc, "Women in 19th-Century Asylums: Three Exemplary Women; A New Brunswick Hero," in *Mad Matters: A Critical Reader in Canadian Mad Studies*, ed. Brenda A. LeFrançois et al. (Canadian Scholars' Press, 2013), 42.
14. St-Amand and LeBlanc, "Women in 19th-Century Asylums," 42.
15. Carla Joinson, "Anti-Insane Asylum Society," Healing, Hell, and the History of American Insane Asylums, n.d., https://hhhasylum.com/anti-insane-asylum-society/.
16. Bob Mullan, *Mad to Be Normal: Conversations with R.D. Laing* (Free Association Books, 1996).
17. R.D. Laing, *The Divided Self* (Viking, 1991), 17.
18. Thomas Szasz, *The Myth of Mental Illness: Foundations of a Theory of Personal Conduct* (Harper Perennial, 2010), 11–13.

19. Szasz, *The Myth of Mental Illness*, 9.

20. Szasz, *The Myth of Mental Illness*, 267–268.

21. Jacob Sullum, "Curing the Therapeutic State: Thomas Szasz Interviewed by Jacob Sullum," *Reason*, July 2000.

22. Leonard Roy Frank, "Tom Szasz: Freedom Fighter," *Madness Network News*, 1972, 12–14.

23. Erving Goffman, *Asylums: Essays on the Social Situation of Mental Patients and Other Inmates* (Anchor Books, 1990), ix–x.

24. Goffman, *Asylums*, 386.

25. Femi Eromosele, "Frantz Fanon in the Time of Mad Studies," *The Journal of New Paradigm Research*, 2020, 6.

26. Luona Lin, Karen Stamm, and Peggy Christidis, "Demographics of the U.S. Psychology Workforce Findings from the 2007–2016 American Community Survey," American Psychological Association, Center for Workforce Studies, 2018.

27. Sherry Hirsch, *Madness Network News* 1, no. 1 (1972): 3.

28. Mel Starkman, "The Movement," in *Mad Matters: A Critical Reader in Canadian Mad Studies*, ed. Brenda A. LeFrançois et al. (Canadian Scholars' Press, 2013), 27.

29. Bradley Lewis, *Moving Beyond Prozac, DSM, and the New Psychiatry* (University of Michigan Press, 2006), 81–98.

30. "Mission Statement—Mad in America," 2021, https://www.madinamerica.com/mission-statement/.

31. Robert Menzies, Brenda A. LeFrançois, and Geoffrey Reaume, "Introducing Mad Studies," in *Mad Matters: A Critical Reader in Canadian Mad Studies*, ed. Brenda A. LeFrançois et al. (Canadian Scholars' Press, 2013), 13.

32. Menzies, LeFrançois, and Reaume, "Introducing Mad Studies," 17.

33. Bonnie Burstow, *Psychiatry Disrupted: Theorizing Resistance and Crafting the r(Evolution)* (McGill-Queen's University Press, 2014), 36.

34. Burstow, *Psychiatry Disrupted*, 36.

SECTION VI

Supernatural Asylums

14

Dracula

The Supernatural in the Asylum

George Higham

Published in 1897, Bram Stoker's *Dracula* is a complex narrative ultimately centered around Doctor Seward's asylum. The madhouse serves as a base of operations for the vampire hunters, led by Dr. Seward and his mentor Dr. Van Helsing. These men of science reluctantly accept that their foe is supernatural, while steadfastly applying their scientific method to both folklore and religion in an effort to defeat this creature of the night. They slowly become aware of Dracula's ability to weaponize madness when their asylum stronghold is breached from within by Seward's pet lunatic, Renfield, secretly a confederate of the vampire count.

The countless film adaptations over the past century routinely abandon Stoker's narrative structure while often combining characters, locations, and motivations—but Renfield's insanity and the madhouse that holds him have remained as iconic to the story as Dracula's Transylvanian castle ruins or his cobweb-covered Carfax Abbey. This essay will compare and contrast Stoker's original asylum with many of the Dracula films adapted from his genre-shaping timeless tale of terror.

That said, we will start with Stoker's story as he intended it, which, we will see, would be forever changed in the mind of popular culture following an unauthorized film version from 1922.

A man of science and a man of action, at 29 years old, Dr. Seward is master of his own asylum. He strives to make a name for himself as a physician of the mind, keeping detailed notes on phonograph cylinders, an innovative method of record-keeping for the novel's 1890s setting.

But Seward is a flawed man. As a failed suitor to Lucy Westenra, the doctor attempts to lose himself in his work. He develops an unhealthy obsession with R.M. Renfield, an inmate of his asylum. Not yet aware of the key role his "pet lunatic" is destined to play in the frightful adventure about to unfold around him, Seward excitedly classifies Renfield as a "zoophagus maniac." Obsessively consuming all manner of lower lifeforms, for Renfield it is about the quantity, not the quality, of his weird dietary impulses. To extend his own life, the madman eats a multitude of insects before moving onto spiders and birds.

Intelligent enough to know that the illness and mystery surrounding his friends lies beyond his understanding, Seward calls upon his mentor, Dr. Van Helsing. Eventually they become aware that the madman in their midst is the herald of Count Dracula, an ancient vampire from the mountains of Transylvania, hell-bent on spreading his dark evil through the heavily populated London area. With losses mounting and more loved ones in danger, the friends band together to stop the evil threat at all costs.

Led by Van Helsing, the team engages in an incredibly logical approach to defeat the supernatural menace. Vampire folklore is researched and studied, teasing out the known strengths and weaknesses of the undead. Lists are made, assets and liabilities are identified, and a plan is formulated to put the victims on the offensive. Even the choices of weapons are impressively logical. Knowing that firearms are futile against the king of the vampires, they recognize that these weapons are nevertheless effective against the natural menaces controlled by this supernatural master: the wolves. The wolves controlled by Dracula would succumb to firepower, as would the band of Gypsies (known today as Romani or Travelers) serving as his henchmen. Stakes, garlic, crucifixes, and holy wafers are employed, but the most useful weapons in their arsenal are the huge knives kept on hand—notably the bowie knife carried by Quincy and the kukri wielded by Harker.

Jonathan Harker is usually present in screen adaptations, while the American Quincy Morris is very rarely seen on the big screen. Stoker's equally rarely filmed climax is the action-packed culmination of a continent-spanning chase that concludes in a bloody battle with Dracula and his Gypsy henchmen as the vampire attempts to flee back to his Transylvanian home following defeat in England.

Dracula was never a love story until it was adapted for the screen. Stoker's female characters were victims of a misogynistic evil that chose them as pawns and as petty revenge against those who hunted him. Stoker's megalomaniacal villain is defeated by cunning and steadfast resolution driven to protect society and certainly fueled by their own thirst for justice after losing some of their own to the vampire. The most common conceit of cinematic adaptations is the attempt to humanize him by giving him a broken, lonely heart along with an air of suave charm. This, along with Stoker's numerous characters and shifting points of view, has resulted in a body of cinema often defined by how different the screen versions are from the printed page.

Ironically, the first screen adaptation, which was unauthorized, remains one of the more faithful to the character of Dracula himself. The film is also guilty of establishing the love-story angle that has dominated the three most popular versions of the tale: *Dracula* (1931), *Dracula* (1979), and *Bram Stoker's Dracula* (1992).

F.W. Murnau's *Nosferatu* (1922) was the brainchild of producer/designer Albin Grau, who conspired with Henrik Galeen to create a rogue adaptation from within Germany, a safe enough distance from Bram Stoker's England where Florence Stoker, his widow, kept a watchful eye on the legacy of his writing as she slowly went broke. Feeble efforts such as simply changing the characters' names while streamlining the complex narrative ultimately failed, and a legendary lawsuit was born. The unfolding legal drama is nearly as complex as Stoker's tale itself, best covered by David J. Skal in his definitive study of Dracula's journey to the silver screen, *Hollywood Gothic*.

Murnau grounded Grau's supernatural story in a natural world of decaying Gothic architecture, avoiding the artifice made popular by Germany's *The Cabinet of Dr. Caligari* in 1919, while still adhering to an Expressionist style. Grau, an occultist in real life, infused the visuals with occult symbols while shifting the film's locale to Wisborg and moving the story's setting back to 1838. He designed Count Orlok (Max Schreck), the barely disguised "Count Dracula" character, as a cadaverous, rodent-like old man. He

In Tod Browning's *Dracula* (1931), the captive, insect-eating "pet lunatic" Renfield (Dwight Frye) grasps the bars of his squalid cell in Dr. Seward's Asylum as he pleads with Count Dracula (Bela Lugosi), who stands outside the photo frame.

introduced a plague subplot wholly befitting the tale while streamlining much of Stoker's plot—also setting a precedent for all future versions.

But regardless of the cuts and changes, there is still a madman in an asylum serving as the vampire's herald. Knock, an estate broker (Alexander Granach), stands in for Renfield while Professor Sievers, the Doctor (Gustav Botz), stands in for Doctor Seward. Knock sends Hutter (Gustav von Wangenheim), aka Harker, to Transylvania for a real estate deal to sell local property to the Count. As in Stoker's novel, Knock becomes more unhinged as the Count's journey brings him nearer and nearer. "Stark raving mad," Knock is confined to a cell within Sievers's madhouse—a rough corner with stone walls and high, barred windows. The cell walls are disturbingly etched with bizarre scrawled symbols and random scratching apparently done by crazed fingernails. Sievers rubs his beard while contemplating Knock, watching him eat flies and shout out "Blood is the Life!"

He is hardly fazed when Knock attacks him, and he has the inmate bound with rough rope following the incident. With Orlok's arrival, Knock strangles the guard and escapes his dungeon-like cell. As the plague overtakes the town, those who survive believe Knock himself to be the vampire and hunt him down after he runs amok over the rooftops and through the fields.

Nosferatu draws a definite parallel between insanity and evil—for Knock is under the (unexplained) influence of Count Orlok from the start, equipping Hutter with a strange contract to deliver to the Count, written in occult symbols. He facilitates the Count's coming to the town of Wisborg, and as such is indirectly responsible for the deaths of seemingly hundreds of villagers. Unlike Stoker's Renfield, Knock is unrepentant. Hog-tied back in his cell as the film concludes, he declares with a note of sadness, "The master is dead."

As Stoker intended Renfield, there was an internal struggle within the man's mind—and when the good in Renfield began to win, Dracula beat him to death within the asylum. Dracula used Renfield to gain entrance into Seward's madhouse, for according to vampire lore the undead may not cross a threshold uninvited. As an inmate within the asylum, Renfield's invitation allowed the Count to breach the stronghold of his enemies. While *Nosferatu* eliminates this subplot, it sets up Knock/Renfield as an outside agent destined to go insane in the many adaptations that followed.

Prior to the game-changing 1931 *Dracula*, one other adaptation would forever alter Stoker's tale. The Hamilton Deane/John L. Balderston stage play (1927) would continue the consolidation of characters and locations while trimming down the plot—and the action. Interestingly, the play was centered around Seward's asylum, using it as the main location for its three acts.[1] The stage play proved to be successful in both London and New York, generating interest from Universal Studios as a property worth pursuing.[2] Universal not only purchased the adaptation rights to the plays, they also managed to secure one of the only stateside prints of *Nosferatu*![3]

With the rights firmly in hand, both *Nosferatu* and the stage plays were used as inspiration for the Universal film *Dracula* (1931), directed by Tod Browning. Stoker's novel had been perceived as an imposing narrative, but these earlier adaptations provided a blueprint for the screenplay.[4] An early sound film, Browning's production played out more like a stage play than a movie, with limited sets and far fewer characters than intended by Stoker.[5] Casting Bela Lugosi as Dracula would be the next drastic change from Stoker's text, one that would forever thereafter cement the association of Dracula as a suave foreigner.[6]

The secondary character-swapping took hold in the narrative, carrying on the consolidation already established in *Nosferatu*, but streamlining further by having Renfield (Dwight Frye at his manic best) travel to Castle Dracula and subsequently go insane. As the sole survivor of the infamous sea voyage to England, Renfield is a raving lunatic by the time Dracula's ship runs aground on the English shoreline. Dr. Seward is now Mina's father, and Renfield is quickly committed to his asylum when found on the ship, becoming his "pet loony." Renfield frequently escapes, apparently with Dracula's help, often stalking the halls of Seward's home, connected to the asylum and situated next door to Dracula's new abode, Carfax Abbey. Renfield confesses to Van Helsing that Dracula has promised him "rats ... thousands, millions of them" for his subservience. While not expressly played out onscreen, it is implied that this entails facilitating Dracula's entrance into Seward's asylum to perform his nefarious acts.

Nearly three decades of spin-offs and sequels followed before the next big-screen Dracula event. While significant within the history of Dracula cinema, Hammer's *Horror of Dracula* (1958) eliminated both Renfield and the asylum setting. While there *is* a Dr. Seward (Charles Lloyd-Pack), the character exists merely as a confused physician unable to assist in any way other than giving Dr. Van Helsing a reason to step in as the more qualified "second opinion." The film remains noteworthy for introducing

Christopher Lee as Dracula, along with Peter Cushing as his nemesis Dr. Van Helsing. *Horror of Dracula* was but one of the Hammer entries in a series of films which brought the reimaginings of Universal's monster movies to life in shocking color. The only nod to Stoker's Dr. Seward comes by way of a quick scene where Van Helsing records his medical notes (about vampires) on a cylinder phonograph, a detail rarely presented in the Dracula movies. Christopher Lee would continue to play Dracula through the Hammer series of Dracula films, taking time out to portray the Count in another production as well—*Count Dracula* (1970).

Once again playing musical chairs with characters and motivations, Jess Franco's *Count Dracula* features a rather subdued Renfield (Klaus Kinski) as an inmate in Dr. Van Helsing's (Herbert Lom) and Dr. Seward's (Paul Muller) asylum. It is here that Jonathan Harker (Fred Williams) is found senseless following his escape from Castle Dracula. The asylum remains the main location throughout the film, while maintaining the concept of being close to Carfax Abbey, the property that Dracula moves into.

Even though Christopher Lee touted the film as the most faithful version of *Dracula* ever made, the story is filled with numerous differences. What *is* faithful, however, is Lee's portrayal of the Count as having gray hair and a mustache, adhering to Stoker's description and a rarity on the silver screen.

A major unexplainable difference has Van Helsing wheelchair-bound due to a stroke. Second in charge, Dr. Seward strives to help Renfield, who remains silent for most of the film. Renfield is kept in a padded cell, but a barred window is within reach, which he pries open and subsequently jumps from, injuring his neck and arm. Seward continues to comfort him to the best of his ability. Regardless of the kind treatment given by Dr. Seward, Renfield attacks Mina (Maria Rohm) at the hypnotic suggestion of Dracula, choking her … but Dracula's mental faculties are strained at the time while he psychically defends himself against Harker and Quincy[7] (Soledad Miranda) as they locate his resting place in Carfax. He causes a horrible attack upon them by ratty, taxidermied creatures while simultaneously controlling Renfield, but loses his mental grasp on both when Harker brandishes a crucifix to defend himself. Even though straitjacketed, Renfield's treatment appears to be otherwise sympathetic, an approach which is not present in most other adaptations.

Within a decade, Kinski would return to the big screen in another adaptation of Stoker's tale—but this time he would be on the other side of the grave. Headlining in Werner Herzog's "remake" of Murnau's famous film, Kinski took on the role of *Nosferatu, the Vampyre* (1979). Every bit as boring as Murnau's version was terrifying, Kinski's performance is once again subdued, appropriate only to the slow pace of the film's narrative. Drs. Seward and Van Helsing are combined into a reluctant, ineffectual Dr. Van Helsing (Walter Ladengast), whose asylum is seen as little more than a single, cramped wood-barred cell where a giggly Renfield (Roland Topor) is kept locked up. Even as things come to a head, the doctor refuses to aid Lucy (Isabelle Adjani), insisting that they research vampire-hunting methodology even when there is not a moment to spare.

Strangely, Herzog declared Murnau's *Nosferatu* the "most important film ever made in Germany," yet (as seen above) he proceeded to change the character's name back to the name in the novel, in an effort to "have a continuity in film history."[8]

That same year also brought John Badham's *Dracula* (1979), famous for upping the ante on the love story and for casting heartthrob Frank Langella as a fangless vampire count. In keeping with the cinematic *Dracula* tradition, the film takes great liberties with the characters and motivations while crediting the Balderston/Deane play, which had been reinterpreted for a Broadway run in the late 1970s. The Broadway play also featured Langella in the title role and was known for the stylized sets designed by Edward Gorey, to the degree that paper "toy theaters" were made available which recreated Gorey's gothic designs in paper miniatures. While not as set-bound as the play, Badham did limit his locations while centering the action around Seward's Whitby Asylum, making this film very asylum-centric. Donald Pleasence appears as a rather ineffectual Dr. Seward, annoyingly eating in almost every scene while playing second fiddle to Laurence Olivier as Dr. Van Helsing.

Seward's asylum is a multi-tiered madhouse, perfectly suited to John Badham's direction, with an eye toward overly gothic and creepy set dressings viewed through a desaturated color palette. Lucy (Kate Nelligan) is Seward's daughter, while Mina (Jan Francis) is the child of Van Helsing. Renfield (Tony Haygarth) goes insane after selling Carfax Abbey to Dracula and helping the vampire move in. The madhouse in which he is committed is truly a place of madness. Suggestive of a human zoo, it is a filthy place populated by background characters which epitomize stereotypes of insanity. The most illogical inclusion is an obviously unstable woman, allowed to keep her infant child with her among the inmates. Obviously, this does not end well.

The next notable contribution to Dracula films came in 1992, courtesy of Francis Ford Coppola. *Bram Stoker's Dracula* (1992) went out of its way to credit the author of the novel in the title, while also going out of its way to deviate from the tale by promoting the tagline, "Love Never Dies."

That said, Coppola does give us what is undoubtedly the most accurate characterization of Dr. Seward ever put to film. In a rare, very accurate depiction, Dr. Seward (Richard E. Grant) is presented as the young 29-year-old physician described by Stoker in the original novel. As in the novel, he is inappropriate in his continuing affections for Lucy after being rejected as a suitor. As in the book, he distracts himself with Renfield (Tom Waits), his "pet lunatic."

Once again, the onscreen asylum is suggestive of a zoo. Seward's "Carfax Asylum" is reminiscent of the giant cage area from *Planet of the Apes* (1968), even sharing scenes in which the inmates are hosed down with powerful blasts of water. In *Apes*, the human prisoner Taylor (Charlton Heston) shouts "It's a madhouse … a MADHOUSE!" as he is mercilessly hosed down by a sadistic ape-guard. While Taylor is distressed by the topsy-turvy world dominated by cruel apes, Coppola's use of a similar architecture is a literal madhouse-asylum.[9]

To ensure that the asylum/zoo metaphor is not lost on the movie audience, Coppola intercuts scenes of both inmates and animals from the London Zoo going berserk during a raging storm as Dracula lands on the shores of England.[10]

Dr. Seward's treatment of Renfield includes goading him on. While not evil, his approach is questionable. The doctor then retreats to his private office to shoot morphine while dictating case notes onto cylinder phonographs, another nod to Stoker's innovative use of technology in his 1897 novel.

Coppola provides countless fanciful touches throughout the film. Tom Waits as Renfield is equipped with weird finger cups wired to a gauntlet, seemingly aiding his ability to catch flies. Harnesses seem to be the dominant theme here, as Seward wears unnaturally wide suspenders and his asylum team wear cages over their heads to protect them from the potentially violent patient/inmates. Believing he was betrayed by

Renfield trying to warn Mina away, Dracula invades Renfield's cell in cloud form and kills him by viciously slamming him into the bars.

A more recent addition to Dracula cinema updates not only the story, but the asylum setting as well. *Renfield* (2023) features Nicholas Hoult as R.M. Renfield and Nicolas Cage as Dracula. Nearly a century of subservience has driven Renfield to the point of desperation, having him fall in with a 12-step group therapy program he had originally planned on using as a hunting ground for the abusive partners of the attendees. He sought to assuage his conscience by eliminating the abusers but soon realizes that he himself is trapped within an abusive codependent relationship. The redemption he seeks while helping them is turned inward, giving him the strength to end his relationship with Dracula, although the vampire count is not one to let his servant walk away so easily. The cleverly comedic approach substitutes modern group therapy via the self-help theater of contemporary treatment of chronically abused people in lieu of the traditional asylum setting.

Throughout the countless movie adaptations of *Dracula*, filmmakers have sought original approaches, often elevating secondary elements from within the narrative to be the focal points of some looser adaptations of Stoker's original concepts. Dracula's nemesis, his underling—even the schooner that transported his coffins to Whitby, England—were all featured as the main subjects of feature films, some quite recent, proving the enduring appeal. *Van Helsing* (2004), *Renfield* (2023), and *The Last Voyage of the Demeter* (2023) are but a few of the films expanding the Dracula universe, while even Nosferatu has maintained his shadowy, clawed grasp on popular culture with remakes in 1979 and 2024 and a fanciful glimpse behind the scenes of the 1922 original by way of E. Elias Merhige's *Shadow of the Vampire* (2000).

With so many aspects of Stoker's novel being mined for movie material over the past century, it is just a matter of time before Seward's asylum takes center stage on the silver screen.

Notes

1. Lyndon W. Joslin, *Count Dracula Goes to the Movies: Stoker's Novel Adapted, 1922–2003*, 2nd Edition (McFarland, 2006), 25.
2. Alain Silver and James Ursini, *The Vampire Film from* Nosferatu *to* Bram Stoker's Dracula, *Revised and Updated* (Limelight Editions, 1993), 50.
3. David J. Skal, *Hollywood Gothic* (Faber and Faber, revised 2004), 150–161.
4. Roy Kinnard, *Horror in Silent Films: A Filmography, 1896–1929* (McFarland, 1995), 137.
5. Donald F. Glut, *The Dracula Book* (Scarecrow Press, 1975), 113.
6. John Edgar Browning and Caroline Joan (Kay) Picart, *Dracula in Visual Media: Film, Television, Comic Book and Electronic Game Appearances, 1921–2010* (McFarland, 2011), 4.
7. One of the very few appearances onscreen of the "Quincy Morris" character. In Stoker's novel, he was an American cowboy-type and suitor of Lucy Westenra. Films such as this one often swap Lucy/Mina, but this one goes as far as giving the English nobleman-suitor Arthur Holmwood the American character's name.
8. Rolf Giesen, *Golem, Caligari, Nosferatu: A Chronicle of German Fantasy Film* (Bear Manor Media, 2021), 61–62.
9. Coppola's unofficial nod to the *Apes* franchise would eventually circle back in 2017's *War for the Planet of the Apes*, which featured knowing winks at the famous director's classic *Apocalypse Now* (1979).
10. Francis Ford Coppola and James V. Hart, *Bram Stoker's Dracula: The Film and the Legend* (Newmarket Press, 1992), 66–67.

15

Session 9

Danvers State Hospital Is the Star of the Show

Brenda S. Gardenour Walter

"It is among the most painful features of insanity, that in its treatment, so many are compelled to leave their families."—Thomas Kirkbride, 1854

"We say haunted, but the house has gone insane."—Ellen Rimbauer in Stephen King's *Rose Red*

The psychological horror film *Session 9* (2001) is set amid the ruins of the State Lunatic Hospital at Danvers, Massachusetts, later known as the Danvers State Hospital, with a focus on the Kirkbride building at the center of the sprawling complex. The two main characters in the film are the asylum itself and Gordon Fleming, the owner of the company charged with asbestos abatement in the Kirkbride structure. Throughout the film, the haunted histories of the asylum and Fleming, two tragic manifestations of failed fatherhood, become increasingly intertwined. Based on the work of Dr. Thomas Story Kirkbride, the Danvers asylum was designed as a type of specialized domestic architecture, a patriarchal *domus* with the power to nurture, protect, and potentially heal those suffering from mental illness. In Kirkbride's vision, residents lived under the loving guidance of the chief physician as father, as members of a family unit in a structure designed to both accommodate and modify their behavior.

In his 1854 treatise, *On the Construction, Organization, and General Arrangements of Hospitals for the Insane*, Kirkbride repeatedly argues that the domestic model of mental healthcare grounded in his architectural design for the asylum depends on hiring a chief physician with the fortitude and stability to rule the complex family within its walls. Kirkbride likewise warns the reader that the total number of residents at the asylum must never exceed 250 people.[1] With more than 250 residents, the strongest chief physician could not provide the necessary love, guidance, and physical care, nor could the architectural *domus* offer nurturing and safety. Despite Kirkbride's repeated warnings, the Danvers asylum, which was originally designed to accommodate 500 patients, became increasingly overcrowded. By 1930, its population had reached 2,073 while its staff and financial resources had dwindled. Kirkbride's vision of the asylum as a nurturing and well-ordered upper-middle-class domicile led by a competent patriarch had proven unsustainable. Understaffed, underfunded, and pushed to the point of breakage, the idealized "good family" home had become an impoverished "broken home" plagued by absentee caregivers, neglect, and physical

This intentionally ambiguous poster for *Session 9* (2001), with its empty chair sitting center stage, lets spectators decide if the unsettling images witnessed at the asbestos-laden Danvers State Hospital are ghostly apparitions or hallucinatory visions.

abuse. The introduction of pharmacotherapy, the process of deinstitutionalization, and the dwindling of patient populations led to the shuttering of Danvers State Hospital in 1992. No longer a home at all, Danvers became a haunted house high atop a hill, seemingly devoid of human life yet alive with persistent memories and the weight of a complex history.

Gordon Fleming's character in *Session 9* is a microcosm of the asylum, reflecting not only the institution's history but also its dysfunctional architectural embodiment. After years of infertility, Gordon and his wife, Wendy, eventually conceive a child. Gordon enters fatherhood with love and hope, but the exhaustion of parenting a colicky baby, running a failing business, and his own advanced age soon overwhelms him. Like the asylum, his mind becomes overcrowded with worries beyond its capacity, a breakage that leads to the physical destruction of his family and the abandonment of his home. Having murdered his wife and child, Gordon secretly moves to the asylum, where his mental health continues to deteriorate while attempting to lead the asbestos abatement team that depends upon him. Isolated from quotidian life within the abandoned asylum, both Gordon and his team members experience slippage.

A broken home, the Kirkbride building magnifies mental illnesses such as nyctophobia (an extreme fear of the dark), obsessive-compulsive disorder, and addiction. One by one, Gordon kills each member of the work family for whom he was responsible, much as he murdered his wife and child. At the film's conclusion, Gordon commits himself to a room in the ward for the criminally insane, where he pastes photos of his family on the wall, thereby recreating a broken home within a broken home. Pushed to the point of breakage, unable to care for their families, both the asylum and Gordon are failed patriarchs who ultimately destroy those they were meant to protect. Residing at the interstices of architectural theory and human suffering, *Session 9* serves as a warped and potentially compassionate lens through which we might view the convoluted history of the insane asylum and its architecture—from Kirkbride's idealism to domestic dysfunction and displacement—in 19th- and 20th-century America.

Domestic Utopias: From Kirkbride to the Suburbs

The State Lunatic Hospital at Danvers was constructed between 1874 and 1878. The plans for the asylum followed the work of Dr. Thomas Story Kirkbride, a Quaker physician specializing in the care of the mentally ill. In his seminal text, *On the Construction, Organization, and General Arrangements of Hospitals for the Insane* (1854), Kirkbride grounds the architectural form and function of the insane asylum in the 19th-century domestic ideals. In the upper-middle-class world of Kirkbride, the structure of the family home was a projection of patriarchal embodiment and power. Like a good father, this rational and mechanistic domain ordered the lives of those living within it, promoting productivity while providing physical and moral protection. The interior of the home was divided into communal spaces such as parlors and dining rooms, and private spaces such as bedrooms and bathrooms.[2]

In keeping with Victorian architectural norms, communal areas were most often located toward the front and center of the house and private areas removed toward the back or hidden upstairs, away from prying eyes.[3] In private areas of the home, family members were segregated into hermetically sealed compartments where bodily activities long considered shameful—sexual activity, defecation, urination, emesis—were cloaked behind doors.[4] The Victorian home was at once a space of exclusion and containment, its thick walls meant to protect inhabitants from chaotic external forces, thereby serving as a container for "safety, privacy, and family."[5]

Subordinated within this patriarchal structure, the matron functioned as the loving angel of the house. The loving motherly spirit within the rigid fatherly body, the matron nurtured her children, guided her household in Christian morality, and reinforced patriarchal ideals. Fatherly structuring and motherly nurturing were believed to produce stable and productive members of the middle class who would go on to perpetuate the good standing of the family name. According to this bourgeois ideal, those raised outside of well-ordered domiciles—especially children born to lower-class working families from "broken" homes—were seen as susceptible to criminality and insanity. Victorian correlations between poverty and criminality are writ large in Charles Booth's *London Poverty Maps* (1886–1903) and persist into the present day.

As a physician and member of the upper middle class, Kirkbride perpetuated contemporary domestic ideologies in his design for the insane asylum. In *On the Construction, Organization, and General Arrangements of Hospitals for the Insane* (1854), Kirkbride argues that the asylum should be located in a semi-rural area, removed from the disorder and filth of urban life. The fenced perimeter of the asylum should contain "30 to 50 acres of pleasure grounds" for the health and benefit of residents and their families, between whom there was fluid contact.[6] As to the building itself, it should be of "cheerful and comfortable appearance," with "everything repulsive and prison-like" being "carefully avoided."[7] The structure itself can be imagined as a series of interlinked domestic spheres, at the center of which was the main house through which all patients entered the asylum. This core structure, or Kirkbride building, was imposing, having multiple floors and large towers that loomed over the complex and grounds. At Danvers, for example, the Kirkbride building featured a phallic central tower, six stories tall, topped by a soaring spire, and flanked by steeply pitched gables in the Gothic-revival style. Built of brick and stone and having an ornate façade, the Kirkbride building was designed to reassure patients that resources were plentiful and that the structure was stable and well ordered. This central structure contained the main kitchen and storerooms on the basement floor; a reception area, offices, a shared library, and parlors for visiting relatives on the main floors; and the private home of the chief physician or superintendent and his family on the upper floors.[8] The Kirkbride building served as the main patriarchal domus. For purposes for control and sexual sanitation, men and women patients were segregated into separate wings. Each wing, in turn, was divided into wards that served specific patient populations. At the farthest end of the wing, on the highest floors, were the most violent and potentially incurable patients. These spaces were designed for protective containment and intensive monitoring by caregivers.

Isolation and mechanical restraint were deemed "evils of no trifling magnitude" and were forbidden in Kirkbride's model of moral care.[9] Ideally, even these patients would begin to recover and move inward and downward through the wings where individual wards became less restrictive and more focused on rehabilitation through domestic integration. The goal was for patients to fully recover and exit the asylum through the same doors that they entered and return to society as productive and stable members of the community.

Kirkbride's asylum was a middle-class patriarchal domus not only in its architectural form but also in its function. The successful treatment of the patients living in the asylum was predicated on the presence of a strong, capable, and loving father in the form of the chief physician or superintendent. Beyond being a highly skilled medical authority, the chief physician must also be a stern head of household able to manage the asylum's "farm, and garden, its pleasure grounds … its varied internal arrangements, its furniture, its table service and the food, the mode in which its domestic concerns are carried on, everything connected with it … in order to secure harmony, economy, and successful results."[10] Despite this great responsibility, the chief physician should rule with silent strength, with power that might be "unseen and unfelt, but a knowledge of its existence will often alone prevent wrangling and difficulties in the household, and secure regularity, good order, and an efficient discipline about the whole establishment."[11] Any perceived weakness in the patriarch's authority might weaken the functioning of the household and result in chaos. For this reason, Kirkbride warns that "a man to whom this amount of power cannot be safely entrusted certainly is not the proper person to be placed at the head of an institution containing 250 insane patients."

Under the direction of the chief physician was the matron, who maintained the "domestic arrangements of the house" and managed the nurses who served as motherly figures on the wards.[12] As in the main house, the wards were sharply divided into public areas where patients could interact, and private areas for sleeping and personal hygiene, thereby ensuring patient dignity as they recovered. Daily care was to be provided by nurses assigned to no more than two patients, ensuring a close and nurturing relationship. In Kirkbride's model, the asylum's wings functioned much like family bedrooms in a large Victorian home, and as a microcosm of the chief physician's patriarchal domus.

The domestic model that drove Kirkbride's vision of therapeutic care has remained salient in the form and function of the nuclear, cishet suburban family home such as that occupied by Gordon Fleming and his young family in *Session 9*. Like Kirkbride's asylum, the suburban family home is a middle-class fortress that functions as a space of exclusion and containment. In keeping with Kirkbride's model, the cishet suburban home is not only a space of ordering, but also a patriarchal *domus* where father knows best. As "king of his castle," the patriarch controls not only his house-body and its perimeter, but also the bodies of those dwelling within it. Under the direction of the strong father, the loving mother raises the children and manages a healthy home where everything has its place. The unspoken cultural belief is that children raised in such "good homes" will experience minimal trauma and grow to be happy and productive adult consumers who contribute to society and perpetuate the mythical American dream.

The very real Danvers State Hospital and Gordon Fleming's fictional home in *Session 9* were both built on middle-class utopian visions of the domestic sphere as a healing space, a nurturing place that could shape the bodies and mental health of those dwelling within them. Through this lens, the construct of the perfect middle-class home becomes a self-soothing narrative to mask domestic violence, neglect, and sexual abuse, all of which are more common than reflected in already horrifying statistics. At an even deeper level, the façade of the "good home" obscures the chaotic nature of embodiment, including the existence of disease and mental illnesses beyond our control. Although the healthiest domestic environment might mitigate some of the symptoms of mental illness, it cannot cure it. A broken home, however, can exacerbate mental illness and cause acute trauma that haunts future generations. Because of the cherished values related to the middle-class "good home" and the stigmatization of those from often impoverished "bad homes," the social reality of domestic dysfunction is often hidden behind white picket fences and neat exteriors, as well as behind the false faces of parental authorities and fathers who do not "know what's best."

Broken Homes: Institutional and Domestic Violence

Thomas Kirkbride's utopian vision of the State Lunatic Hospital at Danvers as a good family home failed almost as it began. Kirkbride believed that nearly all mental illnesses were curable with proper care and, therefore, preferred the term "Hospital for the Insane" rather than "asylum." By shifting the language around institutional care, he hoped to lessen the stigma and horrifying associations attached to insanity and madhouses. His emphasis on moral care meant that patients were no longer restrained, while the domestication of mental illness created an inviting and homely environment for family and visitors. The institution's grounds were open to family, curious visitors, and those who simply wanted to picnic amid the lush landscape at the "Castle on the Hill," enjoying cool summer breezes. Kirkbride's attempts at normalizing institutional care, however, did little to shift public perception of the institutionalized insane. For many, the asylum broadly construed remained a locus of horror, a place of forcible confinement and brutal treatment for those who were lost to society.

The citizens of Danvers, Massachusetts, likewise had fiscal concerns about the asylum, which was subsidized by the state. For those living humble lives in the town at the bottom of the hill, the decadent nature of the asylum, from N.J. Bradlee's grandiose "Domestic Gothic" architecture to its landscaped grounds and well-stocked larder, seemed a waste of money. In 1877, Massachusetts senator E.F. Sanborn argued that "even many a royal palace is neither so large nor so pretentious architecturally as the hospital at Danvers."[13] Kirkbride's vision was, after all, based on an upper-middle-class model of domesticity, something unattainable for most of the people paying for the institution through taxation. By 1890, therefore, the Danvers asylum had become a locus of fear, suspicion, and resentment despite its purported openness.

By the early 20th century, collective concerns about the asylum had become well justified due to overcrowding and underfunding. Kirkbride's hospital architecture was designed to "accommodate 250 patients."[14] The Danvers asylum was designed to accommodate 500 patients, double Kirkbride's recommendation. Throughout the late 19th century and into the 20th, continued economic downturns meant that many families could not afford to care for the suffering mentally ill at home and sent them to Danvers. Additionally, the closure of other regional hospitals brought increasing numbers of chronic cases into the asylum. While the Danvers asylum was state funded, it relied on a significant number of private patients who could pay for care. According to the *Annual Report of the Trustees of the Danvers State Hospital* for 1910, private patients brought in $36,476 of revenue as compared to just over $23,500 for state funded patients.

By the Great Depression in 1930, there were 2,078 patients at Danvers, most of them requiring public assistance. While the institution continued to produce its own food, labor laws limited the work that could be done by patients, thereby reducing the institution's ability to sustain itself. The growing patient population likewise required an increased staff, including physicians and nurses at the forefront of advanced mental health care. The upkeep of the elaborate Victorian Kirkbride building and the vast surrounding complex, which included a nursing school, staff and student housing, occupational therapy sites, and a working farm, presented nightmarish funding and staffing challenges.

Overcrowding, the yearly cutback of government funds, and chronic understaffing led to the collapse of Kirkbride's ideal of moral care and the decay of the patriarchal domus meant to provide domestic healing to the suffering sick. The continued admission of patients to a burgeoning chronic population meant that the domestic structure envisioned by Kirkbride could not function as a space for healing. Nurses and orderlies meant to provide care in these domestic subunits were quickly overburdened, leading to neglect and, in some cases, restraint and physical punishment. Patients who were once seen as children had become objects of control, transforming the family home into a prison. The chief physician, overwhelmed by the demand for care in a financially failing institution, became a nearly absentee father. As a result, the Kirkbride building that was originally designed as a "good home" became an impoverished "broken home" that confined and, in some cases, damaged those within its walls.

With its form and function radically disconnected, the irrational Kirkbride building at Danvers became a locus of insanity that participated in a codependent relationship with its inhabitants, each imprinting dysfunction on the other. Architectural theory postulates that just as buildings can affect human behavior and embodiment, so can humans imprint upon the built environment. As a body within a body, the human organism "spreads out and connects with the environment like an invisible network," with information flowing from body to building and back again.[15] This "singularity of self and world" marks the relationship between body and building as a form of embodied knowledge. The intertwining of human and architectural embodiment is most sustained and intense in our multivalent sensory experience of home. Beyond the visual, auditory, and olfactory is our haptic experience of dwelling space. Our skin brushes against walls, presses into furniture, makes pathways on floors as we wear patterns into a home's surfaces. Like birds, we nestle into spaces, shaping them with our bodies, making them our own, as noted by Sarah Robinson in her study of "Nested Bodies."[16]

At Danvers, patients imprinted themselves onto the structure by creating nests in their rooms, filling them with photographs and drawings, wearing footsteps into the floors, marking the walls with handprints. At the height of overcrowding, the walls and floors of the institution would have borne evidence of bodily leakage—urine, feces, blood—the smells from which would have been masked with bleach and other cleaning solvents. We might imagine the auditory experiences of such an environment, with the sounds of quotidian life punctuated by moans, cries, screams, laughter, and chatter. As the population size at Danvers dwindled due to the introduction of psychotherapeutic drugs and, by the 1970s, the demands of deinstitutionalization, the imprints of former patients and their experiences remained in the building—like old family photos, or ghosts wandering the wards. This visceral presence of history, this weight of human suffering, is one reason why the Danvers asylum has remained a locus of horror in the collective imagination, a place best shuttered and forgotten.

The historical experience of architectural embodiment including the failure of the patriarchal domus and the reciprocal imprinting of the family home upon its members is echoed in the narrative of Gordon in *Session 9*. A microcosm of the asylum's history, Gordon believes in the wholeness of the nuclear family. After years of infertility, he and his wife finally conceive a child, believing that parenthood will bring joy and stability to their lives. The film's opening scenes make it clear that Gordon and his wife are finding parenting difficult, in great part because their child suffers from colic and no one in his household is getting any sleep. Exhausted and overwhelmed, Gordon also faces the financial challenges of providing for his family. As the owner of a small asbestos abatement company, his income is tied to his ability to win bids. Increased competition from larger firms has left Gordon on the edge of bankruptcy, leading him to promise the completion of the Danvers State Hospital project in an unrealistically short time.

Having won the contract bid, Gordon buys flowers for his wife and returns home with the good news, optimistically believing that the influx of funds into his failing household will restore order. In a series of recovered memories throughout the film, the horrifying events of that night are revealed. Gordon arrives home and through the open front door sees his wife in the kitchen, truly exhausted, holding a crying baby. He enters with the flowers, hugs his wife, and the door closes. Through auditory snippets, the viewer learns that his wife spilled hot boiling water on Gordon's leg as she prepared pasta for her family. Pain, exhaustion, and anxiety led Gordon to lash out, killing his wife, child, and the family dog in a fit of rage. Having failed as a husband and a father, Gordon then leaves the house with the flowers, closing the blinds and locking the front door as a means of burying the truth both architecturally and psychologically. Gordon's psychotic break and the domestic violence that ensued are written on the home's interior, with the ruptured and broken bodies of his wife and baby slowly suppurating in the chaotic kitchen. From the street, the home's façade, like a false face, hides the horror within. Once discovered, the house will forever be marked as a "murder house" in local lore, a place stained by moral failure, the most broken of family homes.

Gordon, like the domestic architecture within which he once dwelled, bears a false façade that hides his internal chaos. Unable to return home and face the abject horror of his actions, Gordon moves into the abandoned asylum—from one broken home to another—in a state of dissociation. At the institution, Gordon's asbestos abatement team joins him to form a new family unit, one which he determines to remain in control of. Each member of the skeleton crew working in the Kirkbride at Danvers is an embodiment of irrational masculinity and failed patriarchy. Gordon's business partner and close friend, Phil, has just been jilted by his long-term girlfriend, Amy, to be with a younger man named Hank, who is also a member of the team. Hank jokes disparagingly that Amy wanted a man who could perform sexually, intimating that Phil is inadequately masculine. To cope with his pain, Phil uses marijuana to induce a mild state of dissociation. Young and handsome, Hank is a narcissist who suffers from a gambling addiction. After finding a cache of silver coins in the institution's morgue, he determines to dump his new girlfriend and head to Atlantic City but never gets a chance. Jeff, the youngest member of the team and Gordon's biological nephew, suffers from nyctophobia and is terrified of the dark. Still in his teens, Jeff has not yet reached manhood and is seen as a scared child in need of a night-light.

Mike is a failed law student who now works in a blue-collar world. Still an academic, he is drawn to the records room in the institution's basement where he finds moldering boxes containing fragments of forgotten lives. There he becomes obsessed with the patient file of Mary, a young girl with dissociative identity disorder. As Mike reads documents and listens to tapes of her therapy sessions, he discovers that Simon, one of Mary's male alter egos, stabbed her family to death after her brother broke her porcelain doll. A nested narrative of domestic violence, the brother shatters the baby doll and Simon-Mary slaughters the family in a fit of pain and rage, just as Gordon destroys his nuclear family and, ultimately, his work family at the asylum. Throughout the film, the cracks in Gordon's false façade of normalcy and rationality widen to the point of breakage. As the blistered burns on his leg begin to seep through his pant leg, so too do the horrifying memories of domestic destruction. In a state of slippage, unable to manage his team, he kills his men one by one and sequesters their bodies in solitary spaces within the institution like a father sending naughty children to their squalid rooms. Believing that he has contained the contamination and restored imaginary order within the shattered structure, Gordon moves into Mary's old room in the female wing for the criminally insane. There, he creates a fragmented domestic space nested within a failed domestic institution, pasting the walls with pictures of his family at their infant daughter's baptism, a sacrament that promises rebirth and the washing away of sins, a ritual theologically grounded in the sacrifice of a child.

Domestic Displacement: The Haunted and Homeless

At the conclusion of *Session 9*, the Danvers State Hospital remains an abandoned and chaotic mess, a broken home containing the leaky bodies of Gordon's team and the fragmented memories of those who once lived there. The interweaving of Mary's story and the voices of her alter egos from the session tapes into the film's narrative introduces the possibility that ghosts or demons possessed Gordon and caused him to commit violence. The ruined Kirkbride building with its crumbling turrets and once-decadent ornamentation is an ideal haunted house, especially in an American culture where the

Victorian past has come to signify corruption and decay.[17] Even before its abandonment, the Kirkbride at Danvers was imagined as a haunted house of horrors by writers of the supernatural.[18] For example, H.P. Lovecraft used Danvers as the inspiration for Arkham Asylum in the Cthulhu mythos, a fictional institution that continues to haunt popular culture in the DC *Batman* universe. Despite these overlays, despite the historical conflation of psychosis with the supernatural and the film's intentional ambiguity about this topic, and despite the fact that some readings of this film may emphasize the supernatural over the natural, in this author's view, the haunting in *Session 9* is not paranormal, and the ghost of a mentally ill child is not to blame for the dissolution of Gordon's sanity. Instead, Gordon, his family home, and the asylum are all haunted by mental illness, human suffering, and the horrors of mistreatment both intentional and unintentional. Each is likewise a testament to the detrimental effects of impossibly idealized and oversimplified visions of perfection, be it that of fatherhood, the family home, or mental stability. No amount of patriarchal rationality can order the organic chaos of the human experience or the complexities of being fully alive. Perhaps the most powerful phantasm in *Session 9* is our collective sorrow, guilt, and helplessness in our inability to care for those who suffer from incurable and illegible mental illnesses. Like Gordon, we sit in cemeteries making calls to those we love on broken phones, perched on numbered graves without names, praying for contact.

Unable to return home, legally unable to live at Danvers, Gordon is lost in transmission, trapped between two broken homes. Since deinstitutionalization in the 1970s, this has been the very real experience of many individuals who were once confined to Danvers State Hospital.

After the institution's official closure in 1992, patients requiring continual care were sent to Tewksbury Hospital, while others were sent to group homes or referred to day care facilities. Over time, many former patients fell between cracks in the healthcare and social work systems and became unhoused. For those on the outside, the closure of state hospitals was deemed to be an act of compassion in which those who were once confined were set free from horrifying places. For many residents at Danvers State, however, the institution was the most stable home they had ever known. Despite its significant flaws, it was a space for belonging and community, a sheltered environment with access to necessities such as sanitary facilities, beds, regular meals, and medication. Living on the street, former patients were guaranteed none of these things. Unmedicated and unsupported, some individuals suffering from mental illness found themselves in trouble with local authorities and became incarcerated, thereby exchanging one form of confinement for another.

For decades, former patients would occasionally find their way to the abandoned Kirkbride building at Danvers and live there as squatters in the ruins of their former lives. The forces of gentrification, however, have erased even this sad possibility. In 2006, Avalon Bay, a development firm, began the demolition of Danvers State Hospital, leaving only the brick façade and shell of the Kirkbride building intact. The structure was then renovated as a community center for the upscale condominium complex that was built on the site. In its decadence, the structure remains true to Kirkbride's vision as an upper-middle-class domestic space, although it is no longer accessible to those for whom it was designed. Cast out of the Castle on the Hill, these living ghosts now haunt the streets, reminders of institutional horrors and human vulnerabilities that—much like Gordon—we would much like to forget.

Notes

1. Thomas Story Kirkbride, *On the Construction, Organization, and General Arrangements of Hospitals for the Insane* (1854), https://collections.nlm.nih.gov/bookviewer?PID=nlm:nlmuid-66510280R-bk.
2. Victoria Rosner, *Modernism and the Architecture of Private Life* (Columbia University Press, 2008), 2.
3. Sensual City Studio, *A History of Thresholds: Life, Death, and Rebirth* (JOVIS, 2018), 41.
4. Rosner, *Modernism*, 1.
5. Leslie Kanes Weisman, *Discrimination by Design: A Feminist Critique of the Man-Made Environment* (University of Illinois Press, 1992), 87.
6. Kirkbride, *On the Construction*.
7. Kirkbride, *On the Construction*, 12.
8. Kirkbride, *On the Construction*, 12.
9. Nancy Tomes, *The Art of Asylum Keeping: Thomas Story Kirkbride and the Origins of American Psychiatry* (University of Pennsylvania Press, 1994); Kirkbride, *On the Construction*, 61.
10. Kirkbride, *On the Construction*, 42.
11. Kirkbride, *On the Construction*, 43.
12. Kirkbride, *On the Construction*, 45.
13. E.F. Sanborn, *The Hospital Palace at Danvers* (1877).
14. Kirkbride, *On the Construction*.
15. Thomas Fuchs, "The Phenomenology of Body Memory," *Body Memory, Metaphor, and Movement*, ed. Sabine C. Koch et al. (John Benjamins, 2012), 10–22.
16. Sarah Robinson, "Nested Bodies," in *Mind in Architecture: Neuroscience, Embodiment, and the Future of Design*, ed. Sarah Robinson and Juhani Pallasmaa (MIT Press, 2015).
17. Sarah Burns, "'Better for Haunts': Victorian Houses and the Modern Imagination," *American Art* 26, no. 3 (2012): 2–25.
18. H.P. Lovecraft, *At the Mountains of Madness*, serialized in the February, March, and April 1936 issues of *Astounding Stories*.

Epilogue

Before and After the Asylum

Sharon Packer

The preceding essays revolve around life inside asylums, but that is not necessarily the end of the story, even if this short section is the end of this book. Many filmmakers have tapped into themes about the aftermath of an asylum stay, and divergent plots evolved over the decades. A few famous films even began before entry.

For instance, Georges Méliès' short silent from 1901, named *L'omnibus des toques blancs et noirs* in its original French and retitled as *Off to Bloomingdale Asylum* for American audiences and as *Off to Bedlam* for the British, begins before arrival at the asylum. In the span of a single minute, that fantasy-based film combines comedy and science fiction and anticipates Méliès' better-known *A Trip to the Moon* (1902), which would arrive the next year.

In *Off to Bloomingdale Asylum*, white-costumed clowns ride in on a wagon drawn by a skeletal horse, performing acrobatic tricks and transforming back and forth between traditional white-faced circus clowns and ethically questionable blackface. Blackface is ordinarily associated with minstrel shows and is disdained in the U.S. today, but this switch was probably intended as an inversion of whiteface, and as a way for Méliès the magician to showcase his special effects skills, which are evident in all his other films as well.

More common than arrivals at asylums are escapes from them. This often-exploited meme is sometimes extremely successful, as evidenced by the many afterlives of *Halloween* (1978). Long before John Carpenter came on the scene, multiple adaptations of Wilkie Collins's serialized novel, *The Woman in White* (1860), made their way to stage and screen. This convoluted Victorian tale, which blends Gothic horror and psychological suspense, introduces a heroine who wears all white and who is revealed to be an escapee from a mental asylum. The tangled web that led to her incarceration in the asylum is as intriguing as the aftermath of her escape, and attests to the acclaim accorded Collins's 19th-century "sensation novel."

Two American-made silent films based on Collins's literary work were released in 1912. In 1917, two more American movies were made, and an Austrian silent film by the same name appeared in 1921. The year 1929 saw yet another silent cinematic adaptation, with this one being British. Stephen Morehouse Avery's 1948 Hollywood adaptation stars Sydney Greenstreet, Eleanor Parker, Alexis Smith, and Gig Young. Many television versions of this intriguing Victorian-era story followed in the coming decades, as did

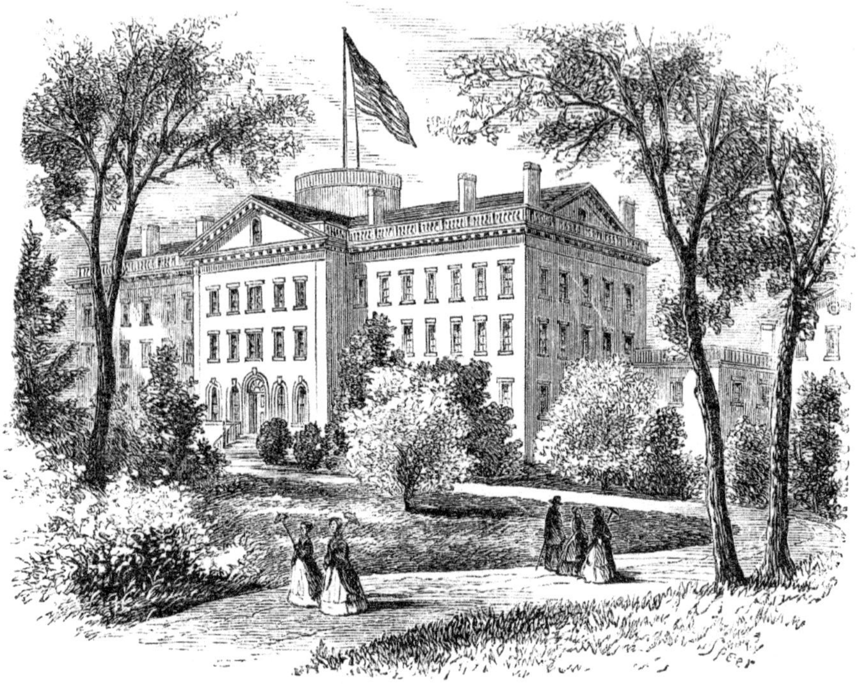

Georges Méliès's short silent film, *Off to Bloomingdale Asylum* (1901), with acrobatic clowns aboard a tram drawn by a skeletal horse, may be fanciful in its execution, but the Bloomingdale Insane Asylum depicted in this drawing actually existed in real life, on Bloomingdale Road in Manhattan's Morningside Heights, near Columbia University (New York Public Library).

video games. The trope of a woman wronged, who is unfairly incarcerated and deemed to be insane, all because of duplicitous actions of exploitative others, appears to have endless appeal.

Some movies about escapes from mental asylums have next to nothing to do with actual life in an insane asylum—as happens in Fritz Lang's noir classic, *Ministry of Fear* (1944). That wartime drama opens with the protagonist's recent release from a mental hospital, before the action starts. This detail anticipates the confusion that the character encounters as the convoluted plot progresses. (This is the very same Fritz Lang who brought us several incarnations of Dr. Mabuse, the sinister psychiatrist par excellence. The *Mabuse* franchise started as early as 1922 and continued several decades after *Ministry of Fear* premiered.)

If we look back at early film, we see several silent shorts that anticipate Carpenter's history-making *Halloween* (1978), which started the slasher craze in the late 1970s. Early in cinema's history, we find *The Escaped Lunatic* (1904), directed by Wallace McCutcheon. D.W. Griffith's *The House of Darkness* (1913) opened before Griffith's much more controversial film, *The Birth of a Nation* (1915), and even before *Caligari* debuted on screen in 1919–1920. The existence of such movies confirms the long-standing intrigue with mental hospital experiences, and the enduring fear of uncontrolled and untreated mental patients let loose and on the lam. As mentioned above, ample literary examples antedate the invention of "moving pictures," some of which later inspired films.

A few films that follow this trope are standard horror fare, such as *Strait-Jacket* (1964), written by Robert Bloch (who wrote *Psycho*), and directed by the same William Castle who brought us *House on Haunted Hill* (1959) and *The Tingler* (1959). Castle also left us with amusing anecdotes about innovative movie theater decorations devised to offset television's convenient home-based appeal, intended to lure audiences back into movie theaters proper. In *Strait-Jacket* (1964), Joan Crawford stars as an axe-murderer who was recently released after a 20-year stint in a mental hospital, where she was remanded after being found NGRI (not guilty by reason of insanity) for murdering her then-husband and his lover. And then she begins again.

Other films on this subject were more serious, such as *Through a Glass Darkly* (1961), directed by Ingmar Bergman. George Cukor's *A Bill of Divorcement* (1932) appeared over a decade before the release of his better-remembered movie, *Gaslight* (1944), another film that centers on psychiatric themes. As overworked as this theme may seem, it has nevertheless been translated into fine filmic interpretations over the years, along with endless entertainment for some, or a nonstop source of chagrin for those who deem such sensational themes exploitative and stigmatizing of mental illness.

Loudermilk's article on "32 Films That Begin with Leaving a Mental Institution" cites many more examples of this subgenre.[1] But since we're on the subject, perhaps we should stop now, and note that this trope of "after the asylum" should be the start of a brand-new book.

Notes

1. A. Loudermilk, "32 Films that Begin with Leaving a Mental Institution," PopMatters, March 13, 2020, https://www.popmatters.com/32-films-begin-mental-institution-2495445831.html.

Filmography

A

American Horror Story: Asylum: Directed by Ryan Murphy and Brad Falchuk, Aired 2012–2013, FX, 2013
Analyze That (2002): Harold Ramis
Analyze This (1999): Harold Ramis
Asylum (1972): Roy Ward Baker
Asylum (2008): David R. Ellis

B

The Batman (2004–2008): Directed by Brandon Vietti, Aired 2004–2008, on Warner Bros.
Batman Arkham Asylum (2009): Rocksteady Studios
Batman: Arkham City (2011): Sefton Hill
Batman: Arkham Knight (2015): Sefton Hill
Batman Begins (2005): Christopher Nolan
Batman Beyond (1999–2000): Directed by Butch Lukic, Aired 1999–2000, on Warner Bros.
Batman Beyond: Return of the Joker (2000): Curt Geda
Batman: Mask of the Phantasm (1993): Eric Radomski and Bruce Timm
A Beautiful Mind (2001): Ron Howard
Bedlam (1946): Mark Robson

C

The Cabinet of Dr. Caligari (1919): Robert Wiene
Caged Heat (1974): Jonathan Demme
The Caretakers (1963): Hal Barlett
Cat People (1942): Jacques Tourneur
A Clockwork Orange (1971): Stanley Kubrick
Close Encounters of the Third Kind (1977): Steven Spielberg
The Couch Trip (1988): Michael Ritchie
The Cure (1917): Charles Chaplin

D

The Dark Knight (2008): Christopher Nolan
Dark Mirror (1946): Robert Siodmak
David and Lisa (1962): Frank Perry
Death Wish II (1982): Michael Winner
Die Hard (1988): John McTiernan
Die Hard 2: Die Harder (1990): Renny Harlin
Die Hard with a Vengeance (1995): John McTiernan
The Doctor's Secret (*Hydrotherapie Fantastique*) (1910): Georges Méliès
Dr. Dippy's Sanitarium (1906): American Mutascope (production company)
Dr. Jekyll and Mr. Hyde (1912): Lucius Henderson
Dr. Jekyll and Mr. Hyde (1920): John S. Robertson
Dr. Jekyll and Mr. Hyde (1931): Rouben Mamoulian
Dr. Jekyll and Sister Hyde (1970): Roy Ward Baker
Dr. Mabuse, der Spieler [*Dr. Mabuse, the Gambler*] (1922): Fritz Lang
Dracula (1931): Tod Browning
Dream of a Hindu Beggar (1902): Georges Méliès
The Dybbuk (1937): Michal Waszynski

E

The Exorcist (1973): William Friedkin

F

Fear Strikes Out (1957): Robert Mulligan
Frances (1982): Graeme Clifford
Frankenstein (1931): James Whale

G

Gaslight (1940): Thorold Dickinson
Gaslight (1944): George Cukor
Girl, Interrupted (1999): James Mangold
Good Burger (1997): Brian Robbins
Good Will Hunting (1997): Gus Van Sant
Gotham (2016): "This Ball of Mud and Meanness." Directed by John Behring, Aired January 2016, on Fox
Gothika (2003): Mathieu Kassovitz

H

Halloween (1978): John Carpenter
Hannibal (2001): Ridley Scott
High Anxiety (1977): Mel Brooks
High Wall (1947): Curtis Bernhardt
Home Before Dark (1958): Mervyn LeRoy
Horrors of the Black Museum (1959): Arthur Crabtree

Horse Girl (2020): Jeff Baena. Netflix
Hot Shots! (1986): Jim Abrahams
House on Haunted Hill (1959): William Castle
House on Haunted Hill [remake] (1999): William Malone

I

I Confess (1953): Alfred Hitchcock
I Never Promised You a Rose Garden (1977): Anthony Page
In Dreams (1999): Neil Jordan
In the Mouth of Madness (1994): John Carpenter
The Island of Dr. Moreau (1977): Don Taylor
The Island of Dr. Moreau (1996): John Frankenheimer
The Island of Lost Souls (1933): Erle C. Kenton
It Conquered the World (1956): Roger Corman
It's Kind of a Funny Story (2010): Anna Boden and Ryan Fleck

J

The Jacket (2005): John Maybury

K

King of Hearts (1966): Philippe de Broca
Klute (1971): Alan J. Pakula

L

Lady in the Dark (1944): Mitchell Leisen

M

Manhunter (1986): Michael Mann
Me, Myself & Irene (2000): Bobby Farrelly and Peter Farrelly
Mindhunter (2017–2019): Directed by David Fincher. Aired 2017 & 2019, Netflix
Mine Own Executioner (1947): Anthony Kimmins
Moon Knight (2022): Marvel

N

A Nightmare on Elm Street (1984): Wes Craven
The Ninth Configuration (1980): William Peter Blatty
Nosferatu (1922): F.W. Murnau
Now, Voyager (1942): Irving Rapper

O

Off to Bloomingdale Asylum (1901): Georges Méliès
One Flew Over the Cuckoo's Nest (1975): Miloš Forman
Our Man Flint (1966): Daniel Mann

P

Possessed (1947): Curtis Bernhardt
Pressure Point (1962): Hubert Cornfield
Prime (2005): Ben Younger
Psycho (1960): Alfred Hitchcock
Psycho (1998): Gus Van Sant

Q

Quills (2000): Philip Kaufman

R

Rain Man (1988): Barry Levinson
Reefer Madness (1936): Louis J. Gasnier
Renfield (2023): Chris McKay
Requiem for a Dream (2000): Darren Aronofsky
Return to Oz (1985): Walter Murch

S

Session 9 (2001): Brad Anderson
Shock (1946): Alfred L. Werker
Shock Corridor (1963): Samuel Fuller
Shutter Island (2010): Martin Scorsese
Side Effects (2013): Steven Soderbergh
The Silence of the Lambs (1991): Jonathan Demme
Silent Hill (2006): Christophe Gans
The Snake Pit (1948): Anatole Litvak
Somewhere in the Night (1946): Joseph L. Mankiewicz
Spellbound (1945): Alfred Hitchcock
Spider (2002): David Cronenberg
Strait-Jacket (1964): William Castle
Suicide Squad (2016): David Ayer
The System of Dr. Tarr and Professor Fether (1912): Maurice Tourneur

T

Ten Days in a Madhouse (2015): Timothy Hines
The Testament of Dr. Mabuse (1933): Fritz Lang
Titicut Follies (1967): Frederick Wiseman
Total Recall (1990): Paul Verhoeven
The Tramp (1915): Charles Chaplin
The Trip (1967): Roger Corman.

U

Unsane (2018): Steven Soderbergh

V

Van Helsing (2004): Stephen Sommers
The Vow (1937): Henryk Szaro

W

The Ward (2010): John Carpenter
What About Bob? (1991): Frank Oz
The Woman in White aka *The Unfortunate Marriage* (1917): Ernest C. Warde

Bibliography

Adorno, T.W. "Chaplin Times Two." *The Yale Journal of Criticism* 9, no. 1 (Spring 1996): 57–61.
Agrest, Diana I. "Architecture from Without: Body, Logic, and Sex." *Assemblage* 7 (1988): 28–41.
Anderson, Carolyn. "The Conundrum of Competing Rights in *Titicut Follies*." *Journal of the University Film Association* 33, no. 1 (Winter 1981): 15–22.
Andrin, M. "Back to the 'Slap': Slapstick's Hyperbolic Gesture and the Rhetoric of Violence." In *Slapstick Comedy*, edited by T. Paulus and R. King. AFI Film Readers Series, 2010.
Annual Report of the Trustees of the Danvers State Hospital. 1910.
Bean, J.M. "The Art of Imitation: The Originality of Charlie Chaplin and Other Moving-Image Myths." In *Slapstick Comedy*, edited by T. Paulus and R. King. AFI Film Readers Series, 2010.
"The Bloomingdale Insane Asylum." *Bloomingdale History* (blog), January 10, 2016. https://bloomingdalehistory.com/2016/01/10/the-bloomingdale-insane-asylum/.
Braslow, Joel T. *Mental Ills and Bodily Cures: Psychiatric Treatment in the First Half of the Twentieth Century*. University of California Press, 1997.
Broe, Dennis. *Film Noir, American Workers and Postwar Hollywood*. University Press of Florida, 2009.
Burns, Sarah. "'Better for Haunts': Victorian Houses and the Modern Imagination." *American Art* 26, no. 3 (2012): 2–25.
Burstow, Bonnie. *Psychiatry Disrupted: Theorizing Resistance and Crafting the r(Evolution)*. McGill-Queen's University Press, 2014.
Cahalan, Susannah. "The Flawed Experiment That Destroyed the World's Faith in Psychiatry." *New Scientist*, February 20, 2020.
Conard, Mark T., ed. *Philosophy of Film Noir*. University Press of Kentucky, 2005.
Cooper, David. *The Death of the Family*. Penguin, 1980.
Cooper, D.G. *Psychiatry and Anti-Psychiatry*. Routledge, 2007.
de Broca, Philippe. 1966. *King of Hearts*. Script by Daniel Boulanger.
Dery, Marc. *The Pyrotechnic Insanitarium: American Culture on the Brink*. Grove Press, 1999.
Durand, Kevin K., and Mary K. Leigh, eds. *Riddle Me This, Batman: Essays on the Universe of the Dark Knight*. McFarland, 2011.
Durante, Salvatore B. "The Historical Significance of *Titicut Follies* in Psychiatric Treatment: An Anti-Censorship Perspective." *Psychological Reports* 126, no. 3 (2023): 1130–1142.
Eisner, Lotte H. *The Haunted Screen: Expressionism in the German Cinema and the Influence of Max Reinhardt*. University of California Press, 1977.
Eromosele, Femi. "Frantz Fanon in the Time of Mad Studies." *World Futures: The Journal of New Paradigm Research* 76, no. 3 (2020): 167–187.
Fakhoury, Walid, and Stefan Priebe. "Deinstitutionalization and Reinstitutionalization: Major Changes in the Provision of Health Care." *Psychiatry* 6, no. 8 (August 2007): 313–316.
Fleischhacker, H.H. "Some Neurological and Neurovegetative Phenomena Occurring During and After Electroshock." *Journal of Nervous and Mental Disease* 102, no. 4 (1945): 185–190.
Forcén, Fernando Espí. "A Hospital for the Mentally Ill in the Middle Ages—Psychiatry in History." *The British Journal of Psychiatry* 208, no. 2 (2016): 103.
Foucault, Michel. *Discipline and Punish: The Birth of the Prison*. Vintage, 1995.
Foucault, Michel. *Madness and Civilization: A History of Insanity in the Age of Reason*. Vintage, 1988.
Frank, Leonard Roy. "Tom Szasz: Freedom Fighter." *Madness Network News* (1972): 12–14.
Fuchs, Thomas. "The Phenomenology of Body Memory." In *Body Memory, Metaphor, and Movement*, edited by Sabine C. Koch, et al. John Benjamins Press, 2012.
Gilman, Charlotte Perkins. "The Yellow Wallpaper." *The New England Magazine*, January 1892.
Gilman, Sander L. *Difference and Pathology: Stereotypes of Sexuality, Race and Madness*. Cornell University Press, 1985.
Gilman, Sander L. *Disease and Representation: Images of Illness from Madness to AIDS*. Cornell University Press, 1988.
Gilman, Sander L. *Seeing the Insane: A Visual and Cultural History of Our Attitudes Toward the Mentally Ill*. Echo Point Books and Media, 2014.
Goffman, Erving. *Asylums: Essays on the Social Situation of Mental Patients and Other Inmates*. Anchor Books, 1961.

Goodwin, John. "The Horror of Stigma: Psychosis and Mental Health Care Environments in Twenty-First Century Horror Film (Part II)." *Perspectives in Psychiatric Care* 50, no. 4 (2014): 224–34.

Gralnick, Alexander. "A Fatality Incident to Electroshock: A Review of the Subject and Autopsy Report." *Journal of Nervous and Mental Disease* 102, no. 5 (November 1945): 483–495.

Grant, Barry Keith. *Ethnography in the First Person: Frederick Wiseman's* Titicut Follies. Wayne State University Press, 2014.

Grob, Gerald N. *Mental Institutions in American Social Policy to 1875.* Routledge, 2008.

Hale, Nathan G. "American Psychoanalysis Since World War II." In *American Psychiatry after World War II, 1944–1994*, edited by Roy W. Menninger and John C. Nemiah. American Psychiatric Press, 2000.

Harman, Graham. *Weird Realism: Lovecraft and Philosophy.* Zero Books, 2012.

Hepworth, Mike. "Privacy, Security, and Respectability: The Ideal Victorian Home." In *Housing and Dwelling: Perspectives on Modern Domestic Architecture*, edited by Barbara M. Lane. Routledge, 2006.

Hine, David, and Jeremy Haun. *Batman: Arkham Reborn.* DC Comics, 2010.

Hirsh, Foster. *The Dark Side of the Screen: Film Noir.* Da Capo Press, 2001.

Honig, Jennifer. "The History of Bridgewater State Hospital." Massachusetts Association for Mental Health. October 2, 2023. https://www.mamh.org/library/the-history-of-bridgewater-state-hospital.

Horwitz, Allan V. "How an Age of Anxiety Became an Age of Depression." *The Milbank Quarterly*, February 2010.

Houellebecq, Michel. *H.P. Lovecraft: Against the World, Against Life.* McSweeney's, 2005.

Ingram, Richard A. "Doing Mad Studies: Making (Non)Sense Together." *Intersectionalities: A Global Journal of Social Work Analysis, Research, Polity, and Practice* 5, no. 3 (2016).

Jackson, Shirley. *The Haunting of Hill House.* Penguin Books, 1984.

Jacobs, S., and H. D'haeyere. "Frankfurter Slapstick: Benjamin, Kracauer, and Adorno on American Screen Comedy." *October* 160 (Spring 2017): 30–50.

Jay, Mike. *This Way Madness Lies: The Asylum and Beyond.* Thames & Hudson, 2016.

Joinson, Carla. "Anti-Insane Asylum Society." Healing, Hell, and the History of American Insane Asylums. https://hhhasylum.com/anti-insane-asylum-society/.

Jones, Mark. "Tentacles and Teeth: The Lovecraftian Being in Popular Culture." In *New Critical Essay on H.P. Lovecraft*, edited by David Simmons. Palgrave, 2013.

Joshi, S.T. *H.P. Lovecraft: A Life.* Necronomicon Press, 1996.

Joshi, S.T. "Lovecraft and a World in Transition." In *Lovecraft and a World in Transition: Collected Essays on H.P. Lovecraft.* Hippocampus Press, 2014.

Jung, C.G. *The Red Book: Liber Novus.* Translated by M. Kyburz and J. Peck. Edited by S. Shamdasani. W.W. Norton, 2009.

Kalinowsky, Lothar, and Paul Hoch. *Somatic Treatments in Psychiatry: Pharmacotherapy, Convulsive, Insulin, Surgical Other Methods*, 2nd ed. Grune & Stratton, 1952.

Keaton, B. *My Wonderful World of Slapstick.* Pickle Partners Publishing, 2015.

Kerkhoff, Jack. *How Thin the Veil: A Newspaper Man's Story of His Own Mental Crackup and Recovery.* Greenberg, 1952.

Kesey, Ken. *One Flew Over the Cuckoo's Nest.* Signet, 1962.

King, Stephen. *Danse Macabre.* Everest House, 1981.

King, Stephen. "Lovecraft's Pillow." Introduction to *H.P. Lovecraft: Against the World, Against Life*, by Michel Houellebecq. Believer Books, 2005.

Kirkbride, Thomas Story. *On the Construction, Organization, and General Arrangements of Hospitals for the Insane.* 1854. https://collections.nlm.nih.gov/bookviewer?PID=nlm:nlmuid-66510280R-bk.

Klöckner, Clemens. "Experience and Memory: The Visualization of World War I by Artists in Vienna and Berlin." In *Vienna-Berlin, The Art of Two Cities.* Prestel, 2013.

Kneeland, Timothy. "ECT as Miracle Maker, Crucifier & Resurrector: Christian Imagery and ECT 1940-Present." Unpublished paper presented at Popular Culture Conference. 1999.

Kneeland, Timothy. "Review: *Hurry Tomorrow.*" http://emro.lib.buffalo.edu/emro/emroDetail.asp?Number=4253.

Kneeland, Timothy, and Carol Warren. *Pushbutton Psychiatry: A History of Electroshock in America.* Praeger, 2002.

Knoll, James L., IV. "In Memoriam—Thomas Stephen Szasz, MD." *Psychiatric Times*, September 13, 2012.

Kolocotronis, Cyril. "The Truth About Electro-Shock Treatments." In *Madness Network News Reader.* Glide Publications, May 1973.

Laham, N. *Currents of Comedy on the American Screen: How Film and Television Deliver Different Laughs for Changing Times.* McFarland, 2009.

Laing, R.D. *The Divided Self: An Existential Study in Sanity and Madness.* Penguin Books, 1965.

Lang, Derrik. "Colorado Massacre Casts Ugly Scar on Batman Mythology." Associated Press, July 26, 2012. https://www.usnews.com/news/entertainment/articles/2012/07/26/colo-massacre-casts-ugly-scar-on-batman-mythology.

Lewis, Bradley. *Moving Beyond Prozac, DSM, and the New Psychiatry: The Birth of Postpsychiatry.* University of Michigan Press, 2006.

Lin, Luona, Karen Stamm, and Peggy Christidis, "Demographics of the U.S. Psychology Workforce Findings from the 2007–2016 American Community Survey." American Psychological Association, Center for Workforce Studies. 2018.

Lovecraft, H.P. "The Call of Cthulhu." In *The Complete Fiction of H.P. Lovecraft*. Chartwell Books, 2016.

Lovecraft, H.P. "The Dreams in the Witch House." In *The Complete Fiction of H.P. Lovecraft*. Chartwell Books, 2016.

Lovecraft, H.P. "The Festival." In *The Complete Fiction of H.P. Lovecraft*. Chartwell Books, 2016.

Lovecraft, H.P. "The Outsider." In *The Complete Fiction of H.P. Lovecraft*. Chartwell Books, 2016.

Lovecraft, H.P. "The Picture in the House." In *The Complete Fiction of H.P. Lovecraft*. Chartwell Books, 2016.

Lovecraft, H.P. "The Shadow Out of Time." In *The Complete Fiction of H.P. Lovecraft*. Chartwell Books, 2016.

Lovecraft, H.P. "The Silver Key." In *The Complete Fiction of H.P. Lovecraft*. Chartwell Books, 2016.

Lovecraft, H.P. "The Thing on the Doorstep." In *The Complete Fiction of H.P. Lovecraft*. Chartwell Books, 2016.

Luhr, William. *Film Noir*. Wiley Blackwell, 2012.

Marnell, Blair. "New CALL OF CTHULHU Game Trailer Embraces Lovecraftian Madness." *Nerdist*, January 23, 2017. https://archive.nerdist.com/new-call-of-cthulhu-game-trailer-embraces-lovecraftian-madness/.

Martin, Kathleen Callanan. *Hard and Unreal Advice: Mothers, Social Science, and the Victorian Poverty Experts*. Palgrave, 2008.

McGovern, Constance M. *Masters of Madness: Social Origins of the American Psychiatric Profession*. University of New England, 1985.

Means-Shannon, Hannah. "The Joker Plays King: Archetypes of the Underworld in Grant Morrison and Dave McKean's *Arkham Asylum: A Serious House on Series Earth*." In *The Joker: A Serious Study of the Clown Prince of Crime*, edited by Robert Moses Peaslee and Robert G. Weiner. University Press of Mississippi, 2015.

Menzies, Robert, Brenda A. LeFrançois, and Geoffrey Reaume. "Introducing Mad Studies." In *Mad Matters: A Critical Reader in Canadian Mad Studies*, edited by Brenda A. LeFrançois, et al. Canadian Scholars' Press, 2013.

Middleton, Robin. "Sickness, Madness and Crime as the Grounds of Reform." *AA Files: Architectural Association School of Architecture* 25 (1993): 14–29.

Miller, Dinah, and Annette Hanson. *Committed: The Battle over Involuntary Psychiatric Care*. Johns Hopkins University Press, 2016.

Miller, Frank, with Klaus Janson and Lynn Varley. *Batman: The Dark Knight Returns*. DC Comics, 1986.

Millet, John A.P., and Eric P. Mosse. "On Certain Psychological Aspects of Electroshock Therapy." *Psychosomatic Medicine* 6 (July 1944): 226–236.

Mohan, Mark. "Frederick Wiseman Talks 'Titicut Follies.'" Oregon Artswatch, April 18, 2016. https://archive.orartswatch.org/frederick-wiseman-talks-titicut-follies/.

Moon, Graham, Robin Kearns, and Alun Joseph. *The Afterlives of the Psychiatric Asylum: Recycling Concepts, Sites and Memories*. Ashgate, 2015.

Moore, Alan, Brian Bolland, and John Higgins. *Batman: The Killing Joke*. DC Comics, 1988.

Morrison, Grant. *Supergods: What Masked Vigilantes, Miraculous Mutants, and a Sun God from Smallville Can Teach Us about Being Human*. Spiegel & Grau, 2011.

Morrison, Grant, and David McKean. *Arkham Asylum: A Serious House on Serious Earth*. DC Comics, 1997.

Morrison, Grant, and David McKean. *Batman: Arkham Asylum 25th Anniversary Paperback—Deluxe Edition*. DC Comics, 2014.

Mullan, Bob. *Mad to Be Normal: Conversations with R.D. Laing*. Free Association Books, 1996, 2003.

Naremore, James. *More than Night: Film Noir in its Contexts*. University of California Press, 2008.

Packer, Sharon. *Cinema's Sinister Psychiatrists*. McFarland, 2012.

Packer, Sharon. *Dreams in Myth, Medicine and Movies*. Praeger, 2002.

Packer, Sharon. "How Anti-Semitism and the Shoah Helped Shape Twentieth Century Psychiatry." In *Anti-Semitism and Psychiatry: Recognition, Prevention, and Interventions*, edited by H.S. Moffic, et al. Springer Nature Switzerland, 2020.

Packer, Sharon, ed. *Mental Illness in Popular Culture*. ABC-Clio, 2017.

Packer, Sharon. *Movies and the Modern Psyche*. Praeger, 2007.

Packer, Sharon. *Neuroscience in Science Fiction Films*. McFarland, 2015.

Packer, Sharon. *Superheroes and Superegos: The Minds Behind the Masks*. Praeger, 2010.

Packer, Sharon, and Daniel Fredrick, eds. *Welcome to Arkham Asylum: Essays on Psychiatry and the Gotham City Institution*. McFarland, 2019.

Packer, Sharon, and Jody Pennington, eds. *A History of Evil in American Popular Culture: What Hannibal Lecter, Stephen King, and Vampires Reveal about America* (2 volumes). ABC-Clio, 2014.

Pallasmaa, Juhani. *The Architecture of Image: Existential Space in Cinema*. Rakennustieto, 2001.

Pallasmaa, Juhani. *The Eyes of the Skin: Architecture and the Senses*. Wiley Press, 2012.

Parks, Alison, Helen Sweeting, Daniel Wight, and Marion Henderson. "Do Television and Electronic Games Predict Children's Psychosocial Adjustment? Longitudinal Research Using the UK Millennium Cohort Study." *Archives of Disease in Children* 98, no. 5 (May 2013): 341–8.

Parteger, William. *Observations on Maniacal Disorders*. For the Author (1792), 123; cited in Andrew Scull, *Madhouse: A Tragic Tale of Megalomania and Modern Medicine*. Yale University Press, 2005.

Peaslee, Robert Moses, and Robert G. Weiner, eds. *The Joker: A Serious Study of the Clown Prince of Crime.* University Press of Mississippi, 2015.

Poe, Edgar Allan. "The System of Dr. Tarr and Prof. Fether." *Graham's Magazine* XXVIII, no. 5 (November 1845).

Poe, Edgar Allan. *Works of Edgar Allan Poe: Sixty-Seven Tales, One Complete Novel, and Thirty-one Poems.* Gramercy, 1990.

Porter, Roy. *Madmen: A Social History of Madhouses, Mad-Doctors and Lunatics: Revealing History.* Tempus, 2006.

Porter, Roy. *Madness: A Brief History.* Oxford University Press, 2002.

Porter, Roy. *A Social History of Madness: The World through the Eyes of the Insane.* Weidenfeld and Nicolson, 1988.

Reiss, Benjamin. *Theaters of Madness: Insane Asylums and Nineteenth-Century American Culture.* University of Chicago Press, 2008.

Roberts, Andrew. "The Lunacy Commission: A Study of Its Origin, Emergence, and Character." Middlesex University. http://studymore.org.uk/01.

Rosenhan, David. "On Being Sane in Insane Places." *Science* 179 (January 1973): 250–258.

Rosner, Victoria. *Modernism and the Architecture of Private Life.* Columbia University Press, 2008.

Rothman, David J. *The Discovery of the Asylum: Social Order and Disorder in the New Republic.* Little, Brown and Company, 1971.

Sadowsky, Jonathan. *Electroconvulsive Therapy in America: The Anatomy of a Medical Controversy.* Routledge, 2017.

St-Amand, Nérée, and Eugene LeBlanc, "Women in 19th-Century Asylums: Three Exemplary Women; A New Brunswick Hero." In *Mad Matters: A Critical Reader in Canadian Mad Studies,* edited by Brenda A. LeFrançois, et al. Canadian Scholars' Press, 2013.

Sanborn, E.F. *The Hospital Palace at Danvers.* 1877. https://www.danverslibrary.org/archive/danvers-state-hospital/.

Santos, Marlisa. *The Dark Mirror: Psychiatry and Film Noir.* Rowman and Littlefield, 2010.

Schlozman, Steven. "What Happened to Mental Illness by the 23rd Century?" In *Star Trek Psychology: The New Frontier,* edited by Travis Langley. Sterling, 2017.

Scull, Andrew. *Madhouse: A Tragic Tale of Megalomania and Modern Medicine.* Yale University Press, 2005.

Scull, Andrew, ed. *Madhouses, Mad-Doctors, and Madmen: The Social History of Psychiatry in the Victorian Era.* University of Pennsylvania Press, 1981.

Scull, Andrew. *Madness in Civilization: A Cultural History of Insanity from the Bible to Freud, from the Madhouse to Modern Medicine.* Princeton University Press, 2015.

Shelby, Spenser. *Dark City: The Film Noir.* McFarland, 1984.

Shorter, Edward. *A History of Psychiatry: From the Era of the Asylum to the Age of Prozac.* Wiley, 1998.

Shorter, Edward, and David Healy. *Shock Therapy: A History of Electroconvulsive Treatment in Mental Illness.* Rutgers University Press, 2007.

Sims, David. "Gotham's Arkham Asylum Is Too Bland to Be Scary." *The Atlantic,* January 6, 2015. https://www.theatlantic.com/entertainment/archive/2015/01/gothams-arkham-asylum-is-too-bland-to-be-scary/384244/.

Singer, Marc. *Grant Morrison: Combining the Worlds of Contemporary Comics.* University Press of Mississippi, 2012.

Snyder, Scott. *Batman Zero Year Savage City.* DC Comics, September 2014.

Spicer, Andrew. *Film Noir.* Routledge, 2016.

Starkman, Mel. "The Movement." In *Mad Matters: A Critical Reader in Canadian Mad Studies,* edited by Brenda A. LeFrançois, et al. Canadian Scholars' Press, 2013.

Staub, Michael E. *Madness Is Civilization: When the Diagnosis Was Social, 1948–1980.* University of Chicago Press, 2011.

Sullum, Jacob. "Curing the Therapeutic State: Thomas Szasz Interviewed by Jacob Sullum." *Reason,* 2000.

Szasz, Thomas, ed. *The Age of Madness: The History of Involuntary Mental Hospitalization.* Jason Aronson, 1974.

Szasz, Thomas. *The Manufacture of Madness.* Syracuse University, 1970.

Szasz, Thomas. *The Myth of Mental Illness.* Harper and Row, 1961.

Tegler, Jan. *B-47 Stratojet: Boeing's Brilliant Bomber.* McGraw-Hill, 2000.

Tomes, Nancy. *The Art of Asylum Keeping: Thomas Story Kirkbride and the Origins of American Psychiatry.* University of Pennsylvania Press, 1994.

Uricchio, William. "The Batman's Gotham City™: Story, Ideology, Performance." In *Comics and the City: Urban Space in Print, Picture and Sequence.* Continuum International, 2010.

Vieira, Mark A. *Into the Dark: The Hidden World of Film Noir, 1941–1950.* Running Press, 2016.

Weisman, Leslie Kanes. *Discrimination by Design: A Feminist Critique of the Man-Made Environment.* University of Illinois Press, 1992.

Wilson, Edmund. "Tales of the Marvellous and the Ridiculous." In *H.P. Lovecraft: Four Decades of Criticism,* edited by S.T. Joshi. Ohio State University Press, 1980.

Wurtz, James F. *The Architecture of Madness: Insane Asylums in the United States.* University of Minnesota Press, 2007.

Wurtz, James F. "'Out of the Asylum': Physical, Mental, and Structural Space in Grant Morrison and Dave McKean's 'Arkham Asylum: A Serious House on Serious Earth.'" *Amerikastudien* 56, no. 4 (2011): 555–71.

Yanni, Carla. "The Linear Plan for Insane Asylums in the United States before 1866." *Journal for the Society of Architectural Historians* 62, no. 1 (March 2003): 24–49.

About the Contributors

Ashley Barry received her Ph.D. in women's, gender, and sexuality studies from Stony Brook University in August 2024. Her dissertation, "In/Sane on Screen: Mad Films and the Psychiatric Gaze," combines Mad Studies with feminist film theory to analyze the discursive and narrative proliferation of psychiatric norms including diagnosis, the sane/insane binary, and representations of trauma. Following her Ph.D., she works as a policy researcher at the New York nonprofit organization College Access: Research and Action through the ACLS Leading Edge Fellowship.

Jeffrey Bullins is a sound designer and educator living in Greensboro, North Carolina. He has worked in the sound department for several horror films and written about various aspects of the genre. He has worked with Dr. Packer previously, contributing essays to her edited collections *Evil in American Pop Culture, Mental Illness in Popular Culture, Welcome to Arkham Asylum*, and *Lenses on Blindness*. Jeffrey's first monograph, *Sound in the American Horror Film*, was published by McFarland in July 2024.

Laura E. Colmenero-Chilberg is a professor of sociology and program coordinator for the MS in strategic leadership at Black Hills State University in Spearfish, South Dakota. An educator for almost all her professional life, she began teaching as a middle/junior high reading/language arts teacher and then as an English and history teacher. Looking to try a new form of teaching, Chilberg tried her hand at corporate training and enjoyed the opportunity of working with adults and coaching team building, communication, HR, and management. Missing the academic life, however, Chilberg returned to school to study a discipline she had minored in—sociology. Three years later she earned her Ph.D. after investigating the images of gender found in contemporary genre fiction, commencing a career-long exploration of the continuing gendered inequality we practice in the United States and around the world.

Jaq Greenspon is a professional writer whose career has had several incarnations. He spent his formative years in Hollywood, where he wrote movies and TV shows as well as numerous books and articles about the entertainment industry. Upon completing his MFA in creative writing from UNLV, he embarked on a career as an educator, eventually leading to an associate professorship at Vytautas Magnus University in Kaunas, Lithuania. He is transitioning his academic work to examine the underappreciated art form of comic books, including working on a Ph.D. dissertation about comic book superheroes and World War II.

David Andrew Harmon is an associate professor of history at Alabama State University. He is the author of *Beneath the Image of the Civil Rights Movement and Race Relations: Atlanta, Georgia, 1946–1981* (Routledge, 1996). With degrees from the University of Tennessee and Emory University, he specializes in post–World War II Southern history with a particular interest in the civil rights movement. He also served as a researcher for the documentary *The Durrs of Montgomery* (Alabama Public Television, 2012).

George Higham, coexisting in a world of both science and art, has spent over 30 years irradiating the dead in addition to engaging in the design and fabrication of illusion tech, often based upon Victorian-era principles. Calling upon his background in special effects and knowledge of film history, his previous works for McFarland include *Wax Museum Movies: A Comprehensive Filmography* (2020) and *Magic and Illusion in the Movies* (2024).

Kristi Rowan Humphreys is a senior lecturer in the department of English at Baylor University in Waco, Texas. In addition to many chapter publications, she has authored the monographs *Housework and Gender in American Television: Coming Clean* and *The Evil Twins of American Television: Feminist Alter Egos Since 1960.*

Timothy W. Kneeland is a professor of history and director of the Center for Public History at Nazareth University. He produces the *Nazareth College Centennial Podcast*, and his most recent publication is *The Routledge History of American Science* (2022). He has authored books and chapter-length studies on politics, policy, and psychiatry, including *Declaring Disaster: Buffalo's Blizzard of '77 and the Creation of FEMA* (2021), *Playing Politics with Natural Disaster: Hurricane Agnes, the 1972 Election, and the Origins of FEMA* (2020), *Democrats and Republicans on Social Issues* (2017), and *Pushbutton Psychiatry: A Cultural History of Electroshock in America* (2008).

H. Steven Moffic, M.D., is currently a pro bono private community psychiatrist, previously based in academic institutions. National and international accolades include the Exemplary Psychiatrist Award from NAMI (1993); Hero of Public Psychiatry commendation from the American Psychiatric Association (2002); Administrative Psychiatrist Award from the American Psychiatric Association (2016); Creative Scholarship Award from the Society for the Study of Psychiatry and Culture (2021); and the Abraham Halpern Humanitarian Award from the American Association for Social Psychiatry (2024). He served as lead editor for a four-volume series on various religions and psychiatry (Springer, 2018–2024).

Sharon Packer, M.D., is a Chicago-born, NY-based physician and psychiatrist who practices psychiatry and supervises psychiatrists-in-training from Icahn School of Medicine at Mount Sinai, NYC. She has authored 200+ journal articles and 20+ book chapters. Her books include *Dreams in Myth, Medicine, & Movies*; *Movies & the Modern Psyche*; *Superheroes and Superegos: The Minds Behind the Masks*; *Cinema's Sinister Psychiatrists*; and *Neuroscience in Science Fiction Films.* She edited *The History of Evil in American Popular Culture*; *Mental Illness in Popular Culture*; *Welcome to Arkham Asylum: Essays on Psychiatry & the Gotham City Institution*; and *Lenses on Blindness.*

Bryan Senn, a full-time psychometrist (now retired, having conducted neuropsychological assessments at Seattle Children's Hospital for over three decades) and part-time writer, has authored scores of articles and a dozen books on cinema, including *Golden Horrors: An Illustrated Critical Filmography of Terror Cinema 1931–1939*; *The Most Dangerous Cinema: People Hunting People on Film*; *The Werewolf Filmography*; *"Twice the Thrills, Twice the Chills": Horror and Science Fiction Double Features 1955–1974*; *Ski Films*; and *Mummy Movies*. He lives in Montana.

Eric J. Sterling holds a Ph.D. from Indiana University and is Distinguished Research Professor at Auburn University at Montgomery, where he has taught for the past 31 years. He is also the director of the master of liberal arts graduate program. He has published four books and more than 100 refereed articles, particularly on the Holocaust, drama, and film studies. His previous publications on film include essays on *Schindler's List*, Robin Williams movies, Robert Zemeckis, Terry Gilliam's *Brazil*, *Beowulf & Grendel*, and Shakespeare adaptations.

W. Harrison Taylor is a professor of history at Alabama State University, where he concentrates primarily on the Reformed tradition in the Anglo-American world during the long 18th century. He is the author of *Unity in Christ and Country: American Presbyterians during the Revolutionary Era, 1758–1801* (University of Alabama Press, 2017) and co-editor of *Revolution as Reformation: Protestant Faith in the Age of Revolutions, 1688–1832* (University of Alabama Press, 2021) and *Faith and Slavery in the Presbyterian Diaspora* (Lehigh University Press, 2016).

Brenda S. Gardenour Walter holds a Ph.D. in medieval history from Boston University. Her research areas include medievalism in dark popular culture, kink studies, and the intersections between the human body, architecture, and the environment in the Anthropocene. She was a professor of history at the Saint Louis College of Pharmacy, where she taught classes in cultural competency and global health. She has worked with nongovernmental organizations to serve communities in Honduras and Haiti, and is now a full-time horticulturalist for Forest Park Forever, an urban nonprofit serving Saint Louis, Missouri.

Index

www.ingramcontent.com/pod-product-compliance
Ingram Content Group UK Ltd.
Pitfield, Milton Keynes, MK11 3LW, UK
UKHW051930100926
8556IPUK00022B/1476

9 781476 690926